OVERCOMING BIBLE DIFFICULTIES

Answers to the So-Called
Errors and Contradictions

EDWARD D. ANDREWS

OVERCOMING BIBLE DIFFICULTIES

Answers to the So-Called Errors and Contradictions

Edward D. Andrews

Christian Publishing House

Cambridge, Ohio

Christian Publishing House

Professional Christian Publishing of the Good News

OVERCOMING BIBLE DIFFICULTIES Answers to the So-Called Errors and Contradictions

Publishing by Christian Publishing House

ISBN-13: 978-0692504697
ISBN-10: 0692504699
BISAC: Religion / Christian Theology / Apologetics

Table of Contents

PREFACE How This Book Works

The Bible is loaded with thousands of difficult, challenging passages--many of which become obstacles in the development of our faith. These difficulties arise out of differences in culture, language, needs, religious and political organization, not to mention between 2,000 and 3,500 years of separation between the Bible author and modern day reader. Calling attention to these difficulties and sifting out the misconceptions, Andrews defends the inerrancy of the Bible, clarifies the so-called errors and what might seem like apparent contradictions. He arms the Christian with what he or she needs to defend their faith in the Bible.

OVERCOMING BIBLE DIFFICULTIES will help its readers

- Be prepared to make a defense (1 Peter 3:15)

- Reasoned from the Scriptures, explaining and proving (Acts 17:3)

- Contend for the faith (Jude 1:3)

- Help those who doubt (Jude 1:22-23)

- Speak Boldly in the Name of Jesus (Acts 9:27-28)

OVERCOMING BIBLE DIFFICULTIES will also offer several chapters on how to effectively evangelize those within their communities, be it neighbors, friends, family, or coworkers. These evangelism chapters will enable its readers to defend their faith, to reason from the Scriptures, explaining and proving, overturning false reasoning, while instructing in sound doctrine.

INTRODUCTION

FIRST, this book will in no way, attempt to cover every so-called error or contradiction in the Bible. There are approximately 3,000 of these supposed errors and contradictions. It would take a book of many pages to consider such an undertaking. There are some exceptional books that do just that as was mentioned in the preface, which are used within as sources, and are highly recommended. Second, please do not be disheartened by such a large number, because there are compelling reasons why we have so many Bible difficulties, not errors or contradictions. This will be discussed further in chapter one. This book is to serve as an essential source in dealing with Bible difficulties. If we offer reasonable responses and satisfactory answers for some of the most popular and challenging passages, it can be inferred that there would be reasonable answers for others as well.

One reason for having such publications as this is the new atheist. The unbeliever of decades past was satisfied to believe that everything came about by chance, through evolution, and not concern himself with what others believed. This is no longer the case. Sadly, today's atheist is more involved in leading the Christian down the path of doubt, while the Christian denominations are almost entirely inactive in evangelizing the unbeliever. Hundreds of atheistic books and videos are flooding the market in an attempt to discredit the Bible, the foundation of the Christian belief system. Another enemy of God's Word is found in the agnostic. An agnostic teaches that it is hard to know whether God exists and that we are unable to accept the Bible as a revelation of that existence. Before we begin defining Bible difficulties, it is best that we better define how we should view available evidence.

Legal Terms as to How We Should Objectively View Evidence

Burden of Proof: The burden of proof falls on the one making the claims. If the Christian is witnessing to another, he has the burden to prove what he says is so if asked for proof. However, if the critic is challenging the Christian, the burden of disproving lies with the critic. The closer the claim is to socially accepted knowledge, less proof is needed, while the further one moves from conventional knowledge, the more evidence is required. I believe that the legal burden of proof offers the best answers to the witnessing of others. It has been refined over the last 200 years to the point of evaluating a life that is held in its balance, just as everlasting life is held in the balance. Below we will list the levels of legal proof and some percentage and wording to indicate the degree of certainty needed. We have used different Bible objects for each one, but any criticism could be plugged into that particular burden of proof.

Warrants Further Investigation

Reasonable (30%): This is a low-level burden of proof in that it is enough to accept something as *reasonably likely*, being so unless proven otherwise by a deeper look, which may bring in more evidence. For example, at this level, it is *reasonably likely* that Jesus Christ lived, died and was resurrected. This may be achieved in the first conversation with the one which we are sharing the good news.

Probable (40%): This is also a low-level burden of proof in that it is enough to accept something as *likely being so* unless proven otherwise by a deeper look, which may bring in more evidence. At this level, it is *probable* that the Bible is the inspired, inerrant Word of God. This may be achieved in the first 2-3 conversations with the one which we are sharing the good news.

Conviction for Claim

Preponderance of Evidence (51%): This is a higher-level burden of proof that makes Noah surviving a worldwide flood *more likely* to be true than not true.

Clear and Convincing Evidence (85%): This is an even higher level of burden of proof that Adam and Eve were historical persons, created by God is substantially *more likely than not*.

Beyond Reasonable Doubt (99%): This is the highest level of burden of proof that over forty major prophecies about Jesus Christ in the Old Testament came true, being beyond reasonable doubt. It must be understood that feeling as though we have no reason doubt is not the same as 100 percent absolute evidence of certainty. If one has doubts that affect their belief of certainty, it is not beyond reasonable doubt. This too must be qualified, because it is reasonable to have doubts on certain aspects of the whole that does not have all the answers as of yet, but it does not affect the level of certainty as a whole.

Evidentialism only becomes self-defeating the moment one tries to raise the level of certainty to the absolute instead of beyond reasonable doubt (sufficient evidence). The argument against the use of evidentialism that the principle simply does not account for the way

4

we come to have most of our beliefs is no real argument at all. A belief that cold weather makes you sick is not the same as believing there is an Almighty God, Creator. Each of us has hundreds of thousands of core beliefs that are accepted as fact until we come across something that tell us otherwise. Ironically, we are told to investigate before buying a car, or especially a house, as it is a big commitment. Yet, are we to equate the acceptance and commitment to Christ the same way we do that a chair will hold our weight or our car will get us to work?

The Bible critic generally exaggerates the level of his evidence, presenting it in a sly fashion. At the same time, he will arbitrarily dismiss the Christian evidence, by declaring that all who believes in God and the Bible are foolish and naive. The simple principle to be observed here is to ask, 'which is more likely to be true based on what you know.' Of course, as one grows in knowledge, that is subject to change. A Christian that falls away due to atheism or agnosticism (like Dr. Bart D. Ehrman) will, after that require absolute evidence rather that evidence beyond a reasonable doubt. From that time on, God must then show him all that his doubting heart desires. The common expression being, "God if you just _____, I will believe."

The Bible critic runs around like a scavenger looking for an error, not reason. As they come upon a pebble of doubt, they throw it out as though it were a boulder of truth against God. Six months later, an archaeologist digging in Bible lands somewhere finds something that utterly and completely removes this critic's evidence. Does the critic even lean a little closer to God? No, because Christian evidence, no matter how weighty, does not exist on the critic's agenda, which is to sow seeds of doubt regarding the Bible's authenticity. Even if the Ark of the Covenant with the Ten Commandments and

5

Aaron's rod that budded were to be located, the critic would still maintain their stand because the unearthing of these objects does not meet their agenda.

For example, the Bible critic will argue from silence, saying 'Belshazzar of the Bible has not been found in secular history, we have no evidence that he ever existed.' Now, say a year later, a piece of a tablet is found that mentions Belshazzar (this has actually happened), and in connection with the historical account in the Bible. Well, that critic does not draw closer to where the evidence is pointing; he throws it out, dismissing it as though he never raised the argument, and runs to look for another. Sadly this circle of madness just keeps going.

SECTION 1 Overcoming Bible Difficulties

This section will explain Bible difficulties, how to overcome them, and evidence that the Bible is the inspired, inerrant Word of God.

The Bible is loaded with thousands of difficult, challenging passages--many of which become obstacles in the development of our faith. These difficulties arise out of differences in culture, language, needs, religious and political organization, not to mention between 2,000 and 3,500 years of separation between the Bible author and modern day reader. Calling attention to these difficulties and sifting out the misconceptions, Andrews defends the inerrancy of the Bible, clarifies the so-called errors and what might seem like apparent contradictions. He arms the Christian with what he or she needs to defend their faith in the Bible.

OVERCOMING BIBLE DIFFICULTIES will help its readers

- Be prepared to make a defense (1 Peter 3:15)

- Reasoned from the Scriptures, explaining and proving (Acts 17:3)

- Contend for the faith (Jude 1:3)

- Help those who doubt (Jude 1:22-23)

- Speak Boldly in the Name of Jesus (Acts 9:27-28)

CHAPTER 1 Bible Difficulties Explained

IT SEEMS THAT the charge that the Bible contradicts itself has been made more and more in the last 20 years. Generally, those making such claims are merely repeating what they have heard, because most have not even read the Bible, let alone done an in-depth study of it. I do not wish, however, to set aside all concerns as though they have no merit. There are many who raise legitimate questions that seem, on the surface anyway, to be about well-founded contradiction. Sadly, these issues have caused many to lose their faith in God's Word, the Bible. The purpose of this books is, to help its readers to be able to defend the Bible against Bible critics (1 Pet. 3:15), to contend for the faith (Jude 1:3), and help those, who have begun to doubt. – Jude 1:22-23.

Before we begin explaining things, let us jump right in, getting our feet wet, and deal with two major Bible difficulties, so we can see that there are reasonable, logical answers. After that, we will delve deeper into explaining Bible difficulties.

Is God permitting Human Sacrifice at Judges 11:30-31?

Judges 11:29-34, 37-41 English Standard Version (ESV)

²⁹ Then the Spirit of the Lord was upon Jephthah, and he passed through Gilead and Manasseh and passed on to Mizpah of Gilead, and from Mizpah of Gilead he passed on to the Ammonites. ³⁰ And Jephthah **made a vow** to the Lord and said, "If you will give the

Ammonites into my hand, [31] then **whatever**[1] comes out from the doors of my house to meet me when I return in peace from the Ammonites shall be the Lord's, and I will offer it up for a burnt offering." [32] So Jephthah crossed over to the Ammonites to fight against them, and the Lord gave them into his hand. [33] And he struck them from Aroer to the neighborhood of Minnith, twenty cities, and as far as Abel-keramim, with a great blow. So the Ammonites were subdued before the people of Israel.

[34] Then Jephthah came to his home at Mizpah. And behold, **his daughter came out** to meet him with tambourines and with dances. She was his only child; besides her he had neither son nor daughter.

[37] So she said to her father, "Let this thing be done for me: leave me alone two months, that I may go up and down on the mountains and weep for my virginity, I and my companions." [38] So he said, "Go." Then he sent her away for two months, and she departed, **she and her companions, and wept for her virginity** on the mountains. [39] And at the end of two months, she returned to her father, who **did with her according to his vow that he had made**. She had never known a man [been intimate with a man], and it became a custom in Israel [40] that the daughters of Israel went year by year to **lament [or commemorate] the daughter** of Jephthah the Gileadite four days in the year.

It is true; to infer that having the idea of an animal sacrifice would really have not been an impressive vow, which the context requires. Human sacrifice would be repugnant, if we are talking about taking a life. Jephthah

---

[1] Whoever

had no sons, so he likely knew it was the daughter, who would come to greet him.

First, the text does not say he killed his daughter. The idea of some that he did kill her is concluded only by an inference. While it is not good policy to interpret backward, using Paul on Judges, he does say humans are to be **"as a living sacrifice."** Therefore, Jephthah could have offered his daughter at the temple, "as a living sacrifice" in service, like Samuel.

This is not to be taken dismissively, because under Jewish backgrounds, it is no small thing to offer a **perpetual virginity** as a sacrifice. This would mean Jephthah's lineage would not be carried on, the family name, was no more.

Second, the context says she went out to weep for two months, not mourn her death. It says, "she left with her friends and **mourned her virginity**."

If she was facing impending death, she could have married, and spent that last two months as a married woman. There would be absolutely no reason for her to mourn her virginity, if she were not facing perpetual virginity. – Exodus 38:8; 1 Samuel 2:22

Third, it was completely forbidden to offer a human sacrifice. – Leviticus 18:21; 20:2-5; Deuteronomy 12:31; 18:10

Imagine an Israelite believing that he could please God with a human sacrifice that was intended to offer up a human life. To do so would have been a rejection of Jehovah's Sovereignty (the very person you are asking for help), and a rejection of the Law that made them a special people. Worse still, this interpretation would have us believe that Jehovah knew this was coming, allowed the vow, and then aided this type of man to succeed over his enemies.

The last point is simple enough. If such a man as one who would make such a vow, in gross violation of the law, and then carry it out; there is no way he would be mentioned by Paul in Hebrews chapter 11.

There is no way God would have granted and helped in Jephthah's initial success knowing the vow that was coming, because both Jehovah and Jephthah would be as bad as the Canaanites. There is no way that God would accept such a vow and then go on to help Jephthah with his enemies yet again. Then, to allow such a vow to be carried out, to then put Jephthah on the wall of star witnesses for God in Hebrews chapter 11.

Does Isaiah 45:7 mean that God Is the Author of Evil?

Isaiah 45:7 King James Version (KJV)

7 I form the light, and create darkness: I make peace, and **create evil**: I the Lord do all these things.

Isaiah 45:7 English Standard Version (ESV)

7 I form light and create darkness,

I make well-being and **create calamity**,

I am the Lord, who does all these things.[2]

Encarta Dictionary: (Evil) (1) morally bad: profoundly immoral or wrong (2) deliberately causing great harm, pain, or upset

---

[2] See Jeremiah 18:11, Lamentations 3:18, and Amos 3:6

QUESTION: Is this view of evil always the case? No, as you will see below.

Some apologetic authors try to say, 'we are not understanding Isaiah 45:7 correctly, because there are other verses that say God is not evil (1 John 1:5), cannot look approvingly on evil (Hab. 1:13), and cannot be tempted by evil. (Jam. 1:13)' Well, while all of these things are Scripturally true, the question at hand is not: Is God evil, can God approvingly look on evil, or can God be tempted with evil? Those questions are not relevant to the one at hand, as God cannot be those things, and at the same time, he can be the yes to our question. The question is, is God the author, the creator of evil?

We would hardly argue that God was **not just** in his bringing "calamity" or "evil" down on Adam and Eve. Thus, we have Isaiah 45:7 saying that God is the creator of "calamity" or "evil."

Let us begin simple, without trying to be philosophical. When God removed Adam and Eve from the Garden of Eden, he sentenced them and humanity to sickness, old age, and death. (Rom. 5:8; i.e., enforce penalty for sin), which was to bring "calamity" or "evil" upon humankind. Therefore, as we can "evil" does not always mean wrongdoing. Other examples of God bringing "calamity" or "evil" are Noah and the flood, the Ten Plagues of Egypt, and the destruction of the Canaanites. These acts of evil were not acts of wrongdoing. Rather, they were righteous and just, because God, the Creator of all things, was administering justice to wrongdoers, to sinners. He warned the perfect first couple what the penalty was for sin. He warned the people for a hundred years by Noah's preaching. He warned the Canaanites centuries before.

Nevertheless, there are times, when God extends mercy, refraining from the execution of his righteous judgment to one worthy of calamity. For example, he warned Nineveh, the city of blood, and they repented, so he pardoned them. (Jon 3:10) God has made it a practice to warn persons of the results of sin, giving them undeservedly many opportunities to change their ways. – Ezekiel 33:11.

God cannot sin; it is impossible for him to do so. So, when did he create evil? Without getting into the eternity of his knowing what he was going to do, and when, let us just say, evil did not exist when he was the only person in existence. We might say the idea of evil existed because he knew what he was going to do. However, the moment he created creatures (spirit and human), the potential for evil came into existence because both have a free will to sin. Evil became a reality the moment Satan entertained the idea of causing Adam to sin, to get humanity for himself, and then acted on it.

God has the right and is just to bring calamity of or evil down on anyone that is an unrepentant sinner. God did not even have to give us the underserved kindness of offering us his Son. God is the author or agent of evil regardless of the source books that claim otherwise. If he had never created free will beings, evil would have never gone from the idea of evil to the potential of evil, to the existence of evil. However, God felt that it was better to get the sinful state out of angel and human existence, recover, and then any who would sin thereafter, he would be justified in handing out evil or calamity to just that person or angel alone.

Who among us would argue that he should have created humans and angels like robots, automatons with no free will? The moment he chose the free will, he moved evil from an idea to a potential, and Satan moved it to a reality. God has a moral nature that does not bring about evil and sin when he is the only person in existence. However, the moment he created beings in his image, who had the potential to sin, he brought about evil. The moment we have a moral code of good and evil that is placed upon one's with free will; then, we have evil.

In English, the very comprehensive Hebrew word ra' is variously translated as "bad," "downcast (sad, NASB)," "ugly," "evil," "grievous (distressing, NASB)," "sore," "selfish (stingy, HCSB)," and "envious," depending upon the context. (Gen 2:9; 40:7; 41:3; Ex 33:4; Deut. 6:22; 28:35; Pro 23:6; 28:22)

Evil as an adjective **describes** the **quality of** a class of people, places, or things, or of a specific person, place, or thing

Evil as a noun, **defines** the **nature** of a class of people, places, or things, or of a specific person, place, or thing (e.g., the evil one, evil eye).

We can agree that "evil" is a thing. Create means to bring something into existence, be it people, places, or things, as well something abstract, for lack of a better word at the moment. We would agree that when God was alone evil was not a reality, it did not exist? We would agree that the moment that God created free will creatures (angels and humans), creating humans in his image, with his moral nature, he also brought the potential for evil into existence, and it was realized by Satan?

Inerrancy: Can the Bible Be trusted?

If the Bible is the Word of God, it should be in complete agreement throughout; there should be no contradictions. Yet, the rational mind must ask, why is it that some passages appear to be contradictions when compared with others? For example, Numbers 25:9 tells us that 24,000 died from the scourge, whereas at 1 Corinthians 10:8, the apostle Paul says it was 23,000. This would seem to be a clear error. Before addressing such matters, let us first look at some background information.

Full inerrancy in this book means that the original writings are fully without error in all that they state, as are the words. The words were not dictated (automaton), but the intended meaning is inspired, as are the words that convey that meaning. The Author allowed the writer to use his style of writing, yet controlled the meaning to the extent of not allowing the writer to choose a wrong word, which would not convey the intended meaning. Other more liberal-minded persons hold with *partial inerrancy*, which claims that as far as faith is concerned, this portion of God's Word is without error, but that there are historical, geographical, and scientific errors.

There are several different levels of inerrancy. *Absolute Inerrancy* is the belief that the Bible is fully true and exact in every way; including not only relationships and doctrine, but also science and history. In other words, all information is completely exact. *Full Inerrancy* is the belief that the Bible was not written as a science or historical textbook, but is phenomenological, in that it is written from the human perspective. In other words, speaking of such things as the sun rising, the four corners of the earth, or the rounding off of number approximations are all from a human perspective. *Limited Inerrancy* is the belief that the Bible is meant only as a reflection of God's purposes and will, so the science and history is the understanding of the author's day, and is limited. Thus, the Bible is susceptible to errors in these areas. *Inerrancy of Purpose* is the belief that it is only inerrant in the purpose of bringing its readers to a saving faith. The Bible is not about facts, but about persons and relationships, thus, it is subject to error. *Inspired: Not Inerrant* is the belief that its authors are human and thus subject to human error. It should be noted that this author holds the position of full inerrancy.

For many today, the Bible is nothing more than a book written by men. The Bible critic believes the Bible to be full of myths and legends, contradictions, and geographical, historical, and scientific errors. University professor Gerald A. Larue had this to say, "The views of the writers as expressed in the Bible reflect the ideas, beliefs, and concepts current in their own times and are limited by the extent of knowledge in those times."[3] On the other hand, the Bible's authors claim that their writings were inspired of God, as Holy Spirit moved them along. We will discover shortly that the Bible critics have much to say, but it is inflated or empty.

2 Timothy 3:16-17 Updated American Standard Version (UASV)

[16] All Scripture is inspired by God and profitable for teaching, for reproof, for correction, for training in righteousness; [17] so that the man of God may be fully competent, equipped for every good work.

---

[3] Gerald Larue, "The Bible as a Political Weapon," *Free Inquiry* (Summer 1983): 39.

2 Peter 1:21 Updated American Standard Version (UASV)

²¹ for no prophecy was ever produced by the will of man, but men carried along by the Holy Spirit spoke from God.

The question remains as to whether the Bible is a book written by imperfect men and full of errors, or is written by imperfect men, but inspired of God. If the Bible is just another book by imperfect man, there is no hope for humankind. If it is inspired of God and without error, although penned by imperfect men, we have the hope of everything that it offers: a rich happy life now by applying counsel that lies within and the real life that is to come, everlasting life. This author contends that the Bible is inspired of God and free of human error, although written by imperfect humans.

Before we take on the critics who seem to sift the Scriptures looking for problematic verses, let us take a moment to reflect on how we should approach these alleged problem texts. The critic's argument goes something like this: 'If God does not err and the Bible is the Word of God, then the Bible should not have one single error or contradiction, yet it is full of errors and contradictions.' If the Bible is riddled with nothing but contradictions and errors as the critics would have us believe, why, out of 31,173 verses in the Bible, should there be only 2-3 thousand Bible difficulties that are called into question, this being less than ten percent of the whole?

First, let it be said that it is every Christian's obligation to get a deeper understanding of God's Word, just as the apostle Paul told Timothy:

1 Timothy 4:15-16 Updated American Standard Version (UASV)

[15] Practice these things, be absorbed in them, so that your progress will be evident to all. [16] Pay close attention to yourself and to your teaching; persevere in these things, for as you do this you will ensure salvation both for yourself and for those who hear you.

Paul also told the Corinthians:

2 Corinthians 10:4-5 Updated American Standard Version (UASV)

[4] For the weapons of our warfare are not of the flesh[4] but powerful to God for destroying strongholds.[5] [5] We are destroying speculations and every lofty thing raised up against the knowledge of God, and we are taking every thought captive to the obedience of Christ,

Paul also told the Philippians:

Philippians 1:7 Updated American Standard Version (UASV)

[7] It is right for me to feel thus about you all, because I hold you in my heart, for you are all partakers with me of grace, both in my imprisonment and in the defense and confirmation of the gospel.

In being able to defend against the modern-day critic, one has to be able to reason from the Scriptures and overturn the critic's argument(s) with mildness. If someone were to approach us about an alleged error or contradiction, what should we do? We should be frank and honest. If we do not have an answer, we should

---

[4] That is *merely human*

[5] That is *tearing down false arguments*

admit such. If the text in question gives the appearance of difficulty, we should admit this as well. If we are unsure as to how we should answer, we can simply say that we will look into it and get back with them, returning with a reasonable answer.

However, do not express disbelief and doubt to your critics, because they will be emboldened in their disbelief. It will put them on the offense and you on the defense. With great confidence, you can express that there is an answer. The Bible has withstood the test of 2,000 years of persecution and is the most printed book of all time, currently being translated into 2,287 languages. If these critical questions were so threatening, the Bible would not be the book that it is.

When you are pursuing the text in question, be unwavering in purpose, or resolved to find an answer. In some cases, it may take hours of digging to find the solution. Consider this: as you resolve these difficulties, you are also building your faith that God's Word is inerrant. Moreover, you will want to do preventative maintenance in your personal study. As you are doing your Bible reading, take note of these surface discrepancies and resolve them as you work your way through the Bible. Make this a part of your prayers as well. I recommend the following program. At the end of this chapter I list several books that deal with difficult passages. As you read your Bible from Genesis to Revelation, do not attempt it in one year; make it a four-year program. Use a good exegetical commentary like *The New International Commentary of the Old and New Testament* (NICOT/NICNT) or *The New American Commentary* set, and *The Big Book of Bible Difficulties* by Norman L. Geisler, as well as *The Encyclopedia of Bible Difficulties* by Gleason Archer.

You should be aware that the originally written books were penned by men under inspiration. In fact, we do not have those originals, what textual scholars call autographs, but we do have thousands of copies. The copyists, however, were not inspired; therefore, as one might expect, throughout the first 1,400 years of copying, thousands of errors were transmitted into the texts that were being copied by imperfect hands that were not under inspiration when copying. Yet, the next 450 years saw a restoration of the text by textual scholars from around the world. Therefore, while many of our best literal translations today may not be inspired, they are a mirror-like reflection of the autographs by way of textual criticism.[6] Therefore, the fallacy could be with the copyist error that has simply not been weeded out. In addition, you must keep in mind that God's Word is without error, but our interpretation and understanding of that Word is not.

In this chapter, we are not going to take the space that we will in later chapters that are dedicated to one difficulty. Here, in short, we will address a number of them. Before looking at a few examples, it should be noted that the Bible is made up of 66 smaller books that were hand-written over a period of 1,600 years, having some 40 writers of various trades such as shepherd, king, priest, tax collector, governor, physician, copyist, fisherman, and tentmaker. Therefore, it should not surprise us that some difficulties are encountered as we casually read through the Bible. Yet, if one were to take a deeper look, one would find that these difficulties are

---

[6] Textual criticism is the study of copies of any written work of which the autograph (original) is unknown, with the purpose of ascertaining the original text. Harold J. Green, Introduction to New Testament Textual Criticism (Peabody, MA: Hendrickson, 1995), 1.

easily explained. Let us take a few pages to examine some passages that have been under attack.

Again, our objective here is not to be exhaustive, not even close. What we are looking to do is cover a few alleged contradictions and a couple of alleged mistakes. This is to give you, the reader, a small sampling of the reasonable answers that you will find in the recommended books at the end of the chapter. Remember, your Bible is a sword that you must use both offensively and defensively. One must wonder how long a warrior of ancient times would last who was not expertly trained in the use of his weapon. Let us look at a few scriptures that support our need to learn our Bible well so will be able to defend what we believe to be true.

When "false apostles, deceitful workmen, disguising themselves as apostles of Christ" were causing trouble in the congregation in Corinth, the apostle Paul wrote that under such circumstances, we are to *tear down their arguments* and *take every thought captive*. (2 Corinthians 10:4, 5; 11:13–15) All who present critical arguments against God's Word, or contrary to it, can have their arguments overturned by the Christian who is able and ready to defend that Word in mildness. – 2 Timothy 2:24–26.

1 Peter 3:15 Updated American Standard Version (UASV)

[15] but sanctify Christ as Lord in your hearts, always being prepared to make a defense[7] to anyone who asks you for a reason for the hope that is in you; yet do it with gentleness and respect;

---

[7] Or *argument*; or *explanation*

Peter says that we need to be prepared to make a *defense*. The Greek word behind the English 'defense' is *apologia*, which is actually a legal term that refers to the defense of a defendant in court. Our English apologetics is just what Peter spoke of, having the ability to give a reason to any who may challenge us, or to answer those who are not challenging us but who have honest questions that deserve to be answered.

2 Timothy 2:24-25 Updated American Standard Version (UASV)

24 For a slave of the Lord does not need to fight, but needs to be kind to all, qualified to teach, showing restraint when wronged **25** with gentleness correcting those who are in opposition, if perhaps God may grant them repentance leading to accurate knowledge[8] of the truth,

Look at the Greek word (*epignosis*) behind the English "knowledge" in the above. "It is more intensive than *gnosis* (1108), knowledge, because it expresses a more thorough participation in the acquiring of knowledge on the part of the learner."[9] The requirement of all of the Lord's servants is that they be able to teach, but not in a quarrelsome way, and in a way to correct his opponents with mildness. Why? Because the purpose of it all is that by God, and through the Christian teacher, one

---

[8] *Epignosis* is a strengthened or intensified form of *gnosis* (*epi*, meaning "additional"), meaning, "true," "real," "full," "complete" or "accurate," depending upon the context. Paul and Peter alone use *epignosis*.

[9] Spiros Zodhiates, *The Complete Word Study Dictionary: New Testament*, Electronic ed. (Chattanooga, TN: AMG Publishers, 2000, c1992, c1993), S. G1922.

may come to repentance and begin taking in an accurate knowledge of the truth.

Inerrancy: Practical Principles to Overcoming Bible Difficulties

Below are several ways of looking at the Bible that enable the reader to see he is not dealing with an error or a contradiction, but rather a Bible difficulty.

Different Points of View

At times, you may have two different writers who are writing from two different points of view.

Numbers 35:14 New International Version (NIV)

¹⁴ Give three on this side of the Jordan and three in Canaan as cities of refuge.

Joshua 22:4 New International Version (NIV)

⁴ Now that the Lord your God has given them rest as he promised, return to your homes in the land that Moses the servant of the Lord gave you on the other side of the Jordan.

Here we see that Moses is speaking about the east side of the Jordan when he says "on this side of the Jordan." Joshua, on the other hand, is also speaking about the east side of the Jordan when he says "on the other side of the Jordan." So, who is correct? Both are. When Moses was penning Numbers the Israelites had not yet crossed the Jordan River, so the east side was "this side," the side he was on. On the other hand, when Joshua penned his book, the Israelites had crossed the Jordan, so the east side was just as he had said, "on the other side of the Jordan." Thus, we should not assume that two different writers are writing from the same perspective.

A Careful Reading

At times, it may simply be a case of needing to slow down and carefully read the account, considering exactly what is being said.

Joshua 18:28 New American Standard Bible (NASB)

²⁸ and Zelah, Haeleph and the Jebusite (that is, Jerusalem), Gibeah, Kiriath; fourteen cities with their villages. This is the inheritance of the sons of Benjamin according to their families.

Judges 1:21 New International Version (NIV)

²¹ The Benjamites, however, did not drive out the Jebusites, who were living in Jerusalem; to this day the Jebusites live there with the Benjamites.

Joshua 15:63 New International Version (NIV)

⁶³ Judah could not dislodge the Jebusites, who were living in Jerusalem; to this day the Jebusites live there with the people of Judah.

Judges 1:8-9 New American Standard Bible (NASB)

⁸ Then the sons of Judah fought against Jerusalem and captured it and struck it with the edge of the sword and set the city on fire. ⁹ Afterward the sons of Judah went down to fight against the Canaanites living in the hill country and in the Negev and in the lowland.

2 Samuel 5:5-9 New American Standard Bible (NASB)

⁵ At Hebron he reigned over Judah seven years and six months, and in Jerusalem he reigned thirty-three years over all Israel and Judah.

⁶ Now the king and his men went toJerusalem against the Jebusites, the inhabitants of the land, and they said to David, "You shall not come in here, but the blind and lame will turn you away"; thinking, "David cannot enter here." ⁷ Nevertheless, David captured the stronghold of Zion, that is the city of David. ⁸ David said on that day, "Whoever would strike the Jebusites, let him reach the lame and the blind, who are hated by David's soul, through the water tunnel." Therefore they say, "The blind or the lame shall not come into the house." ⁹ So David lived in the stronghold and called it the city of David. And David built all around from the Millo and inward.

There is no doubt that even the advanced Bible reader of many years can come away confused because the above accounts seem to be contradictory. In Joshua 18:28 and Judges 1:21, we see that Jerusalem was an inheritance of the tribe of Benjamin, yet the Benjamites were unable to conquer Jerusalem. But in Joshua 15:63 we see that the tribe of Judah could not conquer them either, with the reading giving the impression that it was a part of their inheritance. In Judges 1:8, however, Judah was eventually able to conquer Jerusalem and burn it with fire. Yet, to add even more to the confusion, we find at 2 Samuel 5:5–8 that David is said to have conquered Jerusalem hundreds of years later.

Now that we have the particulars, let us look at it more clearly. The boundary between Benjamin's inheritances ran right through the middle of Jerusalem. Joshua 8:28 is correct, in that what would later be called the "city of David" was in the territory of Benjamin, but it also in part crossed over the line into the territory of Judah, causing both tribes to go to war against this Jebusite city. It is also true that the tribe of Benjamin was unable to conquer the city and that the tribe of Judah eventually did. However, if you look at Judges 1:9 again, you will see that Judah did not finish the job entirely and moved on to conquer other areas. This allowed the remaining ones to regroup and form a resistance that neither Benjamin nor Judah could overcome, so these Jebusites remained until the time of David, hundreds of years later.

Intended Meaning of Writer

First, the Bible student needs to understand the level that the Bible intends to be exact in what is written. If Jim told a friend that 650 graduated with him from high school in 1984, it is not challenged, because it is all too clear that he is using rounded numbers and is not meaning to be exactly precise. This is how God's Word operates as well. Sometimes it means to be exact, at other times, it is simply rounding numbers, in other cases, the intention of the writer is a general reference, to give readers of that time and succeeding generations some perspective. Did Samuel, the author of judges, intend to pen a book on the chronology of Judges, or was his focus on the falling away, oppression, and the rescue by a judge, repeatedly. Now, it would seem that Jeremiah, the author of 1 Kings was more interested in giving his readers an exact number of years.

Acts 2:41 English Standard Version (ESV)

[41] So those who received his word were baptized, and there were added that day about three thousand souls.

As you can see here, numbers within the Bible are often used with approximations. This is a frequent practice even today, in both written works and verbal conversation.

Acts 7:2-3 English Standard Version (ESV)

² And Stephen said:

"Brothers and fathers, hear me. The God of glory appeared to our father Abraham when he was in Mesopotamia, before he lived in Haran, ³ and said to him, 'Go out from your land and from your kindred and go into the land that I will show you.'

If you were to check the Hebrew Scriptures at Genesis 12:1, you would find that what is claimed to have been said by God to Abraham is not quoted word-for-word; it is simply a paraphrase. This is a normal practice within Scripture and in writing in general.

Numbers 34:15 English Standard Version (ESV)

¹⁵ The two tribes and the half-tribe have received their inheritance beyond the Jordan east of Jericho, toward the sunrise."

Just as you would read in today's local newspaper, the Bible writer has written from the human standpoint, how it appeared to him. The Bible also speaks of "to the end of the earth" (Psalm 46:9), "from the four corners of the earth" (Isa 11:12), and "the four winds of the earth" (Revelation 7:1). These phrases are still used today.

Unexplained Does Not mean Unexplainable

Considering that there are 31,173 verses in the Bible, encompassing 66 books written by about 40 writers, ranging from shepherds, to kings, an army general, fishermen, tax collector, a physician and on and on, and being penned over a 1,600 year period, one does find a few hundred Bible difficulties (about one percent). However, 99 percent of those are explainable. Yet no one wants to be so arrogant to say that he can explain them all. It has nothing to do with the inadequacy of God's Word, but is based on human understanding. In many cases, science or archaeology and the field of custom and culture of ancient peoples has helped explain difficulties in hundreds of passages. Therefore, there may be less than one percent left to be answered, yet our knowledge of God's Word continues to grow.

Guilty Until Proven Innocent

This is exactly the perception that the critic has of God's Word. The legal principle of being "innocent until proven guilty" afforded mankind in courts of justice is withheld from the very Word of God. What is ironic here is that this policy has contributed to these Bible critics looking foolish over and over again when something comes to light that vindicates the portion of Scripture they are challenging.

Daniel 5:1 English Standard Version (ESV)

[1] King Belshazzar made a great feast for a thousand of his lords and drank wine in front of the thousand.

Bible critics had long claimed that Belshazzar was not known outside of the book Daniel; therefore, they argue that Daniel was mistaken. Yet it hardly seems prudent to argue error from absence of outside evidence. Just because archaeology had not discovered such a person did not mean that Daniel was wrong, or that such a person did not exist. In 1854, some small clay cylinders were discovered in modern-day southern Iraq, which would have been the city of Ur in ancient Babylonia. The cuneiform documents were a prayer of King Nabonidus for "Bel-sar-ussur, my eldest son." These tablets also showed that this "Bel-sar-ussur" had secretaries as well as a household staff. Other tablets were discovered a short time later that showed that the kingship was entrusted to this eldest son as a coregent while his father was away.

He entrusted the 'Camp' to his oldest (son), the firstborn [Belshazzar], the troops everywhere in the country he ordered under his (command). He let (everything) go, entrusted the kingship to him and, himself, he [Nabonidus] started out for a long journey, the (military) forces of Akkad marching with him; he turned towards Tema (deep) in the west."[10]

Ignoring Literary Styles

The Bible is a diverse book when it comes to literary styles: narrative, poetic, prophetic, and apocalyptic; also containing parables, metaphors, similes, hyperbole, and other figures of speech. Too often, these alleged errors are the result of a reader taking a figure of speech as literal, or reading a parable as though it is a narrative.

Matthew 24:35 English Standard Version (ESV)

35 Heaven and earth will pass away, but my words will not pass away.

If some do not recognize that they are dealing with a figure of speech, they are bound to come away with the wrong meaning. Some have concluded from Matthew 24:35 that Jesus was speaking of an eventual destruction of the earth. This is hardly the case, as his

---

[10] J. Pritchard, ed., *Ancient Near Eastern Texts* (1974), 313.

listeners would not have understood it that way based on their understanding of the Old Testament. They would have understood that he was simply being emphatic about the words he spoke, using hyperbole. What he was conveying is that his words are more enduring than heaven and earth, and with heaven and earth being understood as eternal, this merely conveyed even more so that Jesus' words could be trusted.

Two Accounts of the Same Incident

If you were to speak to officers that take accident reports for their police department, you would find that there is cohesion in the accounts, but each person has merely witnessed aspects that have stood out to them. We will see that this is the case as well with the examples below, which is the same account in two different gospels:

Matthew 8:5 English Standard Version (ESV)

⁵ When he had entered Capernaum, a centurion came forward to him, appealing to him,

Luke 7:3 English Standard Version (ESV)

³ When the centurion heard about Jesus, he sent to him elders of the Jews, asking him to come and heal his servant.

Immediately we see the problem of whether the centurion or the elders of the Jews spoke with Jesus. The solution is not really hidden from us. Which of the two accounts is the more detailed account? You are correct if you said Luke. The centurion sent the elders of the Jews to represent him to Jesus, so; that whatever response Jesus might give, it would be as though he were addressing the centurion; therefore, Matthew gave his readers the basic thought, not seeing the need of mentioning the elders of the Jews aspect. This is how a representative was viewed in the first century, just as some countries see ambassadors today as being the very person they represent. Therefore, both Matthew and Luke are correct.

Man's Fallible Interpretations

Inspiration by God is infallible, without error. Imperfect man and his interpretations over the centuries, as bad as many of them have been, should not cast a shadow over God's inspired Word. The entire Word of God has one meaning and one meaning only for every penned word, which is what God willed to be conveyed by the human writer he chose to use.

The Autograph Alone Is Inspired and Inerrant

It has been argued by conservative scholars that only the autograph manuscripts were inspired and inerrant, not the copying of those manuscripts over the next 3,000 years for the Old Testament and 1,500 years for the New Testament. While I would agree with this position as well, it should be noted that we do not possess the autographs, so to argue that they are inerrant is to speak of nonexistent documents. However, it should be further understood that through the science of textual criticism, we can establish a mirror reflection of the autograph manuscripts. B. F. Westcott, F. J. A. Hort, F. F. Bruce, and many other textual scholars would agree with Norman L Geisler's assessment: "The New Testament, then, has not only survived in more manuscripts than any other book from antiquity, but it has survived in a purer form than any other great book—*a form that is 99.5 percent pure.*"[11]

An example of a copyist error can be found in Luke's genealogy of Jesus at Luke 3:35–37. In verse 37, you will find a Cainan, and in verse 36, you will find a second Cainan between Arphaxad (Arpachshad) and Shelah. As one can see from most footnotes in different study Bibles, the Cainan in verse 36 is seen as a scribal error, and is not found in the Hebrew Old Testament, the Samaritan Pentateuch, or the Aramaic Targums, but is found in the Greek Septuagint. (Genesis 10:24; 11:12, 13; 1 Chronicles 1:18, but not 1 Chronicles 1:24) It seems quite unlikely that it was in the earlier copies of the Septuagint, because the first-century Jewish historian Josephus lists Shelah next as the son of Arphaxad, and Josephus normally followed the Septuagint.[12] So one might ask why this second Cainan is found in the translations at all if this is the case? The manuscripts that do contain this second Cainan are some of the best manuscripts that are used in establishing the original text: 01 B L A^1 33 (Kainam); A 038 044 0102 A^{13} (Kainan).

Look at the Context

Many alleged inconsistencies disappear by simply looking at the context. Taking words out of context can distort their meaning. *Merriam-Webster's Collegiate Dictionary* defines context as "the parts of a discourse that surround a word or passage and can throw light on

[11] Norman L. Geisler and William E. Nix: *A General Introduction to the Bible* (Chicago, Moody Press, 1980), 367. (Emphasis is mine.)

[12] *Jewish Antiquities*, I, 146 [vi, 4].

its meaning."[13] Context can also be "the circumstances or events that form the environment within which something exists or takes place." If we were to look in a thesaurus for a synonym, we would find "background" for this second meaning. At 2 Timothy 2:15, the apostle Paul brings home the point of why context is so important: "Do your best to present yourself to God as one approved, a worker who has no need to be ashamed, rightly handling the word of truth."

Ephesians 2:8-9 English Standard Version (ESV)

[8] For by grace you have been saved through faith. And this is not your own doing; it is the gift of God, [9] not a result of works, so that no one may boast.

James 2:26 English Standard Version (ESV)

[26] For as the body apart from the spirit is dead, so also faith apart from works is dead.

So, which is it? Is salvation possible by faith alone as Paul wrote to the Ephesians, or is faith dead without works as James wrote to his readers? As our subtitle brings out, let us look at the context. In the letter to the Ephesians, the apostle Paul is speaking to the Jewish Christians who were looking to the works of the Mosaic Law as a means to salvation, a righteous standing before God. Paul was telling these legalistic Jewish Christians that this is not so. In fact, this would invalidate Christ's ransom, because there would have been no need for it if one could achieve salvation by meticulously keeping the Mosaic Law. (Rom. 5:18) But James was writing to those in a congregation who were concerned with their status

---

[13] Merriam-Webster, Inc: *Merriam-Webster's Collegiate Dictionary*. Eleventh ed. (Springfield, Mass.: Merriam-Webster, Inc. 2003).

before other men, who were looking for prominent positions within the congregation, and not taking care of those that were in need. (Jam. 2:14–17) So, James is merely addressing those who call themselves Christian, but in name only. No person could truly be a Christian and not possess some good works, such as feeding the poor, helping the elderly. This type of work was an evident demonstration of one's Christian personality. Paul was in perfect harmony with James on this. – Romans 10:10; 1 Corinthians 15:58; Ephesians 5:15, 21–33; 6:15; 1 Timothy 4:16; 2 Timothy 4:5; Hebrews 10:23-25.

Inerrancy: Are There Contradictions?

Below I will follow this pattern. I will list the critic's argument first, followed by the text of difficulty, and conclude with an answer to the critic. What should be kept at the forefront of our mind is this: one is simply looking for the best answer, not absoluteness. If there is a reasonable answer to a Bible difficulty, why are the critics able to set them aside with ease? Because they start with the premise that this is not the Word of God, but only a book by imperfect men and full of contradictions; thus, the bias toward errors has blinded their judgment.

Critic: The critic would argue that there was an Adam and Eve, and an Abel who was now dead, so, where did Cain get his wife? This is one of the most common questions by Bible critics.

Genesis 4:17 New English Translation (NET Bible)

¹⁷ Cain had marital relations with his wife, and she became pregnant and gave birth to Enoch. Cain was building a city, and he named the city after his son Enoch.

Answer: If one were to read a little further along, they would come to the realization that Adam had a son named Seth; it further adds that Adam "became father to sons *and daughters.*" (Genesis 5:4) Adam lived for a total of 800 years after fathering Seth, giving him ample opportunity to father many more sons and daughters. So it could be that Cain married one of his sisters. If he waited until one of his brothers and sisters had a daughter, he could have married one of his nieces once she was old enough. In the beginning, humans were closer to perfection; this explains why they lived longer and why at that time there was little health risk of genetic defects in the case of children born to closely related parents, in contrast to how it is today. As time passed, genetic defects increased and life spans decreased. Adam lived to see 930 years. Yet Shem, who lived after the Flood, died at 600 years, while Shem's son Arpachshad only lived 438 years, dying before his father died. Abraham saw an even greater decrease in that he only lived 175 years, while his grandson Jacob was 147 years when he died. Thus, due to increasing imperfection, God prohibited the marriage of closely related people under the Mosaic Law because of the likelihood of genetic defects.—Leviticus 18:9.

Critic: If God is here hardening Pharaoh's heart, what exactly makes Pharaoh responsible for the decisions he makes?

Exodus 4:21 Revised Standard Version (RSV)

[21] And the Lord said to Moses, "When you go back to Egypt, see that you do before Pharaoh all the miracles which I have put in your power; but I will harden his heart, so that he will not let the people go.

Answer: This is actually a prophecy. God knew that what he was about to do would contribute to a stubborn and obstinate Pharaoh, who was going to be unwilling to change or give up the Israelites so they could go off to worship their God. Therefore, this is not stating what God is going to do; it is prophesying that Pharaoh's heart will harden because of the actions of God. The fact is, Pharaoh allowed his own heart to harden because he was determined not to agree with Moses' wishes or accept Jehovah's request to let the people go. Moses tells us at Exodus 7:13 (ESV) that "Pharaoh's heart was hardened, and he would not listen to them, as the Lord had said." Again, at 8:15 we read, "When Pharaoh saw that there was a respite, he hardened his heart and would not listen to them, as the Lord had said."

Critic: The Israelites had just received the Ten Commandments, with one commandment being: "You shall not make for yourself a carved image, or any likeness of anything that is in heaven above, or that is in the earth beneath, or that is in the water under the earth." Therefore, how is the bronze serpent not a violation of this commandment?

Numbers 21:9 English Standard Version (ESV)

⁹ So Moses made a bronze serpent and set it on a pole. And if a serpent bit anyone, he would look at the bronze serpent and live.

Answer: First, an idol is "a representation or symbol of an object of worship; *broadly*: a false god."[14] Second, it should be noted that not all images are idols. The bronze serpent was not made for the purpose of worship, or for some passionate devotion or veneration.

---

[14] Merriam-Webster, Inc: *Merriam-Webster's Collegiate Dictionary*. Eleventh ed. (Springfield, Mass.: Merriam-Webster, Inc., 2003).

There were times, however, when images were created with absolutely no intention of it receiving devotion, veneration, or worship, yet were later made into objects of veneration. That is exactly what happened with the copper serpent that Moses had formed in the wilderness. Many centuries later, "in the third year of Hoshea son of Elah, king of Israel, Hezekiah the son of Ahaz, king of Judah, began to reign. He removed the high places and broke the pillars and cut down the Asherah. And he broke in pieces the bronze serpent that Moses had made; for until those days the people of Israel had made offerings to it (it was called Nehushtan)."—2 Kings 18:1, 4.

Critic: Deuteronomy 15:11 (NET) says: "*There will never cease to be some poor people in the land*; therefore, I am commanding you to make sure you open your hand to your fellow Israelites who are needy and poor in your land." Is this not a contradiction of Deuteronomy 15:4? Will there be no poor among the Israelites, or will there be poor among them? Which is it?

Deuteronomy 15:4 New English Translation (NET Bible)

⁴ However, there should not be any poor among you, for the Lord will surely bless you in the land that he is giving you as an inheritance,

Answer: If you look at the context, Deuteronomy 15:4 is stating that if the Israelites obey Jehovah's command to take care of the poor, "there should not be any poor among" them. Thus, for every poor person, there will be one to take care of that need. If an Israelite fell on hard times, there was to be a fellow Israelite ready to step in to help him through those hard times. Verse 11 stresses the truth of the imperfect world since the rebellion of Adam and inherited sin: there will always be poor among mankind, the Israelites being no different. However, the difference with God's people is that those who were well off were to offset conditions for those who fell on difficult times. This is not to be confused with the socialistic welfare systems in the world today. Those Jews were hard-working men, who labored from sunup to sundown to take care of their families. But if disease overtook their herd or unseasonal weather brought about failed crops, an Israelite could sell himself into the service of a fellow Israelite for a period of time; thereafter, he would be back on his feet. And many years down the road, he may very well do the same for another Israelite who fell on difficult times.

Critic: Joshua 11:23 says that Joshua took the land according to what God had spoken to Moses and handed it on to the nation of Israel as planned. However, in Joshua 13:1, God is telling Joshua that he has grown old and much of the Promised Land has yet to be taken possession of. How can both be true? Is this not a contradiction?

Joshua 11:23 English Standard Version (ESV)

[23] So Joshua took the whole land, according to all that the Lord had spoken to Moses. And Joshua gave it for an inheritance to Israel according to their tribal allotments. And the land had rest from war.

Joshua 13:1 English Standard Version (ESV)

13 Now Joshua was old and advanced in years, and the Lord said to him, "You are old and advanced in years, and there remains yet very much land to possess.

Answer: No, it is not a contradiction. When the Israelites were to take the land, it was to take place in two different stages: the nation as a whole was to go to war and defeat the 31 kings of this land; thereafter, each

Israelite tribe was to take their part of the land based on their individual actions. (Joshua 17:14–18; 18:3) Joshua fulfilled his role, which is expressed in 11:23, while the individual tribes did not complete their campaigns, which is expressed in 13:1. Even though the individual tribes failed to live up to taking their portion, the remaining Canaanites posed no real threat. Joshua 21:44, *ASV*, reads: "Jehovah gave them rest round about."

Critic: The critic would point out that John 1:18 clearly says that "*no one has ever seen God*," while Exodus 24:10 explicitly states that Moses and Aaron, Nadab and Abihu, and seventy of the elders of Israel "*saw the God of Israel*." Worse still, God informs them in Exodus 33:20: "You cannot see my face, for man shall not see me and live." The critic with his knowing smile says, 'This is a blatant contradiction.'

John 1:18 New American Standard Bible (NASB)

[18] No one has seen God at any time; the only begotten God who is in the bosom of the Father, He has explained *Him*.

Exodus 24:10 New American Standard Bible (NASB)

[10] and they saw the God of Israel; and under His feet there appeared to be a pavement of sapphire, as clear as the sky itself.

Exodus 33:20 English Standard Version (ESV)

[20] But," he [God] said, "you cannot see my face, for man shall not see me and live."

Answer: Exodus 33:20 is one-hundred percent correct: No human could see Jehovah God and live. The apostle Paul at Colossians 1:15 tell us that Christ is the image of the invisible God, and the writer informs us at

Hebrews 1:3 that Jesus is the "exact representation of His nature." Yet if you were to read the account of Saul of Tarsus (the apostle Paul), you would see that a mere partial manifestation of Christ's glory blinded Saul – Acts 9:1–18.

When the Bible says that Moses and others have seen God, it is not speaking of *literally* seeing him, because first of all He is an invisible spirit person. It is a *manifestation* of his glory, which is an act of showing or demonstrating his presence, making himself perceptible to the human mind. In fact, it is generally an angelic representative that stands in his place and not him personally. Exodus 24:16 informs us that "the glory of the Lord dwelt on Mount Sinai," not the Lord himself personally. When texts such as Exodus 24:10 explicitly state that Moses and Aaron, Nadab and Abihu, and seventy of the elders of Israel "*saw the God of Israel*," it is this "glory of the Lord," an angelic representative. This is shown to be the case at Luke 2:9, which reads: "And *an angel of the Lord* appeared to them, and *the glory of the Lord shone around them* [the shepherds], and they were filled with fear."

Many Bible difficulties are cleared up elsewhere in Scripture; for example, in the New Testament you will find a text clarifying a difficulty from the Old Testament, such as Acts 7:53, which refers to those "who received the law *as delivered by angels* and did not keep it." Support comes from Paul at Galatians 3:19: "Why then the law? It was added because of transgressions, until the offspring should come to whom the promise had been made, and it was put in place through angels by an intermediary." The writer of Hebrews chimes in at 2:2 with "For since the message *declared by angels* proved to be reliable, and every transgression or disobedience received a just retribution. . . ." As we travel back to

Exodus again, to 19:19 specifically, we find support that it was not God's own voice, which Moses heard; no, it was an angelic representative, for it reads: "Moses was speaking and God was answering him with a voice." Exodus 33:22–23 also helps us to appreciate that it was the back of these angelic representatives of Jehovah that Moses saw: "While my glory passes by . . . Then I will take away my hand, and you shall see my back, but my face shall not be seen."

Exodus 3:4 states: "God called to him out of the bush, 'Moses, Moses!' And he said, 'Here I am.'" Verse 6 informs us: "I am the God of your father, the God of Abraham, the God of Isaac, and the God of Jacob." Yet, in verse 2 we read: "And the angel of the Lord appeared to him in a flame of fire out of the midst of a bush." Here is another example of using God's Word to clear up what seems to be unclear or difficult to understand at first glance. Thus, while it speaks of the Lord making a direct appearance, it is really an angelic representative. Even today, we hear such comments, as 'the president of the United States is to visit the Middle East later this week.' However, later in the article it is made clear that he is not going personally, but it is one of his high-ranking representatives. Let us close with two examples, starting with,

Genesis 32:24-30 English Standard Version (ESV)

[24] And Jacob was left alone. And a man wrestled with him until the breaking of the day. [25] When the man saw that he did not prevail against Jacob, he touched his hip socket, and Jacob's hip was put out of joint as he wrestled with him.[26] Then he said, "Let me go, for the day has broken." But Jacob said, "I will not let you go unless you bless me." [27] And he said to him, "What is your name?" And he said, "Jacob."[28] Then he said," Your

name shall no longer be called Jacob, but Israel, for you have striven with God and with men, and have prevailed."²⁹ Then Jacob asked him, "Please tell me your name." But he said, "Why is it that you ask my name?" And there he blessed him. ³⁰ So Jacob called the name of the place Peniel, saying, "For I have seen God face to face, and yet my life has been delivered."

It is all too obvious here that this man is simply a materialized angel in the form of a man, another angelic representative of Jehovah God. Moreover, the reader of this book should have taken in that the Israelites as a whole saw these angelic representatives, and spoke of them as though they were dealing directly with Jehovah God himself.

This proved to be the case in the second example found in the book of Judges where an angelic representative visited Manoah and his wife. Like the above mentioned account, Manoah and his wife treated this angelic representative as if he were Jehovah God himself: "And Manoah said to the angel of the Lord, 'What is your name, so that, when your words come true, we may honor you?' And the angel of the Lord said to him, 'Why do you ask my name, seeing it is wonderful?' Then Manoah knew that he was the angel of the Lord. And Manoah said to his wife, "We shall surely die, *for we have seen God*." – Judges 13:3–22.

Inerrancy: Are There Mistakes?

I have addressed the alleged contradictions, so it would seem that our job is done here, right? Not hardly. Yes, there are just as many who claim that the Bible is full of mistakes.

Critic: Matthew 27:5 states that Judas hanged himself, whereas Acts 1:18 says that "falling headlong he burst open in the middle and all his bowels gushed out."

Matthew 27:5 English Standard Version (ESV)

⁵ And throwing down the pieces of silver into the temple, he departed, and he went and hanged himself.

Acts 1:18 English Standard Version (ESV)

¹⁸ (Now this man acquired a field with the reward of his wickedness, and falling headlong he burst open in the middle and all his bowels gushed out.

Answer: Neither Matthew, nor Luke made a mistake. What you have is Matthew giving the reader the manner in which Judas committed suicide. On the other hand, Luke is giving the reader of Acts, the result of that suicide. Therefore, instead of a mistake, we have two texts that complement each other, really giving the reader the full picture. Judas came to a tree alongside a cliff that had rocks below. He tied the rope to a branch and the other end around his neck, and jumped over the edge of the cliff in an attempt at hanging himself. One of two things could have happened: (1) the limb broke plunging him to the rocks below, or (2) the rope broke with the same result, and he burst open onto the rocks below.

Critic: The apostle Paul made a mistake when he quotes how many people died.

Numbers 25:9 English Standard Version (ESV)

⁹ Nevertheless, those who died by the plague were twenty-four thousand.

1 Corinthians 10:8 English Standard Version (ESV)

⁸ We must not indulge in sexual immorality as some of them did, and twenty-three thousand fell in a single day.

Answer: We must keep in mind the above principle that we spoke of, the *Intended Meaning of the Writer*. We live in a far more precise age today, where specificity is highly important. However, we round large numbers off (even estimate) all the time: "there were 237,000 people in Time Square last night." The simplest answer is that the number of people slain was in between 23,000 and 24,000, and both writers rounded the number off. However, there is even another possibility, because the book of Numbers specifically speaks of "all the chiefs of the people" (25:4-5), which could account for the extra 1,000, which is mentioned in Numbers 24,000. Thus, you have the people killing the chiefs of the people and the plague killing the people. Therefore, both books are correct.

Critic: After 215 years in Egypt, the descendants of Jacob arrived at the Promised Land. As you recall they sinned against God and were sentenced to forty years in the wilderness. But once they entered the Promised Land, they buried Joseph's bones "at Shechem, in the piece of land that *Jacob bought* from the sons of Hamor the father of Shechem," as stated at Joshua 24:32. Yet, when Stephen had to defend himself before the Jewish religious leaders, he said that Joseph was buried "in the tomb that *Abraham had bought* for a sum of silver from the sons of Hamor." Therefore, at once it appears that we have a mistake on the part of Stephen.

Acts 7:15-16 English Standard Version (ESV)

¹⁵ And Jacob went down into Egypt, and he died, he and our fathers,¹⁶ and they were carried back to Shechem

44

and laid in the tomb that Abraham had bought for a sum of silver from the sons of Hamor in Shechem.

Genesis 23:17-18 English Standard Version (ESV)

[17] So the field of Ephron in Machpelah, which was to the east of Mamre, the field with the cave that was in it and all the trees that were in the field, throughout its whole area, was made over [18] to Abraham as a possession in the presence of the Hittites, before all who went in at the gate of his city.

Genesis 33:19 English Standard Version (ESV)

[19] And from the sons of Hamor, Shechem's father, he [Jacob] bought for a hundred pieces of money the piece of land on which he had pitched his tent.

Joshua 24:32 English Standard Version (ESV)

[32] As for the bones of Joseph, which the people of Israel brought up from Egypt, they buried them at Shechem, in the piece of land that Jacob bought from the sons of Hamor the father of Shechem for a hundred pieces of money. It became an inheritance of the descendants of Joseph.

Answer: If we look back to Genesis 12:6-7, we will find that Abraham's first stop after entering Canaan from Haran was Shechem. It is here that Jehovah told Abraham: "To your offspring I will give this land." At this point Abraham built an altar to Jehovah. It seems reasonable that Abraham would need to purchase this land that had not yet been given to his offspring. While it is true that the Old Testament does not mention this purchase, it is likely that Stephen would be aware of such by way of oral tradition. As Acts chapter seven demonstrates, Stephen had a wide-ranging knowledge of Old Testament history.

Later, Jacob would have had difficulty laying claim to the tract of land that his grandfather Abraham had purchased, because there would have been a new generation of inhabitants of Shechem. This would have been many years after Abraham moved further south and Isaac moved to Beersheba, and including Jacob's twenty years in Paddan-aram (Gen 28:6, 7). The simplest answer is that this land was not in use for about 120 years because of Abraham's extensive travels and Isaac's having moved away, leaving it unused; likely it was put to use by others. So, Jacob simply repurchased what Abraham had bought over a hundred years earlier. This is very similar to the time Isaac had to repurchase the well at Beersheba that Abraham had already purchased earlier. – Genesis 21:27–30; 26:26–32.

Genesis 33:18–20 tells us that 'Jacob bought this land for a hundred pieces of money, from the sons of Hamor.' This same transaction is also mentioned at Joshua 24:32, in reference to transporting Joseph's bones from Egypt, to be buried in Shechem.

We should also address the cave of Machpelah that Abraham had purchased in Hebron from Ephron the Hittite. The word "tomb" is not mentioned until Joshua 24:32, and is in reference to the tract of land in Shechem. Nowhere in the Old Testament does it say that Abraham bought a "tomb." The cave of Machpelah obtained by Abraham would eventually become a family tomb, receiving Sarah's body and, eventually, his own, and those of Isaac, Rebekah, Jacob, and Leah. (Genesis 23:14–19; 25:9; 49:30, 31; 50:13) Gleason L. Archer, Jr., concludes this Bible difficulty, saying:

The reference to a *mnema* ("tomb") in connection with Shechem must either have been proleptic [to anticipate] for the later use of that shechemite tract for

Joseph's tomb (i.e., 'the tomb that Abraham bought' was intended to imply 'the tomb location that Abraham bought"); or else conceivably the dative relative pronoun *ho* was intended elliptically [omission] for *en to topo ho onesato Abraam* ("in the place that Abraham bought") as describing the location of the *mnema* near the Oak of Moreh right outside Shechem. Normally Greek would have used the relative-locative adverb *hou* to express 'in which' or 'where'; but this would have left *onesato* ("bought") without an object in its own clause, and so *ho* was much more suitable in this context. (Archer 1982, 379–81)

Another solution could be that Jacob is being viewed as a representative of Abraham, for he is the grandson of Abraham. This was quite appropriate in Biblical times, to attribute the purchase to Abraham as the Patriarchal family head.

Critic: 2 Samuel 24:1 says that God moved David to count the Israelites, while 1 Chronicles 21:1 Satan, or a resister did. This would seem to be a clear mistake on the part of one of these authors.

2 Samuel 24:1 English Standard Version (ESV)

[1] Again the anger of the Lord was kindled against Israel, and he incited David against them, saying, "Go, number Israel and Judah."

1 Chronicles 21:1 English Standard Version (ESV)

[1] Then Satan stood against Israel and incited David to number Israel.

Answer: In this period of David's reign, Jehovah was very displeased with Israel, and therefore he did not prevent Satan from bringing this sin on them. Often in Scripture, it is spoken of as though God did something

47

when he allowed an event to take place. For example, it is said that God 'hardened Pharaoh's heart' (Exodus 4:21), when he actually allowed the Pharaoh's heart to harden.

Inerrancy: Are There Scientific Errors?

Many truths about God are beyond the scope of science. Science and the Bible are not at odds. In fact, we can thank modern day science, as it has helped us to better under the creation of God, from our solar system, to the universes, to the human body and mind. What we find is a level of order, precision, design and sophistication, which points to a Designer, the eyes of many Christians, to an Almighty God, with infinite intelligence and power. The apostle Paul makes this all too clear, when he writes, "For his invisible attributes, namely, his eternal power and divine nature, have been clearly perceived, ever since the creation of the world, in the things that have been made. So they are without excuse."—Romans 1:20.

Back in the seventeenth century, the world-renowned scientist Galileo proved beyond any doubt that the earth was not the center of the universe, nor did the sun orbit the earth. In fact, he proved it to be the other way around (no pun intended), with the earth revolving around the sun. However, he was brought up on charges of heresy by the Catholic Church and ordered to recant his position. Why? From the viewpoint of the Catholic Church, Galileo was contradicting God's Word, the Bible. As it turned out, Galileo and science were correct and the Church was wrong, for which it issued a formal apology in 1992. However, the point we wish to make here is that in all the controversy, the Bible was never in the wrong. It was a misinterpretation on the part of the Catholic Church, and not a fault with the Bible. One will find no place in the Bible that claims the sun orbits the earth. So where would the Church get such an idea? The Church got such an idea from Ptolemy (b. about 85 C.E.), an ancient astronomer, who argued for such an idea.

As it usually turns out, the so-called contradiction between science and God's Word lies at the feet of those who are interpreting Scripture incorrectly. To repeat the sentiments of Galileo when writing to a pupil—Galileo expressed the same sentiments: "Even though Scripture cannot err, its interpreters and expositors can, in various ways. One of these, very serious and very frequent, would be when they always want to stop at the purely literal sense."[15] I believe that today's scholars, in hindsight, would have no problem agreeing.

While the Bible is not a science textbook, it is scientifically accurate when it touches on matters of science.

The Circle of the Earth Hangs on Nothing

Isaiah 40:22 Updated American Standard Version (UASV)

²² It is he who sits above the **circle of the earth**,
   and its inhabitants are like grasshoppers;
who stretches out the heavens like a curtain,
   and spreads them like a tent to dwell in.

More than 2,500 years ago, the prophet Isaiah wrote that the earth is a circle or sphere. First, how would it be possible for Isaiah to know the earth is a circle or sphere, if not from inspiration? *Scientific America*

---

[15] Letter from Galileo to Benedetto Castelli, December 21, 1613.

writes, "As countless photos from space can attest, Earth is round–the "Blue Marble," as astronauts have affectionately dubbed it. Appearances, however, can be deceiving. Planet Earth is not, in fact, perfectly round."[16] Scientifically speaking, the sun is not perfectly, absolutely 100 percent round but in everyday speech, this verse is both acceptable and accurate, when we keep in mind it is written from a human perspective, not from a scientific perspective. Moreover, Isaiah was not discussing astronomy; he was simply making an inspired observation that man came to realize once he was in space, looking back at the earth, it is round. See the section about title, "Intended Meaning of Writer."

Job 26:7 Updated American Standard Version (UASV)

⁷ "He stretches out the north over empty space
and hangs the earth on nothing.

Here the author describes the earth as hanging upon nothing. Many have never heard of the Greek mathematician and astronomer Eratosthenes. He was born in about 276 B.C.E. and received some of his education in Athens, Greece. In 240 B.C., the "Greek astronomer, geographer, mathematician and librarian Eratosthenes calculates the Earth's circumference. His data was rough, but he wasn't far off."[17] While man very early on used their God given intelligence to arrive at some

---

[16] Charles Q. Choi (April 12, 2007). Scientific America. Strange but True: Earth Is Not Round. Retrieved Monday, August 03, 2015.

http://www.scientificamerican.com/article/earth-is-not-round/

[17] Alfred, Randy (June 19, 2008). "June 19, 240 B.C.E: The Earth Is Round, and It's This Big". Wired. Retrieved Monday, August 03, 2015.

outstanding conclusion that were actually very accurate, we learn two points here. Eratosthenes was a very astute scientist, while Isaiah, who wrote some 500 years earlier, was no scientist at all. Moreover, Moses, who wrote the book of Job over 1,230 years before Eratosthenes, knew that the earth hung upon nothing.

How Is the Sun Standing Still Possible?

Joshua 10:13 Updated American Standard Version (UASV)

[13] And the sun stood still, and the moon stopped, until the nation avenged themselves of their enemies.

Is this not written in the Book of Jashar? The sun stopped in the midst of heaven and did not hurry to set for about a whole day.

The Canaanites had besieged the Gibeonites, a group of people that gained Jehovah God's backing because they had faith in Him. In this battle, Jehovah helped the Israelites continue their attack by causing "the sun [to stand] still, and the moon stopped, until the nation took vengeance on their enemies." (Jos 10:1-14) Those who accept God as the creator of the universe and life can accept that he would know a way of stopping the earth from rotating. However, there are other ways of understanding this account. We must keep in mind that the Bible speaks from an earthly observer point of view, so it need not be that he stopped the rotation. It could have been a refraction of solar and lunar light rays, which would have produced the same effect.

Psalm 136:6 Updated American Standard Version (UASV)

[6] to him who spread out the earth above the waters, for his lovingkindness is everlasting;

51

Hebrews 3:4 Updated American Standard Version (UASV)

⁴ For every house is built by someone, but the builder of all things is God.

2 Kings 20:8-11 Updated American Standard Version (UASV)

⁸ And Hezekiah said to Isaiah, "What shall be the sign that Jehovah will heal me, and that I shall go up to the house of Jehovah on the third day?" ⁹ And Isaiah said, "This shall be the sign to you from Jehovah, that Jehovah will do the thing that he has spoken: shall the shadow go forward ten steps or go back ten steps?" ¹⁰ And Hezekiah answered, "It is an easy thing for the shadow to decline ten steps; no, but let the shadow turn backward ten steps." ¹¹ And Isaiah the prophet cried to Jehovah, and he brought the shadow on the steps back ten steps, by which it had gone down on the steps of Ahaz.

How is it that the stars fought on behalf of Barak?

Judges 5:20 Updated American Standard Version (UASV)

²⁰ The stars fought from heaven,
from their courses they fought against Sisera.

Judges 4:15 Updated American Standard Version (UASV)

¹⁵ And Jehovah routed Sisera and all his chariots and all his army with the edge of the sword before Barak; and Sisera alighted from his chariot and fled away on foot.

In the Bible, you have Biblical prose, and Biblical poetry.

Prose: language that is not poetry: (1) writing or speech in its normal continuous form, without the rhythmic or visual line structure of poetry **(2)** ordinary style of expression: writing or speech that is ordinary or matter-of-fact, without embellishment.

Poetry: literature in verse: (1) literary works written in verse, in particular verse writing of high quality, great beauty, emotional sincerity or intensity, or profound insight **(2) beauty or grace:** something that resembles poetry in its beauty, rhythmic grace, or imaginative, elevated, or decorative style.

We have a beautiful example of both of these forms of writing-communication in chapters four and five of the book of Judges. Judges Chapter 4 is a prose account of Deborah and Barak, while Judges Chapter 5 is a poetic account. As we have learned from the above, poetry is less concerned with accuracy than evoking emotions. Poetry has a license to say things like what we find in of 5:20, which is in the poetry chapter: "from heaven the stars fought." This can be said and the reader is expected to not take the language literally. What we can surmise from it though, is that God was acting against Sisera in some way, there was divine intervention.

Procedures for Handling Biblical Difficulties

1. You need to be completely convinced a reason or understanding exists.

2. You need to have total trust and conviction in the inerrancy of the Scripture as originally written down.

3. You need to study the context and framework of the verse carefully, to establish what the author meant by the words he used. In other words, find the beginning and the end of the context that your passage falls within.

4. You need to understand exegesis: find the historical setting, determine author intent, study key words, and note parallel passages. You need to slow down and carefully read the account, considering exactly what is being said

5. You need to find a reasonable harmonization of parallel passages.

6. You need to consider a variety of trusted Bible commentaries, dictionaries, lexical sources, encyclopedias, as well as books on Bible difficulties.

7. You should investigate as to whether the difficulty is a transmissional error in the original text.

8. You must always keep in mind that the historical accuracy of the biblical text is unmatched; that thousands of extant manuscripts some of which date back to the second century B.C. support the transmitted text of Scripture.

9. We must keep in mind that the Bible is a diverse book when it comes to literary styles: narrative, poetic, prophetic, and apocalyptic; also containing parables, metaphors, similes, hyperbole, and other figures of speech. Too often, these alleged errors are the result of a reader taking a figure of speech as literal, or reading a parable as though it is a narrative.

10. The Bible student needs to understand what level that the Bible intends to be exact in what is written. If Jim told a friend that 650 graduated with him from high school in 1984, it is not challenged, because it is all

too clear that he is using rounded numbers and is not meaning to be precise.

CHAPTER 2 Some Types of Bible Difficulties

By R. A. Torrey

Updated by Edward D. Andrews

All the difficulties found in the Bible can be included under ten general headings:

The Text from which our English Bible was Translated

No one, as far as I know, holds that the English translation of the Bible is absolutely infallible and inerrant. The doctrine held by many is that the Scriptures as originally given were absolutely infallible and inerrant, and that our English translation is a *substantially accurate* rendering of the Scriptures as originally given.

We do not possess the original manuscripts of the Bible. These original manuscripts were copied many times with great care and exactness, but naturally, some errors crept into the copies that were made. We now possess so many good copies that by comparing one with another, we can tell with great precision just what the original text was. Indeed, for all practical purposes the original text is now settled.

Update: After Torrey's death in 1928, we have made the extremely important discovery over 100 papyrus manuscripts that date before 300 C.E. Quite a few date to the second century, with one small fragment being dated to about 125 C.E. The modern textual scholar can now say with certainty that we have establish the Greek New Testament to a ninety-nine percent reflect of the originally publish book(s). Moreover, we have more than 100 English translations today, with many of them being a very good representation of the Hebrew and Greek in English: NASB, ESB, HCSB, LEB, and others. **Edward D. Andrews**

There is not one important doctrine, which hangs upon any doubtful reading of the text. However, when our Authorized Version (KJV) was published in 1611, some of the best manuscripts were not within reach of the translators, and the science of textual criticism was not so well understood as it is today, and so the translation was made from an imperfect text. Not a few of the apparent difficulties in the Bible arise from this source.

For example, we are told in John 5:4 that "an angel went down at a certain season into the pool, and troubled the water: whosoever then first after the troubling of the water stepped in was made whole of whatsoever disease he had." This statement for many reasons seems improbable and difficult to believe, but upon investigation, we find that it is all a mistake of the copyist. Some early copyist, reading John's account, added in the margin his explanation of the healing properties of this intermittent medicinal spring. A late copyist embodied this marginal note in the body of the text, and so it came to be handed down and got into the Authorized Version (KJV). Very properly, it has been omitted from the Revised Version.

Note: It is omitted from almost all of our modern-day translations as well, with the exception of the NASB and the HCSB, which retained it out of esteem to the KJV. **Edward D. Andrews**

The discrepancies in figures in different accounts of the same events as, for example, the differences in the ages of some of the kings as given in the text of Kings and Chronicles, doubtless arise from the same cause, errors of copyists. Such an error in the matter of figures would be very easy to make, as in the Hebrew; letters, and letters that appear very much alike have a very different value as figures denote numbers. For example, the first letter in the Hebrew alphabet denotes one, and with two little points above it, no larger than flyspecks, it denotes a thousand. The twenty-third or last letter of the Hebrew alphabet denotes four hundred, but the eighth letter of the Hebrew alphabet that looks very much like it and could be easily mistaken for it, denotes eight. A very slight error of the copyist would therefore make an utter change in figures. The remarkable thing when one contemplates the facts in the case is that so few errors of this kind have been made.

Inaccurate Translations

For example, in Matthew 12:40 Jonah is spoken of as being in "the whale's belly." Many a skeptic has made a mockery over the thought of a whale with the peculiar construction of its mouth and throat swallowing a man. However, if the skeptic had only taken the trouble to look the matter up, he would have found the word translated "whale" really means "sea monster" [or great fish] without any definition as to the character of the sea monster. We will take this up more in detail in considering the story of Jonah. Therefore, the whole difficulty arose from the translator's mistake and the skeptic's ignorance. Many skeptics today are so densely ignorant of matters clearly understood by many Sunday school children that they are still harping in the name of scholarship on this supposed error in the Bible.

False Interpretations of the Bible

What the Bible teaches is one thing, and what men interpret it to mean is oftentimes something widely different. Many difficulties that we have with the Bible arise not from what the Bible actually says, but from what men interpret it to mean.

A striking illustration of this is found in Genesis 1. If we were to take the interpretation put upon this chapter by many, it would indeed be difficult to reconcile it with much that modern science regards as established. However, the difficulty is not with what Genesis 1 says, but with the interpretation put upon it. There is no contradiction whatever between what is really proven by science and what is really said in Genesis 1.

Another difficulty of the same character is with Jesus' statement that He would be three days and three nights in the heart of the earth. Many interpreters would have us believe that He died Friday and rose early Sunday morning, and the time between these two is far from being three days and three nights. However, it is a matter of biblical interpretation, and the trouble is not with what the Bible actually says, but with the interpretation that men put upon the Bible. We will take this matter up at length below by Edward D. Andrews.

Matthew 12:40 How many days was Jesus in the tomb?

Some argue for three days, based on Jesus' words,

Matthew 12:40 English Standard Version (ESV)

[40] For just as Jonah was three days and three nights in the belly of the great fish, so will the Son of Man be three days and three nights in the heart of the earth.

This would seem to suggest a full 72 hours. However, we should not set aside similar expressions that may allow us to get at the intent of the words. Many times in Scripture, three days does not always mean a full 72 hours of three days. For example, look at the words of Rehoboam,

1 Kings 12:5, 12 English Standard Version (ESV)

⁵ He said to them, "Go away for three days, then come again to me." So the people went away. ¹² So Jeroboam and all the people came to Rehoboam the third day, as the king said, "Come to me again the third day."

You see that the king told the people to go away for three days, and then return to him. But you also will notice that they returned on the third day, which was not a full 72 hours of three days. Now, consider what Jesus said of himself, something that Scripture repeatedly says,

Luke 24:46 English Standard Version (ESV)

⁴⁶ and said to them, "Thus it is written, that the Christ should suffer and **on the third day** rise from the dead

Now, if he had remained in the grave for a full 72 hours of three days, it mean that he would have been raised on the fourth day. Jewish days ran from sundown to sundown. Jesus died on Friday afternoon about 3:00 p.m., Nisan 14, 33 C.E.

- Jesus' death Friday Nisan 14, about 3:00 p.m. (Matt 27:31-56; Mk 15:20-41; Lu 23:26-49; Jn 19:16-30)

- Jesus was in Tomb before sundown Friday evening (Matt 27:57-61; Mk 15:42-47; Lu 23:50-56; Jn 19:31-42)

- Jesus in tomb all of Nisan 15th from sundown Friday to sundown Saturday, which began Nisan 16 (Matt 27:62-66)

- Jesus resurrected early Sunday morning of Nisan 16th (Matt 28:1; Mk 16:1; Lu 24:1; Jn 20:1)

Therefore, Jesus was dead and in the tomb for at least a period of time on Friday Nisan 14, was still in the tomb during the course of the whole day of Nisan 15, and spent the nighttime hours of Nisan 16 in the tomb.

- Now after the Sabbath, toward the dawn of the first day of the week, Mary Magdalene and the other Mary went to see the tomb. (Matt 28:1)

- When the Sabbath was past, Mary Magdalene, Mary the mother of James, and Salome bought spices, so that they might go and anoint him. (Mk 16:1)

- But on the first day of the week, at early dawn, they went to the tomb, taking the spices they had prepared. (Lu 24:1)

- Now on the first day of the week Mary Magdalene came to the tomb early, while it was still dark, and saw that the stone had been taken away from the tomb. (Jn 20:1)

Certain women came to the tomb on Sunday morning, it was still dark, he had already been resurrected. Thus, Jesus had been in the tomb for parts of three days.

A Wrong Conception of the Bible

Many think that when we say the Bible is the Word of God, of divine origin and authority, we mean that God is the speaker in every utterance it contains; but this is not what is meant at all. Oftentimes, it simply records what others say, i.e., what good men say, what bad men say, what inspired men say, what uninspired men say, what angels and demons say, and even what the devil says. The record of what they said is from God and absolutely true, but what those other persons are recorded as saying may be true or may not be true. It is true that they said it, but what they said may not be true.

For example, the devil is recorded in Genesis 3:4 as saying, "You will not surely die." It is true that the devil said it, but what the devil said is not true, but an infamous lie that shipwrecked our race. That the devil said it is God's Word, but what the devil said is not God's word but the devil's word. It is God's Word that this was the devil's word.

Very many careless readers of the Bible do not notice who is talking, God, good men, bad men, inspired men, uninspired men, angels or devil. They will tear a verse right out of its context regardless of the speaker and say, "There, God said that." However, God said nothing of the kind. God's Word says that the devil said it or a bad man said it or a good man said it or an inspired man said it, or an uninspired man said it, or an angel said it. What God says is true, namely, that the devil said it, or a bad man, or a good man, or an inspired man, or an uninspired man, or an angel. However, what they said may or may not be true.

It is very common to hear men quote what Eliphaz, Bildad or Zophar said to Job as if it were necessarily

God's own words because it is recorded in the Bible, in spite of the fact that God disavowed their teaching and said to them, "you have not spoken of me what is right" (Job 42:7). It is true that these men said the thing that God records them as saying, but often they gave the truth a twist and said what is not right. A very large share of our difficulties thus arises from not noticing who is speaking. The Bible always tells us, and we should always note it. Below, under the subheadings of "the Case of Job" and "The Comforters" Andrews demonstrates how the erroneous interpretations come about.

The Case of Job

What we have covered thus far will help us understand one of the more complex books of the Bible, the book of Job.

Job was a "blameless and upright man, who fears God and turns away from evil." Job was living the happy life; he had seven sons and the daughters. He was a wealthy landowner. "He possessed 7,000 sheep, 3,000 camels, 500 yoke of oxen, and 500 female donkeys, and very many servants, so that this man was the greatest of all the people of the east." (1:3) Even so, he is not a materialistic person; he was simply following a proverb like the above, 'if you work hard, your efforts will be blessed.'

Job 1:13-19; 2:7-8 English Standard Version (ESV)

[13]Now there was a day when his sons and daughters were eating and drinking wine in their oldest brother's house, [14]and there came a messenger to Job and said, "The oxen were plowing and the donkeys feeding beside them, [15]and the Sabeans fell upon them and took them and struck down the servants with the edge of the sword,

and I alone have escaped to tell you." [16]While he was yet speaking, there came another and said, "The fire of God fell from heaven and burned up the sheep and the servants and consumed them, and I alone have escaped to tell you." [17]While he was yet speaking, there came another and said, "The Chaldeans formed three groups and made a raid on the camels and took them and struck down the servants with the edge of the sword, and I alone have escaped to tell you." [18]While he was yet speaking, there came another and said, "Your sons and daughters were eating and drinking wine in their oldest brother's house, [19]and behold, a great wind came across the wilderness and struck the four corners of the house, and it fell upon the young people, and they are dead, and I alone have escaped to tell you." [2:7]So Satan went out from the presence of the LORD and struck Job with loathsome sores from the sole of his foot to the crown of his head. [8]And he took a piece of broken pottery with which to scrape himself while he sat in the ashes.

The Comforters

Job 4:7-8 English Standard Version (ESV)

[7]"Remember: who that was innocent ever perished? Or where were the upright cut off? [8]As I have seen, those who plow iniquity and sow trouble reap the same.

Eliphaz in an attempt at dealing with Job's atrocities assumes Job's tragedies are a result of his own actions. Eliphaz has reasoned wrong by taking a proverb and making it an absolute. In essence, he asks Job, 'do those that are innocent die? When have those that live a righteous life been destroyed?' Eliphaz goes on by saying, 'my experience suggests that it is those who are doing wrong and entertain bad that will get back what they

64

gave out.' In other words, Eliphaz is assuming that only the wicked reap bad times.

Job 5:15 English Standard Version (ESV)

[15]But he saves the needy from the sword of their mouth and from the hand of the mighty.

Eliphaz again assumes that Job is at fault. Eliphaz is assuming that it was Job's great riches, which were ill gotten, and this is why he is suffering. Is Eliphaz's statement wrong in and of itself? No, God does rescue the poor from the oppressive, by their following his counsel on the right way to live. However, this is no absolute; saying all who live by God's will and purposes will never be mistreated. Moreover, the whole idea is misplaced, in that maybe Job is the rich oppressor and this is his punishment from God.

Job 8:3-6 English Standard Version (ESV)

[3]Does God pervert justice? Or does the Almighty pervert the right? [4]If your children have sinned against him, he has delivered them into the hand of their transgression.[5]If you will seek God and plead with the Almighty for mercy, [6]if you are pure and upright, surely then he will rouse himself for you and restore your rightful habitation.

Bildad too is stating true statements, but in absolute terms that are misplaced when it comes to Job, or anyone. Certainly, God does not pervert justice. Therefore, Bildad is right on that, but his application and understanding is what is twisted, as he assumes that children died because they had sinned, and justice was being meted out to them. Again, in verse 5-6, we have a true thought, in that if one is in an impure state, and turns to God with pleadings, he will restore them.

65

However, in verses 5-6, Bildad is assuming that Job is unrighteous, because he sees that proverb as an absolute.

As can be seen from the above, one must be aware that proverbs are not absolutes, but are general truths. True enough, there are likely a couple of exceptions to this rule, but that would not negate this rule, and approach of correct interpretation of proverbs.

In the Psalms, we have sometimes, what God said to man and that is always true; but on the other hand, we often have what man said to God, and that may or may not be true. Sometimes, and far oftener than most of us see, it is the voice of the speaker's personal vengeance or despair. This vengeance may be and often is prophetic, but it may be the wronged man committing his cause to Him to whom vengeance belongs (Romans 12:19), and we are not obliged to defend all that he said. In the Psalms, we have even a record of what the fool said, "There is no God" (Psalm 14:1). Now it is true that the fool said it, but the fool lied when he said it. It is God's Word that the fool said it, but what God reports the fool as saying is not God's own word at all but the fool's own word.

Therefore, in studying our Bible, if God is the speaker we must believe what He says. If an inspired man is the speaker, we must believe what he says. If an uninspired man is the speaker, we must judge for ourselves, it is perhaps true, perhaps false. If it is the devil who is speaking, we do well to remember that he was a liar from the beginning; but even the devil may tell the truth sometimes.

The Language in Which the Bible was Written

The Bible is a book of all ages and for all kinds of people, and therefore it was written in the language that continues the same and is understood by all, the language of the common people and of appearances. It was not written in the terminology of science.

Thus, for example, what occurred at the Battle of Gibeon (Joshua 10:12–14) was described in the way it appeared to those who saw it, and the way in which it would be understood by those who read about it. There is no talk about the refraction of the sun's rays, and so forth, but the sun is said to have "*stood still*" (or tarried) in the midst of heaven. It is one of the perfections of the Bible that it was not written in the terminology of modern science. If it had been, it would never have been understood until the present day, and even now it would be understood only by a few. Furthermore, as science and its terminology are constantly changing, the Bible if written in the terminology of the science of today would be out of date in a few years; but being written in just the language chosen, it has proved the Book for all ages, all lands and all conditions of men.

Other difficulties from the language in which the Bible was written arise from the fact that large portions of the Bible are poetical and are written in the language of poetry, the language of feeling, passion, imagination and figure. Now if a man is hopelessly matter-of-fact, he will inevitably find difficulties with these poetical portions of the inspired Word.

For example, in Psalm 18 we have a marvelous description of a thunderstorm, but let the dull, matter-of-fact fellow get hold of that, for example, verse 8: "Smoke went up from his nostrils, and devouring fire from his mouth; glowing coals flamed forth from him," and he will be head over heels in difficulty at once. However, the trouble is not with the Bible, but with his own stupid, thickheaded plainness.

Our Defective Knowledge of the History, Geography and Usages of Bible Times

For example, in Acts 13:7 Luke speaks of "the deputy" (more accurately "the proconsul," see English Standard Version) of Cyprus. Roman provinces were of two classes, imperial and senatorial. The ruler of the imperial provinces was called a propraetor, of a senatorial province a proconsul. Up to a comparatively recent date, according to the best information we had, Cyprus was an imperial province and therefore its ruler would be a propraetor, but Luke calls him a proconsul. This certainly seemed like a clear case of error on Luke's part, and even the conservative commentators felt forced to admit that Luke was in slight error, and the destructive critics were delighted to find this "mistake." Further and more thorough investigation has brought to light the fact that just at the time of which Luke wrote the senate had made an exchange with the emperor whereby Cyprus had become a senatorial province, and therefore its ruler was a proconsul. Luke was right after all, and the literary critics were themselves in error.

Repeatedly further researches and discoveries, geographical, historical and archaeological, have vindicated the Bible and put to shame its critics. For example, the book of Daniel has naturally been one of the books that unbelievers and destructive critics have most hated. One of their strongest arguments against its authenticity and truthfulness was that such a person as Belshazzar was unknown to history, that all historians agreed that Nabonidus was the last king of Babylon, and that he was absent from the city when it was captured. Therefore, Belshazzar must be a purely mythical character, and the whole story legendary and not historical. Their argument seemed very strong. In fact, it seemed unanswerable. However, Sir H. Rawlinson discovered at Mugheir and other Chaldean sites clay cylinders on which Belshazzar (Belsaruzar) is named by Nabonidus as his eldest son. Doubtless he reigned as regent in the city during his father's absence, an indication of which we have in his proposal to make Daniel third ruler in the kingdom (Daniel 5:16). He himself being second ruler in the kingdom, Daniel would be next to him. So the Bible was vindicated again.

The critics asserted most positively that Moses could not have written the Pentateuch because writing was unknown in his day. However, recent discoveries have proved beyond a question that writing far antedates the time of Moses. So the critics have been compelled to give up their argument, though they have had the bad grace to hold on stubbornly to their conclusion.

The Ignorance of Conditions under Which Books Were Written and Commands Given

For example, to one ignorant of the conditions, God's commands to Israel as to the extermination of the Canaanites seem cruel and horrible. However, when one understands the moral condition to which these nations had sunk, the utter hopelessness of reclaiming them and the weakness of the Israelites themselves, their extermination seems to have been an act of mercy to all succeeding generations and to themselves.

The Many-Sidedness of the Bible

The broadest-minded man is one-sided, but the truth is many-sided, and the Bible is all-sided. Therefore, to our narrow thought one part of the Bible seems to contradict another.

For example, religious men as a rule are either Calvinistic or Arminian in their mental makeup. In addition, some portions of the Bible are decidedly Calvinistic and present great difficulties to the Arminian type of mind, while other portions are decidedly Arminian and present difficulties to the Calvinistic type of mind. However, both sides are true. Many men in our day are broad-minded enough to be able to grasp at the same time the Calvinistic side of the truth and the Arminian side of the truth; but some are not, so the Bible perplexes, puzzles and bewilders them. The trouble is not with the Bible, but with their own lack of capacity for comprehensive thought.

Expansion: These schools of doctrinal positions are initially established religious leaders and their followers, such as John Calvin and Jacob Arminius. There are even more, such as the Lutheran, from Martin Luther, The Wesleyan, from John Wesley, and the Mennonites, from Menno Simons, and Society of Friends (Quakers) under George Fox. Actually, I would disagree with Torrey here, I believe that he should have used his earlier point of argument, it boils down to the truth of the Bible as being absolute, but man may misinterpret that truth. Therefore, it will lay concealed until discovered. This misinterpretation does not refute the infallibility or inerrancy of Scripture. Actually, doctrine plays no part in inerrancy of Scripture. Whether one believes the earth was created in six literal 24-hour days, or six creative periods called days, has no impact on the doctrine of inerrancy. The Bible is inerrant and one of those interpretations is wrong and the other is correct. This has to do with the person interpreting the Bible, not the inerrancy of the Bible. **Edward D. Andrews**

Therefore, Paul seems to contradict James, and James seems sometimes to contradict Paul; and what Paul says in one place seems to contradict what he says in another place. However, the whole trouble is that our narrow minds cannot take in God's large truth.

The Bible has to do with the Infinite, and our Minds are Finite

It is necessarily difficult to put the facts of infinite being into the limited capacity of our finite intelligence, just as it is difficult to put the ocean into a pint cup. To this class of difficulties belong those connected with the Bible doctrines of the Trinity and of the divine-human nature of Christ. To those who forget that God is infinite, the doctrine of the Trinity seems like the mathematical monstrosity of making one equal three. However, when one bears in mind that the doctrine of the Trinity is an attempt to put into forms of finite thought the facts of infinite being, and into material forms of expression the facts of the spirit, the difficulties vanish. The simplicity of the Unitarian conception of God arises from its shallowness.

The Dullness of our Spiritual Perception

The man who is farthest advanced spiritually is still so immature that he cannot expect to see everything yet as an absolutely holy God sees it, unless he takes it upon simple faith in Him. To this class of difficulties belong those connected with the Bible doctrine of eternal punishment. It often seems to us as if this doctrine cannot be true, must not be true, but the whole difficulty arises from the fact that we are still so blind spiritually that we have no adequate conception of the awfulness of sin, and especially of the awfulness of the sin of rejecting the infinitely glorious Son of God. However, when we become so holy, so like God, that we see the enormity of sin as He sees it, we shall have no difficulty with the doctrine of eternal punishment.

Expansion: Torrey is like many other Calvinist or Lutheran minded individuals, he wishes to follow the evidence, but instead, desires to call those, who do not find this doctrine Biblical, spiritually blind. I hope that even the most conservative reader can see that as dismissive. Without arguing the evidence, I will say that once again, the truth is biblical, and we must follow it objectively, and not allow theological bias to cloud our judgment. I am recommending that you read, WHAT DOES THE BIBLE REALLY SAY ABOUT HELLFIRE? Eternal Torment? Is Hellfire Just? Is Hellfire Part of Divine Justice? by Edward D. Andrews[18]

As we look back over the ten classes of difficulties, we see they all arise from our imperfection, and not from

---

[18]

http://www.christianpublishers.org/apps/webstore/products/show/5346167

the imperfection of the Bible. The Bible is perfect, but we, being imperfect, have difficulty with it. As we grow more and more into the perfection of God, our difficulties grow ever less and less, and so we are forced to conclude that when we become as perfect as God is, we shall have no more difficulties whatever with the Bible.

CHAPTER 3 Dealing With Bible Difficulties

By R. A. Torrey

Updated By Edward D. Andrews

Honestly

Whenever you find a difficulty in the Bible frankly, acknowledge it. Do not try to obscure it. Do not try to dodge it. Look it square in the face. Admit it frankly to whoever mentions it. If you cannot give a good, square, honest explanation, do not attempt any at all. Those, who in their zeal for the infallibility of the Bible have attempted explanations of difficulties that do not commend themselves to the honest, fair-minded man, have done untold harm. People have concluded that if these are the best explanations, then there are really no explanations at all, and the Bible instead of being helped has been injured by the unintelligent zeal of foolish friends. If you are not really convinced that the Bible is the Word of God, you can far better afford to wait for an honest solution of a difficulty than you can afford to attempt a solution that is evasive and unsatisfactory.

Humbly

Recognize the limitations of your own mind and knowledge, and do not for a moment imagine that there is no solution just because you have found none. There is, in all probability, a very simple solution, even when you can find no solution at all.

Determinedly

Make up your mind that you will find the solution if you can by any amount of study and hard thinking. The difficulties of the Bible are our heavenly Father's challenge to us to set our brains to work. Do not give up searching for a solution because you cannot find it in five minutes or ten minutes. Ponder over it and work over it for days if necessary. The work will be more beneficial than the solution does. There is a solution somewhere, and you will find it if you will only search for it long enough and hard enough.

Fearlessly

Do not be frightened when you find a difficulty, no matter how unanswerable or how insurmountable it appears at first sight. Thousands of men have encountered just such difficulties, and still the old Book has withstood the test of time, being the bestseller that will never be touched, in the untold billions of copies. The Bible that has stood eighteen centuries of rigid examination, and of incessant and awful assault, is not likely to go down before your discoveries or before the discharges of any modern critical guns. To one who is at all familiar with the history of critical attacks on the Bible, the confidence of those modern critics who think they are going to annihilate the Bible at last is simply amusing.

Patiently

Do not be discouraged because you do not solve every problem in a day. If some difficulty persistently defies your very best efforts at a solution, lay it aside for a while. Later it will likely be resolved, and you will wonder how you were ever perplexed by it.

Scripturally

If you find a difficulty in one part of the Bible, look for another scripture to throw light upon it and dissolve it. Nothing explains scripture like scripture. Repeatedly people have come to me with some difficulty in the Bible that had greatly staggered them, and asked for a solution. I have been able to give a solution by simply asking them to read some other chapter and verse, and the simple reading of that scripture has thrown such light upon the passage in question that all the mists have disappeared and the truth has shone as clear as day.

Prayerfully

It is simply wonderful how difficulties dissolve when one looks at them on his knees. Not only does God open our eyes in answer to prayer to behold wonderful things out of His law, but He also opens our eyes to look straight through a difficulty that seemed impenetrable before we prayed. One great reason why many modern Bible scholars have learned to be destructive critics is because they have forgotten how to pray.

CHAPTER 4 Some Bible Difficulties in the Book of Exodus

Exodus 1:15 How could two Hebrew midwives deliver the children of so many women?

When we look at Exodus 12:37 and Numbers chapters 1-4, there were about 600,000 men besides women and children, which would mean a total of about three million. This would mean that there must have been hundreds of thousands of women at the age to potentially have children. Pharaoh is said to have spoken to the midwives Shiphrah and Puah. How is it possible for these two midwives to deliver children for so many women?

It is like any profession, in which a leader would deal with those that he had placed in charge of the midwives. The Egyptian society was one of the more organized. The Pharaohs had someone serving in the position of oversight in almost every conceivable profession. Of course, the Pharaoh would not personally assign people to oversight positions, he would have an administer of affairs, the position that Joseph served at while he was in Egypt. (Gen 41:37-44, 46) The administer of affairs would likely have had a person over the nation of Israel, who was responsible to assign the Hebrews professions and report to him.

Exodus 1:15 How could God bless Hebrew midwives for defying the Pharaoh's decree?

The Hebrew women Shiphrah and Puah, who likely were the heads of the midwife profession, over the other midwives, did not carry out king of Egypt's order. They apparently did not instruct the midwives under them as ordered. The result was: "The people multiplied and grew very strong." Romans 13:1 says that we are commanded to "be subject to the governing authorities. For there is no authority except from God, and those that exist have been instituted by God."

While the above is true, the is a rule that was applicable for Christians, and was not in existence at the time of the midwives dealing with Pharaoh. Even so, no Scripture is an island. They must be understood in conjunction with the Bible as a whole. Are we to just blindly follow anything that a government requires, based on Roman 13:1. No. Acts 5:29 gives us a balanced principle, "But Peter and the apostles answered, 'We must obey God rather than men.'" If the government is asking a servant of God to do anything that would cause him or her to violate God's laws, the servant should not obey. Notice the response of the midwives, "But **the midwives feared God** and did not do as the king of Egypt commanded them, but let the male children live." (Ex 1:17)

We might understand that they wanted to obey God rather than the Egyptian King, but what of their lying?

Exodus 1:18-19 English Standard Version (ESV)

[18] So the king of Egypt called the midwives and said to them, "Why have you done this, and let the male children live?" [19] The midwives said to Pharaoh, "Because the Hebrew women are not like the Egyptian women, for they are vigorous and give birth before the midwife comes to them."

While malevolent lying is certainly condemned in the Bible, this does not mean that a person is under compulsion to disclose truthful information to people who are not entitled to it. We can see that the midwives were favored by Jehovah God for all of their actions, "And because the midwives feared God, he gave them families." (Ex 1:21)

Exodus 3:1 What kind of priest was Jethro?

In the days of Abraham, Isaac, Jacob, the patriarchal times [a culture in which men were the ones who lead the family, especially the oldest living male]. Jethro, Moses' father-in-law, a Kenite, was the patriarchal head of the Midianite tribe. The Midianites were actually related to the Israelites, as they were descendants of Keturah. Therefore, it is quite possible that they might have been familiar with the worship of Jehovah, the Israelite God. Genesis 25:1-2

Exodus 3:22 How could a God that is the epitome of love command the Israelites to plunder the Egyptians for their riches?

Exodus 3:22 English Standard Version (ESV)

[22] but each woman shall ask of her neighbor, and any woman who lives in her house, for silver and gold

jewelry, and for clothing. You shall put them on your sons and on your daughters. **So you shall plunder the Egyptians**."

We must look at the whole text, because the reality is that Jehovah had commanded the Israelites to "ask" their neighbor. To plunder is to gain or acquire something by superior strength, generally by force. By their asking them, they would not be plundering in the sense that we understand the English equivalent, but the result is the same as if they had. Also, it should be mentioned that the Hebrew here is used in a figurative sense, as this was a request, not a forceful taking, and they received what they had asked for. Of course, it is true that the Egyptians were motivated by the ten plagues that they had just experienced at the hands of the Israelite God.

However, to address the idea of whether a loving God, who was simply using force, to free his people from slavery, was now exploiting that fear for the riches of the land, this is not the case at all. What the Israelites received was long overdue. For centuries the Israelites had been abused as slaves, working in a physically, mentally, emotionally and spiritually abusive environment, for nothing more than barely enough food to exist, while the Pharaoh's treasure house grew. In a modern day perspective, we can just view it as the Israelites received their back pay.

Exodus 4:11 How is it that Jehovah "makes mute or deaf or sighted or blind?"

There have been times in Scripture, where Jehovah had the right to cause blindness and muteness. (Genesis 19:11; Luke 1:20-22, 62-64) Those are the only cases where he is directly responsible, and thus this text should not be understood as a saying that he is responsible for all such cases through human history. Of course, he is indirectly responsible for all cases, because he all imperfection to enter into humankind. Blindness and muteness are a result of inherited sin. (Job 14:4; Romans 5:12) However, the direct responsibility falls on the angel known as Satan the Devil, as well as Adam and Eve, when they rebelled in the Garden of Eden. (Gen 3:1-6) Thus, since God has permitted sin to enter into the world, he can speak of himself as making ones 'mute or deaf or sighted or blind.' His allowing sin to enter into humankind is another difficulty that has been discussed at Genesis 3:24.

Exodus 4:16 How was Moses to Be God to Aaron?

Moses represented Jehovah God to the Israelites, as well as any other people they came into contact with. Moses was given miraculous powers and authority by Jehovah God. Therefore, Aaron served as a representative of Moses, Like Moses had done for Jehovah. Elohim, the Hebrew word for God, means 'mighty one' or 'powerful one.' Moses was mighty and powerful as a result of the miraculous powers he was given. When Moses received his instruction to go before the older men of Israel or Pharaoh, he would give those same instructions to Aaron, who would then serve as his spokesman. (Ex 2:23; 4:10-17) Jehovah even spoke of Aaron as Moses' prophet at Exodus 7:1. Just as Moses was directed by Jehovah God, Aaron was directed by Moses. Finally, also at Exodus 7:1, we read, "Jehovah said to Moses, 'See, I have made thee as God to Pharaoh.'" In other words, Moses had far greater power than Pharaoh because his support came from Jehovah, while Pharaoh had his power and support from Satan.

Exodus 5:2 Who was the Exodus Pharaoh?

Genesis 15:13-16 Lexham English Bible (LEB)

[13] And he said to Abram, "[You must surely know] that your descendants shall be as aliens in a land [not their own]. And they shall serve them and they shall oppress them **four hundred years**. [14] And also that the nation which they serve I will judge. Then afterwards they shall go out with great possessions. [15] And as for you, you shall go to your ancestors in peace; you shall be buried in a good old age. [16] And the fourth generation shall return here, for the guilt of the Amorites [is not yet complete]."

The 400-year oppression had to await the promised seed. Shortly after God's statement about the 400 years of oppression, when Abraham was 86 years old (1932 B.C.E.), his Egyptian concubine gave birth to his son, Ishmael. However, it was 14 years later (1918 B.C.E.) that Sarah bore him a son, Isaac, and God chose this son as the one who would produce the coming promised seed. However, God's time had not yet come for giving Abraham or his seed the land of Canaan, and so they were, as foretold, 'strangers and exiles on the earth.'— Gen 16:15, 16; 21:2-5; Heb 11:13.

When did the 400 years of oppression begin, and when did it end? While Jewish tradition begins the 400 years at the birth of Isaac, the more accurate biblical evidence come when Isaac is 5 years old and Ishmael is 19, as the start of the oppression. It was "at that time he who was born according to the flesh [Ishmael] persecuted him who was born according to the Spirit [Isaac]." (Gal 4:29) Ishmael, who was part Egyptian, in distrust and detestation, began "mocking." (YLT; RSV, ftn)[19] at Isaac, the young child, this amounting to much more than a mere children's quarrel. (Gen 21:9) This incident occurred in 1913 B.C.E. Therefore, the 400-year period of oppression began in 1913 B.C.E. and ended at the exodus of 1513 B.C.E.

The pharaohs, who are named in the Bible are Shishak, So, Tirhakah, Nechoh, and Hophra. Some have considered Zerah the Cushite as a ruler of Egypt. Other pharaohs are left nameless. Because of the confused state of Egyptian chronology it is not probable to connect these pharaohs to those of secular history with confidence. These nameless pharaohs include: The one who tried to take Sarah (Gen 12:15-20); the pharaoh who placed Joseph in authority (Gen 41:39-46); the pharaoh (or pharaohs) of the period of oppression of the Israelites prior to Moses' return from Midian (Ex chaps 1, 2); the pharaoh ruling during the Ten Plagues and at the time of the Exodus (Ex 5-14); the pharaoh who gave refuge to Hadad of Edom in David's time (1Ki 11:18-22); the father of the Egyptian wife of Solomon (1Ki 3:1); and the pharaoh who struck down Gaza during the time of the prophet Jeremiah (Jer 47:1).

---

[19] Young's Literal Translation and the Revised Standard Version

Exodus 6:3 In what way had God's name not been made known to Abraham, Isaac, and Jacob?

Exodus 3:13 American Standard Version (ASV)

¹³ And Moses said to God, Behold, when I come unto the children of Israel, and shall say unto them, The God of your fathers hath sent me unto you; and they shall say to me, <u>What is his name? What shall I say to them?</u>

Exodus 6:3 American Standard Version (ASV)

³ and I appeared to Abraham, to Isaac, and to Jacob, as God Almighty; <u>but by my name Jehovah I was not known to them.</u>

How can Exodus 3:13 and 6:13 be accurate, because the patriarchs knew used the divine name Jehovah? . . .

Genesis 2:4 American Standard Version (ASV)

⁴ These are the generations of the heavens and of the earth when they were created, in the day that <u>Jehovah God</u> made earth and heaven. (see also 5, 7, 8-9, and 15)

As well as . . .

Genesis 4:1 American Standard Version (ASV)

¹ And the man knew Eve his wife; and she conceived, and bare Cain, and said, I have gotten a man <u>with the help of Jehovah</u>. (see also 3, 4, 6, and 9)

Jehovah chose his own name, one rich in meaning. "Jehovah" literally means "He Causes to Become." The divine name certainly was not new. The divine name was known and used clear back in the beginning with Adam and Eve. The Patriarchs also knew and used the divine name, as well as received promises from Jehovah. However, keeping in mind the meaning of God's name, "He Causes to Become," the patriarchs did not know Jehovah in an experiential way, as the one that would cause the promises to be fulfilled. (Genesis 12:1, 2; 15:7, 13-16; 26:24; 28:10-15.) They knew the promises, but Moses was about to experience the results. No matter what was to get in the way of Moses and the Israelites, no matter the difficulties they faced, Jehovah was going to become whatever they needed, to deliver them from slavery and into the Promised Land.

Exodus 6:9 Did the Israelites listen to Moses, or did they ignore his words?

Exodus 4:31 American Standard Version (ASV)

³¹ And the people believed: and when they heard that Jehovah had visited the children of Israel, and that he had seen their affliction, then they bowed their heads and worshipped.

Exodus 6:9 American Standard Version (ASV)

⁹ And Moses spoke so to the children of Israel: but they did not listen to Moses for anguish of spirit, and for cruel bondage.

How can both of the above texts be true? Did the children of Israel listen to Moses or not? Obviously, they were in an emotional state, having served as slaves their entire lives, and to hear that their God, Jehovah was going to bring about their release was very overwhelming. Therefore, they were initially excited by such news, and listened to Moses every word. However, when this release was not immediate, they became disheartened, and annoyed with Moses, choosing to no longer listen to him.

Exodus 6:10-13 Did Moses receive his call in Egypt or Midian?

Exodus 3:10 English Standard Version (ESV)

[10] Come, I will send you to Pharaoh that you may bring my people, the children of Israel, out of Egypt."

Exodus 4:19 American Standard Version (ASV)

[19] And Jehovah said to Moses in Midian, Go, return into Egypt; for all the men are dead that sought your life.

Exodus 6:10-11 American Standard Version (ASV)

[10] And Jehovah spoke to Moses, saying, [11] Go in, speak to Pharaoh king of Egypt, that he let the children of Israel go out of his land.

Initially, Moses was commissioned in Egypt (ch 3-4). However, Pharaoh rejected Moses (ch 5), and Moses himself was reluctant to take on the task (4:1, 10). Therefore, it became necessary for God to reassure Moses and restate his call in Exodus 6.

Exodus 6:16-20 How is it possible that the Israelites were in Egypt for 430 years, when there were only three generations between Levi and Moses?

The period from Abraham's move to Canaan until Jacob's going down into Egypt was 215 years. This figure is arrived at from the following facts: 25 years between

Abraham's departure from Haran to the birth of Isaac (Gen 12:4; 21:5); from then to the birth of Jacob was 60 years (Gen 25:26); and Jacob was 130 at the time of his entry into Egypt (Gen 47:9); thus giving a total of 215 years (from 1943 to 1728 B.C.E.). This means that an equal period of 215 years was thereafter spent by the Israelites in Egypt (from 1728 to 1513 B.C.E.).

Again, we must keep in mind that Jehovah told Abraham that in the fourth generation his descendants would return to Canaan. (Gen 15:16) In the entire 430 years from the time when the Abrahamic covenant took effect to the Exodus there were more than four generations, even bearing in mind the long life spans that they enjoyed during that time, according to the record. However, it was only 215 years that the Israelites were in fact, in Egypt. The 'four generations' following their entering Egypt can be calculated in this way, using as an example just one tribe of Israel, the tribe of Levi: (1) Levi, (2) Kohath, (3) Amram, and (4) Moses.—Ex 6:16, 18, 20.

Exodus 6:26-27 How is it possible that Moses wrote this when it speaks of him in third person?

Exodus 6:26-27 English Standard Version (ESV)

[26] **These are** the Aaron and Moses to whom the Lord said: "Bring out the people of Israel from the land of Egypt by their hosts." 27 It was **they** who spoke to Pharaoh king of Egypt about bringing out the people of Israel from Egypt, this Moses and this Aaron.

We must consider the context of the account, and that means going back to verse 14, which is a historical account of the genealogies of Moses and Aaron's ancestors. The customary way of writing, would then require that the writer refer to himself in third person, if he is referenced. This is the common practice throughout history. The record needed to be clear as to the genealogy of the one whom God had chosen to bring Israel out of slavery of Egypt, for future generations of Hebrews. This would have not been quite the case with "It was Aaron and I to whom Jehovah said" or "Aaron and I were the ones speaking to Pharaoh."

Exodus 7:1 How was Moses made "God to Pharaoh"?

Exodus 7:1 American Standard Version (ASV)

[1] And Jehovah said to Moses, See, I have made you as **God to Pharaoh**; and Aaron your brother shall be thy prophet.

The title *elohim* [God, god] draws attention to strength, might, power, and Jehovah God gave Moses divine power and authority over Pharaoh. Therefore, he had no reason to fear that Egyptian king. In other words, Moses had far greater power than Pharaoh did because his support came from Jehovah, while Pharaoh had his power and support from Satan.

Exodus 7:11 How could the wise men and sorcerers of Pharaoh Perform the same feats of power that God did through Moses?

Puzzled by this miracle, Pharaoh summoned his wise men and sorcerers. With the help of demon powers, these men were able to do something similar with their own rods. You can see from Revelation 16:14 below that Satan and his demonic spirit creatures have the power, because they are creatures above mankind in strength and power, to perform counterfeit miracles, in an effort to deceive.

Revelation 16:14 Lexham English Bible (LEB)

[14] For they are the spirits of demons performing signs that go out to the kings of the whole inhabited world, to gather them for the battle of the great day of God the All-Powerful.

Exodus 7:19-20 How could the Israelites escape this plague when it affected the whole of Egypt?

Some commentators as well as other Bible difficulty books have tried to argue, "the Hebrew language the normal word for all is not necessarily absolute."[20] In other words, not all of the water of Egypt was affected. (See Exodus 9:25; 10:5.) However, there is another option that agrees with the facts. Exodus 7:24 says: "And all the Egyptians dug along the Nile for water to drink, for they could not drink the water of the Nile." Therefore, they still had access to unaffected water, by digging wells around the Nile. Moreover, this likely where the Egyptian wise men and sorcerers were able to get their waters to repeat the same miracle of turning water into blood, which discouraged Pharaoh from releasing the Hebrews.

---

[20] Thomas Howe; Norman L. Geisler. Big Book of Bible Difficulties, The: Clear and Concise Answers from Genesis to Revelation (Kindle Locations 900-901). Kindle Edition.

Exodus 8:26-27 Why did Moses say that Israel's sacrifices would be "an abomination to the Egyptians"?

Many different animals were venerated in Egypt. The reference of sacrifices therefore supplied force and persuasion to Moses' resolve that Israel be permitted to go away to sacrifice to Jehovah.

Exodus 9:6, 19-21 If all the livestock of the Egyptians died; then, how is that some survived?

In verse 6 of chapter nine, we are told that "all the livestock of the Egyptians died" in the **fifth plague**. However, verse 19 of the same chapter instructs them concerning the **eighth plague**, to "get your livestock and all that you have in the field into safe shelter." If **all** the livestock died in the fifth plague, how could there be any left for the eighth plague?

First, it should be mentioned that, in both the Old and New Testament, the original language words for "all" is commonly used as hyperbole, an exaggeration to make a point, and seldom means a literal everything, but rather the vast majority. Second, the plague was limited to the livestock "in the field" (vs. 3), not what may have been in stalls.

Exodus 11:33 How Could Moses praise himself and still be considered meek?

First, it is obvious that Moses did not write every word of the Pentateuch. Why? The section that relates his death would be something that Joshua could have added after Moses' death. (Deuteronomy 34:1–8) In addition, to the critic, it would hardly seem very meek to pen these words about yourself: "Now the man Moses was very meek, more than all people who were on the face of the earth." (Numbers 12:3, ESV) Nevertheless, consider that Jesus said of himself: "I am gentle and lowly in heart" (Matthew 11:29, ESV), which no one would fault Jesus with as though he were boasting. Both Moses and Jesus were simply stating a fact. The amount of possible material that may have been added by Joshua, another inspired writer is next to nothing, and does not negate Moses' authorship.

Exodus 12:29 Who were actually the firstborn?

The firstborn would not include females. (Numbers 3:40-51) This is obvious from the fact that later, when an exchange was made by giving the Levites over to Jehovah, only the males were counted. (Numbers 3:40-51) Pharaoh, himself would have been a firstborn, yet he was not killed. The reason being, he had his own household (Ex 12:12). It was not to be the family head but the firstborn son of the household, who died as a result of the tenth plague.

Some would argue that because of the stamen in verse 30 "for there was not a house where someone was not dead," that there had to be daughters involved as well. Well, we need not take this statement as an absolute, but more as hyperbole, emphasizing and highlighting the extent and reach of the justice. Moreover, this applied to the whole household, which would include all people under the patriarchal head, even grandchildren.

Exodus 12:29 How are we to understand that God, who is the epitome of love, could slay every firstborn in Egypt?

Exodus 12:29-30 English Standard Version (ESV)

²⁹ At midnight the Lord struck down all the firstborn in the land of Egypt, from the firstborn of Pharaoh who sat on his throne to the firstborn of the captive who was in the dungeon, and all the firstborn of the livestock. ³⁰ And Pharaoh rose up in the night, he and all his servants and all the Egyptians. And there was a great cry in Egypt, for there was not a house where someone was not dead.

When we consider that the Egyptian people had no control over Pharaoh's decision to not let Israel go, how are we to understand that God, could slay every firstborn in Egypt, who is the epitome of love? Part of the answer lies only a few verses away, 12:38, which states that "And a mixed multitude [of Egyptians] went up also with them; and flocks, and herds, even very much cattle."

The firstborn of the Egyptians, who, after the first nine plagues decided that they were with the only true God, Jehovah, were not slayed. Therefore, we cannot say that the other Egyptians were not responsible, because they still stubbornly chose to cling to Pharaoh as their god. Like others, at any given time, every Egyptian could have avoided the plagues, by siding with Moses' God. Moreover, those who sided with Pharaoh could have changed his mind on the issue by having a complete uprising, and causing him to alter his decision, or having him removed. Notice that after the tenth Plague, the Egyptians chose to involve themselves, whereas they had not before.

Exodus 12:33 English Standard Version (ESV)

[33] The Egyptians were urgent with the people to send them out of the land in haste.

There is nothing prior to this point that shows the Egyptians making it know to Pharaoh that they wanted the Israelites out of the land. They were likely more concerned with losing their slaves. Therefore, they are not as innocent as some would presume. The punishment was for the horrendous treatment of God's people, by the whole of Egypt, not just the Pharaoh and his household. Below is just one incident of the Egyptian effort to keep the Israelites powerless.

Exodus 1:16, 22 English Standard Version (ESV)

[16] "When you serve as midwife to the Hebrew women and see them on the birthstool, if it is a son, you shall kill him, but if it is a daughter, she shall live." [22] Then Pharaoh commanded all his people, "Every son that is born to the Hebrews you shall cast into the Nile, but you shall let every daughter live."

Exodus 12:14 By what internal evidence does the Bible fix the date of Israel's Exodus from Egypt?

Exodus 12:40-41 New American Standard Bible (NASB)

[40] Now the time[a] that the sons of Israel lived in Egypt was four hundred and thirty years. [41] And at the end of four hundred and thirty years, to the very day, all the hosts of the Lord went out from the land of Egypt.

Footnotes:

a. Exodus 12:40 Or *of the sons of Israel who dwelt*

In looking at the expression "Who dwelt," the Hebrew verb is plural, and the relative pronoun 'asher´, 'who,' can apply to the 'sons of Israel' as opposed to the 'dwelling.' The Greek Septuagint renders 12:40, "But the dwelling of the sons of Israel which they dwelt **in the land of Egypt and in the land of Canaan** [was] four hundred and thirty years long." (Bold mine) In addition, the Samaritan *Pentateuch* reads, ". . . in the land of Canaan and in the land of Egypt." The first century Jewish Historian Josephus wrote in *Jewish Antiquities*, "They left Egypt in the month of Xanthicus, on the fifteenth day of the lunar month; four hundred and thirty years after our forefather Abraham came into Canaan, but two hundred and fifteen years only after Jacob removed into Egypt."[21] It is all too clear that the 430-year period encompasses 215 years from the time Abraham enters Canaan, and 215 years in Egypt, starting from the time Jacob moves to Egypt. We now turn to the Apostle Paul, who also shows that this 430-year period began when Abraham crossed the Euphrates and entered into the Promise Land, validating the Abrahamic covenant and ended at the Israelites Exodus out of Egypt.

Galatians 3:16-18 New American Standard Bible (NASB)

[16] Now the promises were spoken to Abraham and to his seed. He does not say, "And to seeds," as *referring* to many, but *rather* to one, "And to your seed," that is, Christ. [17] What I am saying is this: the Law, which came four hundred and thirty years later [same year as the Exodus], does not invalidate [the Abrahamic] covenant previously ratified by God, so as to nullify the

---

[21] Flavius Josephus and William Whiston, *The Works of Josephus: Complete and Unabridged* (Peabody: Hendrickson, 1987).

promise. [18] For if the inheritance is based on law, it is no longer based on a promise; but God has granted it to Abraham by means of a promise.

Now, we simply measure chronologically from the time that Abraham entered the Land of Canaan, validating, until the Israelite exodus from Egypt.

- **Genesis 12:4-5** ESV) [4] ... Abram was **seventy-five years old** when he departed from Haran. (At this time the Abrahamic covenant goes into effect.)

- **Genesis 21:5** (ESV) [5] Abraham was a hundred years old when his son Isaac was born to him. (**25 years**)

- **Genesis 25:26** (ESV) [26] ... Isaac was **sixty years old** when she bore them. (**60 years**)

- **Genesis 47:9** (ESV) [9] And Jacob said to Pharaoh, "The days of the years of my sojourning are **130 years** ..."

- Total (215 years) in the land of Canaan

- The other 215 years were spent in Egypt.

Exodus 14:21-29 How is it that 2-3 million people were able to cross the Red Sea in a mere 24 hours?

We need not always assume the most difficult setting when we are presented with a difficulty. First, the text is not absolute in the it was just that one day. Exodus 14:21 states that, "Moses stretched out his hand over the sea; and Jehovah caused the sea to go back by a strong east wind all the night, and made the sea dry land, and the waters were divided." Now, verse 22 of chapter 14 does seem to give the reader the impression that they crossed the next morning, "and the children of Israel went into the midst of the sea upon the dry ground: and the waters were a wall unto them on their right hand, and on their left." Thereafter, verse 24 states, "and it came to pass in the morning watch, that Jehovah looked forth upon the army of the Egyptians through the pillar of fire and of cloud, and threw the Egyptian army into a panic." Then, verse 26 states, "Then Jehovah said to Moses, 'Stretch out your hand over the sea, that the water may come back upon the Egyptians, upon their chariots, and upon their horsemen.'" The account does not offer an indication of time, so there is no need to assume that the Israelites crossed in that morning alone.

Second, we need not assume that they crossed in some single file line, even though much artwork suggest such. The crossing could have been 1-3 miles wide. Therefore, the Israelites could have crossed in as little as 3-6 hours. We can picture an organized type army march, with no panic, or trampling of people. The Israelites had entered the sea bed and were far into the crossing, when Jehovah moved the cloud that had been blocking them off from the Egyptians, to the front, allowing the Egyptians to see them. The size of the opening is highlighted here, because the very large Egyptian army entered the sea bed, bent on recapturing their slaves. Then, we are told that "in the morning watch [about **2:00 a.m. to 6:00 a.m.**], that Jehovah looked forth upon the army of the Egyptians through the pillar of fire and of cloud, and threw the Egyptian army into a panic." (14:24)

By the time of sunrise, the Israelites, were safely on the eastern side of the Red Sea. Then, 'Moses stretched out his hand over the sea, so that the water may come back upon the Egyptians, upon their chariots, and upon their horsemen.' (14:26) At this "the sea returned to its normal course when the morning appeared. And as the Egyptians fled into it, Jehovah threw the Egyptians into the midst of the sea." (14:27) Here again, we see another indicator of a wide opening into the Red Sea, because if it had been a narrow opening, there would be no need to mention any attempt at fleeing the sea caving in on them, because it would have been instantaneous.

The Bible critics argue that the Hebrew *yamsuph* ("Red Sea") literally means "sea of rushes, or, reeds, bulrushes," and as a result the Israelites crossed, not the arm of the Red Sea known as the Gulf of Suez, but a sea of reeds, a swampy place such as the Bitter Lakes region. However, the Septuagint renders *yamsuph* with the Greek *erythra thalassa*, meaning, literally, "Red Sea." Moreover, both Luke (quoting Stephen in Acts) and the Apostle Paul use this same Greek word in their referring to the Exodus account.—Ac 7:36; Heb. 11:29.

Additionally, the account would have been nothing special if they crossed in a marsh, not to mention the impossibility of how the Egyptian army could have been covered by the Red Sea. (Heb. 11:29; Ex 15:5) Thus, it is evident that such an overwhelming inundation would be impossible in a marsh. Besides, in a shallow marsh dead bodies would not wash up on the seashore, as actually took place, so that "Israel saw the Egyptians dead on the seashore." (Ex 14:22-31) Moses and Joshua wrote of this breathtaking miracle, but it was Paul, who said the Israelites had been baptized into Moses by way of the cloud and the Red Sea. This means that the waters that were held up on both sides had to be above their heads, with the cloud above them. (1 Co 10:1, 2)

Exodus 20:5a Why is Almighty God Jealous?

Jehovah defines himself as "a jealous God."[22] (Ex 20:5; De 4:24; 5:9; 6:15) He also says: "for thou shall worship no other god: for Jehovah, whose name is Jealous, is a jealous God." (Ex 34:14, ASV) What would the Almighty God need to be jealous of and how are we to understand that Jealousy? He certainly does not need to be envious of any other, as they are created being by him. He is the owner of everything, and gives generously to all who love him, so it is no selfishly jealous, an imperfect human characteristic. His jealousy is a zeal or an enthusiastic passion for his holy name (personal name and reputation), to which he himself has said: "Therefore thus says the Lord Jehovah: Now will I bring back the captivity of Jacob, and have mercy upon the whole house of Israel; and I will be jealous for my holy name. Eze 39:25

Exodus 20:5b Does Jehovah God punish the guilt of the parents on the children on the third and on the fourth generations of those hating him?

We must consider the context. Jehovah instituted the Law covenant with the Israelite nation, to which they agreed to be obedient. They said as one,

Exodus 19:8 American Standard Version (ASV)

⁸ And all the people answered together, and said, All that Jehovah hath spoken we will do. And Moses reported the words of the people unto Jehovah.

---

[22] Or, "a God exacting exclusive devotion (zealous); a God not tolerating rivalry." Heb., 'El qanna"; Gr., Theos' zelotes'.

The whole nation of Israel entered themselves into this covenant with Jehovah God, where if they were obedient, Jehovah blessed the nation in many ways; however, if they disobeyed, he simply removed his special blessing, and they would be subject to the difficulties of life like any other nation. Thus, Exodus 20:5 is not directed to individuals, but the nation as a whole.

When the Israelite nation remained obedient to the covenant, they benefited by the blessings that Jehovah bestowed upon them. (Lev. 26:3-8) However, when they were disobedient, the opposite took place, as a result of his removing his extra blessings that he was bestowing on them (a protective hedge about them), they were subject to the elements that every other nation was subject too. (Judg. 2:11-18) When the nation as a whole disobeyed, there was undoubtedly a number that remained obedient to the Law, regardless of what the whole was doing. (1 Ki. 19:14, 18) However, the blessing came as a result of the nation's obedience, so when the majority lost that blessing, the few would feel the loss as well. However, Jehovah still expressed loving-kindness toward them. (Jer. 52:3-11, 27)

Furthermore, there were times that the Nation of Israel became not only disobedient, but unashamedly, grossly rebellious in the extreme in their violation of Jehovah's Law. At times they would be conquered by other petty nations that surrounded them, such as the days of the Judges. In another case, northern Israel was conquered by Assyria and taken captive, while Southern Judah was taken captive by Babylon for seventy years. Of course, this would have affect the individual as well. Thus, there was three to four generations that suffered because of the nation's gross sin, just as Exodus 20:5 said would happen.

In addition, the Scriptures contain moments where individual families suffered as a result of the parents disobedience. For example, you have the High Priest Eli, who offended Jehovah, because he failed to punish, or even remove his worthless, immoral sons as priests. (1 Sam. 2:12-16, 22-25) Clearly, Eli had "honored [his] sons more than [Jehovah] by making [themselves] fat from the best of all the offerings of [God's] people Israel." Thus, it was decreed that the family of Eli would be cut off from the high priesthood, which began with Eli's great-grand-son, Abiathar. (1 Sam. 2:29-36; 1 Ki. 2:27)

1 Kings 2:27 Lexham English Bible (LEB)

[27] So Solomon banished Abiathar from being priest to Yahweh, thus fulfilling the word which [Jehovah] had spoken concerning the house of Eli in Shiloh.

Jehovah is the Creator and the designer of life, who has the right to exercise his authority over his creation. Moreover, he does so in according to his righteous and just standards. Just like anything else in this life that Adam and Eve helped us into, we are subject to the results of other's actions. Even so, those who remain obedient, Jehovah "hears the cry of distress from the needy." Yes, individuals, who remain faithful and look to Jehovah, will receive his favor by their being obedient to his Word, our guide through this wicked age. (Job 34:28) And there are times, when some that are being used by God to carry out his will and purposes, are afflicted by the actions of the many, to which he will miraculously bring relief. However, we must understand, this is the extreme exception to the rule of allowing man to walk on his own.

SECTION 2 Apologetic Evangelism

Apologetic Evangelism "is tilling the soil of people's hearts of people's minds and hearts to help them be more willing to listen to the truth._ - Norman L. Geisler

Evangelism is the work of a Christian evangelist, which seeks to persuade other people to become Christian, especially by sharing the basics of the Gospel, but also the deeper message of biblical truths. Today the Gospel is almost an unknown, so what does the Christian evangelist do? **Preevangelism** is laying a foundation for those who have no knowledge of the Gospel, giving them background information, so that they are able to grasp what they are hearing. The Christian evangelist is preparing their mind and heart so that they will be receptive to the biblical truths. In many ways, this is known as apologetics.

Christian apologetics [Greek: *apologia*, "verbal defense, speech in defense"] is a field of **Christian theology** which endeavors to offer a reasonable and sensible basis for the **Christian faith** , defending the faith against objections. It is reasoning from the Scriptures, explaining and proving, as one instructs in sound doctrine, many times having to overturn false reasoning before he can plant the seeds of truth. It can also be earnestly contending for the faith and saving one from losing their faith, as they have begun to doubt. Moreover, it can involve rebuking those who contradict the truth. It is being prepared to make a defense to anyone who asks the Christian evangelist for a reason for the hope that is in him or her.— Jude 1.3, 21-23; 1 Pet 3.15; Acts 17:2-3; Titus 1:9

What do we mean by **obligated** and what we mean by **evangelism** are at the heart of the matter and are indeed related to each other.

EVANGELISM: An evangelist is a proclaimer of the gospel or good news, as well as all biblical truths. There are levels of evangelism, which is pictured in first-century Christianity. All Christians evangelized in the first century, but a select few fit the role of a full-time evangelist (Ephesians 4:8, 11-12), like Philip and Timothy.

Both Philip and Timothy are specifically mentioned as evangelizers. (Ac 21:8; 2 Tim. 4:5) Philip was a full-time evangelist after Pentecost, who was sent to the city of Samaria, having great success. An angel even directed Philip to an Ethiopian Eunuch, to share the good news about Christ with him. Because of the Eunuch's already having knowledge of God by way of the Old Testament, Philip was able to help him understand that the Hebrew Scriptures pointed to Christ as the long awaited Messiah. In the end, Philip baptized the Eunuch. Thereafter, the Spirit again sent Philip on a mission, this time to Azotus and all the cities on the way to Caesarea. (Ac 8:5, 12, 14, 26-40) Paul evangelized in many lands, setting up one congregation after another. (2 Cor. 10:13-16) Timothy was an evangelizer or missionary, and Paul placed distinct importance on evangelizing when he gave his parting encouragement to Timothy. – 2 Timothy 4:5; 1Timothy 1:3.

The office of apostle and evangelist seem to overlap in some areas, but could be distinguished in that apostles traveled and set up congregations, which took evangelizing skills, but also developed the congregations after they were established. The evangelists were more of a missionary, being stationed in certain areas to grow and develop congregations. In addition, if we look at all of the apostles and the evangelists, plus Paul's more than one hundred traveling companions, it seems very unlikely that they could have had Christianity at over one million by the 125 C.E. This was accomplished because all Christians were obligated to carry out some level of evangelism.

OBLIGATED: In the broadest sense of the term for evangelizer, all Christians are obligated to play some role as an evangelist.

- *Basic Evangelism* is <u>planting</u> seeds of truth and <u>watering</u> any seeds that have been planted. [In the basic sense of this word (euaggelistes), this would involve all Christians.] In some cases, it may be that one Christian planted the seed, which were initially rejected, so he was left in a good way because the planter did not try to force the truth down his throat. However, sometime later he faces something in life that moves him to reconsider those seeds, and another Christian water what had already been planted. This evangelism can be carried out in all of the methods that are available: informal, house-to-house, street, phone, internet, and the like. What amount of time is invested in the evangelism work is up to each Christian to decide for themselves.

- *Making Disciples* is having any role in the process of getting an unbeliever from his unbelief state to the point of accepting Christ as his Savior and being baptized. Once the unbeliever has become a believer, he is still developed until he has become strong. Any Christian could potentially carry this one person through all of the developmental stages. On the other hand, it may be that several have some part. It is like a person that specializes in

103

a certain aspect of a job, but all are aware of the other aspects, in case they are called on to carry out that aspect. Again, each Christian must decide for themselves what role they are to have, and how much of a role, but should be prepared to fill any role needed.

• *Part-Time or* Full-Time Evangelist is one who sees this as their calling and chooses to be very involved as an evangelist in their local church and community. They may work part-time to supplement their work as an evangelist. They may be married with children, but they realize their gift is in the field of evangelism. If it is the wife, the husband would work toward supporting her work as an evangelist and vice-versa. If it were a single person, he or she would supplement their work by being employed part-time, but also the church would help as well. This person is well trained in every aspect of bringing one to Christ.

• *Congregation Evangelists* should be very involved in evangelizing their communities and helping the church members play their role at the basic levels of evangelism. There is nothing to say that one church could not have many within, who have the calling of an evangelist, which would and should be cultivated.

CHAPTER 5 Always Being Prepared to Make a Defense

1 Peter 3:15 Updated American Standard Version (UASV)

¹⁵ but sanctify Christ as Lord in your hearts, always being prepared to make a defense[23] to anyone who asks you for a reason for the hope that is in you; yet do it with gentleness and respect;

When one, who is sincerely interested in our beliefs as a follower of Christ, asks for a reason as to why we believe this or that, we must defend those beliefs with sound biblical answers. When Peter says that we need always to be prepared to make a defense to anyone who asks us for a reason for the hope that is in us, to whom does this apply? Who is supposed to be able to make a defense? Does this apply just to Bible scholars, pastors, elders, priests, church leaders, or all Christians? If we return to the first verse of Peter's letter, he writes, "To those who reside as aliens, scattered throughout Pontus, Galatia, Cappadocia, Asia, and Bithynia, who are chosen." (1 Pet. 1:1, NASB) The ones, who resided as aliens, were Christians living among the Jews and pagan Gentiles of Asia Minor. Thus, the first letter of Peter, especially 1:3 through 4:1 was directed to those who had just been recently been baptized. Thus, Peter expected all Christians, even newly baptized ones to be able to defend the hope that lies within all Christians, offering reasonable, logical answers to those who are genuinely interested.

---

[23] Or *argument*; or *explanation*

This first letter of Peter was penned about 62-64 C.E., meaning that these early Christians in Asia Minor, like others throughout the Roman Empire, were living under very difficult time, being persecuted on two fronts: by the Jews and the pagan population. The early Christians were mostly converts from Judaism, who now followed Jesus as the way, the truth, and the life. After that, pagans were being converted over to Christianity. The Jewish population viewed the Christians as an apostate form of Judaism, who were stumbling their fellow brothers and sisters. The pagan nations were angered because the Christians had given up their former lifestyle and had now become a new person. To the world, these Christians had undergone a life change that was viewed as apostasy from pagan religion and Judaism, and this was a crime! Because Christians refused to be a part of the world, the world hated them, just as it had hated Jesus. (1 Pet. 1.18; 2:1; 4:4) Even worse, Satan himself became enraged at this new Christian faith. Peter warned, "Be sober-minded; be watchful. Your adversary the devil prowls around like a roaring lion, seeking someone to devour."

What counsel within this first letter of Peter would keep these new ones safe, so that they would not return to their former ways? Peter exhorts, "Keep your conduct among the Gentiles honorable, so that when they speak against you as evildoers, they may see your good works and glorify God on the day of visitation."[24] (2:12) Peter goes on to inform them that in those difficult times, they needed to be "be sound in mind[25] and be sober-minded[26]

---

[24] I.e. Christ's second coming to judge

[25] to have understanding about practical matters and thus be able to act sensibly—'to have sound judgment, to be sensible, to use good sense, sound judgment.'– GELNTBSD

in prayers." (4:7) Again, they needed to be "sober-minded; be watchful" because Satan was 'seeking to devour' them as well. (5:8) Satan uses the enticement of old friends of the world, who were "living in sensuality, lusts, drunkenness, orgies, drinking parties, and lawless idolatry." (4:3) Defending one's hope under normal circumstances is difficult enough, let alone such situations as these. It has even become far more difficult these days and as Paul said that "in the last days difficult times will come," as "evil men and impostors will proceed from bad to worse."–2 Timothy 3:1, 13.

There is one more obligation for these new Christians if they are to maintain their right standing before God and strengthen their faith. Yes, they must also declare and defend their hope. Peter's use of the word "hope" is nearly the same with his use of the word "faith" (1 Pet. 1:3, 13, 21). On this, Thomas R. Schreiner writes, "Believers are to be ready constantly to respond to those who ask about their faith. What Peter emphasized is that they were to be prepared to provide a "defense" (NRSV, *apologia*–rendered "answer" by NIV) to those who ask about the Christian faith." (Schreiner 2003, p. 175) These new Christians were taught the correct course of conduct by the preaching of the Gospel, through which they had accepted the Christian faith, i.e., "the hope." Peter makes this clear when he writes, "It was revealed to them [the prophets] that they were serving not themselves but you, in the things that have now been announced to you through those who preached the good news to you by the Holy Spirit sent from heaven." (1 Pet 1:12) This now placed what

---

[26] to be in control of one's thought processes and thus not be in danger of irrational thinking–'to be sober-minded, to be well composed in mind.'–GELNTBSD

obligation on them. Peter went on to command that they "prepare [their] minds for action." (1:13) What action is Peter talking about? He says, "That [they] may proclaim the excellencies of him who called you out of darkness into his marvelous light." (2:9) When should these ones "proclaim the excellencies"? Peter gives the answer in our main text, "always being prepared to make a defense ... for a reason for the hope that is in you."–1 Peter 3:15

We have far worse conditions today than existed in Asia Minor of 2,000 years ago. Satan is still walking around Christianity like a roaring lion, seeking to devour true Christians. However, he knows his time is far shorter, and he has become desperate in his plight to take as many followers of Jesus Christ with him as possible. The world today under the influence of Satan caters to the fleshly desires of the fallen flesh unlike no other time prior to, because technology has the means of reaching billions in the privacy of their own home. The need to evangelize in our own communities has grown as well because so many are abandoning the faith, and many young ones are not taking up the faith of their parents or grandparents. Christians need to be busy in these last days, sharing the good news, helping a new generation come out of the darkness.

1 Peter 1:13-15 English Standard Version (ESV)

[13] Therefore, preparing your minds for action, and being sober-minded, set your hope fully on the grace that will be brought to you at the revelation of Jesus Christ. [14] As obedient children, do not be conformed to the passions of your former ignorance, [15] but as he who called you is holy, you also be holy in all your conduct,

Defending the Hope That Is In You

We must begin with the fact that we must know accurately what the Bible says on different Bible doctrines and be able to offer substantial reasons for the faith. As to the biblical truths, we do not want to remain a spiritual babe. "For everyone who partakes only of milk is not accustomed to the word of righteousness, for he is an infant. But solid food is for the mature, who because of practice have their senses trained to discern good and evil. Therefore leaving the elementary teaching about the Christ, let us press on to maturity." (Hebrews 5:13-6:1) We can consider a Bible example of one, who lack a deeper knowledge, through no fault of his own, correcting it once it was brought to his attention, namely, Apollos. The account is below; notice how he can defend the faith much better after he received the way of God more accurately, he eagerly helps others discover this hope.

Acts 18:24-28 English Standard Version (ESV)

²⁴ Now a Jew named Apollos, a native of Alexandria, came to Ephesus. He was an eloquent man, competent in the Scriptures. ²⁵ He had been instructed in the way of the Lord. And being fervent in spirit, he spoke and taught accurately the things concerning Jesus, though he knew only the baptism of John. ²⁶ He began to speak boldly in the synagogue, but when Priscilla and Aquila heard him, they took him aside and explained to him the way of God more accurately. ²⁷ And when he wished to cross to Achaia, the brothers encouraged him and wrote to the disciples to welcome him. When he arrived, he greatly helped those who through grace had believed, ²⁸ for he powerfully refuted

the Jews in public, showing by the Scriptures that the Christ was Jesus.

Just as was true of Priscilla and Aquila, Christian evangelists should be able to share the faith accurately to unbelievers, to those who have started to doubt, and to those in Christian denominations that are not on the true path of salvation. If we are to accomplish these things, we must have an accurate, full, true knowledge of God's Word. Paul wrote to the brothers in Colossae, "For this reason also, since the day we heard of it, we have not ceased to pray for you and to ask that you may be filled with the accurate knowledge[27] of his will in all spiritual wisdom and understanding, so as to walk in a manner worthy of the Lord, fully pleasing to him bearing fruit in every good work and increasing in the accurate knowledge[28] of God." – Colossians 1:9-10

This sharing of the Gospel is not just some basic biblical truth of Jesus's life and ministry, death, resurrection and ascension. Moreover, this is not just being able to string many good sounding words together, but rather words that will lead others to the same hope that we hold so dearly. The principle behind Paul's words to the Corinthians makes this point nicely. He wrote, "I would rather speak five words with my mind in order to instruct others, than ten thousand words in a tongue." – 1 Corinthians 14:19

---

[27] *Epignosis* is a strengthened or intensified form of *gnosis* (*epi*, meaning "additional"), meaning, "true," "real," "full," "complete" or "accurate," depending upon the context. Paul and Peter alone use *epignosis*.

[28] *Epignosis* is a strengthened or intensified form of *gnosis* (*epi*, meaning "additional"), meaning, "true," "real," "full," "complete" or "accurate," depending upon the context. Paul and Peter alone use *epignosis*.

Yes, Christians looking to share biblical truths with others should seek to do so with words of understanding. They should possess an accurate, full and true knowledge about the Father, the Son , The Holy Spirit, the Kingdom of God, and the Father's will and purpose for mankind, as well as the many other laws and principles found in Scripture. Certainly, if we are going to be successful in sharing or defending our beliefs, we must first fully understand them ourselves. Have we bought out the time and applied our mind meditatively in a study of God's Word so that we can effectively share it with others? Paul exhorted his young traveling companion, Timothy, "Do your best to present yourself to God as one approved, a worker who has no need to be ashamed, rightly handling the word of truth." (2 Tim. 2:15) On this the following commentaries write,

> God bestows his approval on the one who exhibits truth, love, and godliness in daily living, and who correctly handles the word of truth. The false teachers were mishandling God's words, using them for their own benefit. Timothy was commissioned to handle the words of God correctly. All preaching should present the truth clearly, cutting through erroneous ideas or inaccurate opinions.[29]

> Third, this same workman (specifically, Timothy but by application today all believers) was to be accurate in delivering the message of truth. The truth is the gospel. Paul showed concern that Timothy would present the gospel

---

[29] Knute Larson, I & II Thessalonians, I & II Timothy, Titus, Philemon, vol. 9, Holman New Testament Commentary (Nashville, TN: Broadman & Holman Publishers, 2000), 286.

without perverting or distorting it. He was not to be turned aside by disputes about words or mere empty prattle.[30]

Paul develops this concept in the striking phrase ... Paul's use of [*epaischunomai, aischunomai,* and *aischune*] means "unashamed" in the sense that he does not need to be ashamed of his work. The participle orthotomounta qualifies [*ergates*] and together with the words that follow specifically describes how Timothy may be unashamed: by being a worker who handles accurately the word of truth.

The material that this worker is to handle correctly is "the word of truth" ... Only when he handles it correctly will he be unashamed ... The rendering given in several of the modern translations, using a combination of the verb "handle" and some adverb such as "accurately" (NASB), "rightly" (RSV), or "correctly" (NIV), for the compound verb [*orthotomounta*] with the phrase "the word of truth" as the direct object captures this relationship quite well.[31]

If we are going to be "a worker who has no need to be ashamed, rightly handling the word of truth," we must not always rely on others as being more effective,

---

[30] Thomas D. Lea and Hayne P. Griffin, 1, 2 Timothy, Titus, vol. 34, The New American Commentary (Nashville: Broadman & Holman Publishers, 1992), 215.

[31] George W. Knight, The Pastoral Epistles: a Commentary on the Greek Text, New International Greek Testament Commentary (Grand Rapids, MI; Carlisle, England: W.B. Eerdmans; Paternoster Press, 1992), 411–412.

when we are called upon to share or defend our beliefs. Yes, God expects each of us to be capable of supporting our hope with Scripture. We do not want to fall under those who Paul mentioned to Timothy, "always learning and never able to arrive at a knowledge of the truth." (2 Tim. 3:7) We do not want to remain a spiritual babe for our entire Christian life. What do we think of children, who never really grow up and live with their parents off and on for their entire life? When we think of the many different professions in life, such as medicine, law, science, engineer, mechanic and so on, we know that our hands are held throughout our education, but once in the real world, we are expected to be self-reliant. Even Paul said of himself, "When I was a child, I spoke like a child, I thought like a child, I reasoned like a child. When I became a man, I gave up childish ways." – 1 Corinthians 13:11.

If we ever expect to defend our hope effectively, i.e., the faith, we are going to have to study daily. This should not trouble us because it does not take hours every day, but at least 30 minutes or more. The amount that can be accomplished in 30 minutes a day, after 365 days, will be far more than we might have ever expected. A Christian should study the Bible (not just read) a minimum of thirty minutes a day, he should also prepare the lessons assigned for the Bible study at the church and any other service that allows him to prepare ahead of time. A Christian should participate in any comment sessions that are allowed at their particular church, as this gives them practice in effectively sharing biblical truths. Also, A Christian should attend every Christian meeting, as it offers them an opportunity to build others up. A Christian should share every new thing they learn in their personal studies with at least one new friend, which gives them practice at effectively communicating biblical truths.

We must have a deep understanding of the biblical truths that we share and defend, which is going to be presented to all kinds of different persons. Our studying daily needs to be a time on the day when we will not be disturbed. We want to turn the phone off, any music, television, and meditatively go through God's Word. The daily study will be our greatest tool for helping us to share and defend the Word of God and out faith effectively. Paul counsels Titus and by extension us as well, "let our people learn to devote themselves to good works, so as to help cases of urgent need, and not be unfruitful." (Titus 3:14) If we are studying daily, preparing for meetings, answering at meetings, attending all meetings, sharing a new biblical truth with friends, we will be able to apply Paul's thoughts to the Colossians as well. He wrote "Let your speech always be gracious, seasoned with salt, so that you may know how you ought to answer each person." – Colossians 4:6

Using the Bible to Defend Our Hope

It should be noted that many today hold back from sharing or defending their Christian faith. Those who do, tend to do so without using the Bible. If we want to defend our hope successfully, we need to have our Bible as the primary evidence of that hope. Our hope lies within God's Word, so we need to use God's Word to defend it. We must persuade with reason from God's Word, not from what we feel, think, or believe. It should be, 'the Word of God says,' Paul wrote,' 'Jesus said,' 'God said,' not 'I feel,' 'I think,' or 'I believe.' It is our effective use of the Bible when we communicated biblical truths to others that are going to convince the right-hearted ones of the truth and the way. One way that we will become more skilled is by our using our Bible at every opportunity: in our personal study of course, in sharing new truths with friends, and especially in looking up every Scripture that is cited in our religious services. Another way is to start paying attention to how commentaries and other study tools, as well as our pastors, elders tie Scriptures together contextually to establish their biblical point. If you were going to share the hope of salvation, could you walk a listener through 5-10 Scriptures that would paint a picture of that hope? Will our listener tell a friend of what they learned, and say, "He straight to his Bible and showed it to me directly!"

If we are sharing or defending biblical truths, we must do so correctly, persuasively, and in such a way that it is easy to grasp. This means that we know it well ourselves, and we have prepared well by communicating in more relaxed moments, which made us better communicators. For example, can we explain the resurrection hope at this very moment to another if they asked? Will our explanation be from the Bible? Will it be what the author meant by the words he used? Will it be persuasive? Will it be easy to follow and understand? If not, then, how can we honestly say we have a resurrection hope? Is there not irony that many young girls can tell you everything about Taylor Swift, but little if anything about their heavenly Father? The same is true of adult males, who can tear a car apart blindfolded, but cannot string along a handful of verses that defend their resurrection hope. And yes, adult females have an immense amount of knowledge about subject matters that interest them, yet likely cannot support their resurrection hope any better. The above are a bit of a stereotype, which is noted, but it makes the point that we prepare for worldly things with far more vigor than we prepare to share and defend the faith.

If we are going to have any success in defending our Christian faith, we must be able to overcome the objections of others. We will find that the same objections are repeatedly used. Therefore, we will eventually, be able to overcome the standard objections easily. However, a couple words of caution. First, we do not want to become complacent in our response to common objections; because the listener needs to feel as though they are getting an emotionally involved response, not some automatize, robotic response, as if we feel like, 'here we go again.' Second, do not be complacent in thinking that every objection is going to be the common ones. If someone has an objection that we have never addressed, just simply say, "you raise a very good point, and the next time we speak, I will give you a logical and reasonable answer." When we research his objection, do so to the point that we know it inside and out. Moreover, be aware that 99 percent of all Bible difficulties have logical, reasonable answers. On this, R. A. Torrey writes, "Humbly. Recognize the limitations of your own mind and knowledge, and do not for a moment imagine that there is no solution just because you have found none. There is, in all probability, a very simple solution, even when you can find no solution at all."[32] In the end, there are answers, so meditate on the objection that has been raised, search through the literature, looking for Scripture and arguments to refute the objection in defense of the faith. Out of many thousands of Bible difficulties that have answers as to why they are, in fact, Bible difficulties and not errors, mistakes or contradictions, there are but a handful that has yet to be answered. This does not mean there is no answer, just that the information needed may be lacking,

---

[32] http://www.christianpublishers.org/handling-bible-difficulties

or it is something we will have to wait on until, a greater mind comes along, or until the second coming of Christ. However, really, if science had answers to many thousands of issues, but only a few remained unanswered, we would never hear the end of it. It is amazing that we have what we have considering we are dealing with a book where parts of it were penned 2,000 years ago while other parts were written 3,500 years ago.

As a proclaimer and defender of the faith, always be on the alert for points that can be used to overcome objections that we have heard, or what logically sounds like an objection one might raise. Whether we are studying a book, working on the our Bible reading with a commentary or sitting in a pew listening to a talk from our elder or pastor, have our mind attuned to such things. Say, we ae sitting at church, the pastor or elder makes an excellent point that overcomes a particular Bible objection (The Bible is not practical for our day, or there are so many different interpretations, who can know the truth), so we write it down in out notebook, because, yes, we have a notebook and pen. This will further implant the point in our mind. Now, we take it a step further. Find three different people after the meeting and say, "I really enjoyed what the pastor or elder had to say about the objection that the Bible is not practical for our day." Then, we should proceed to reiterate what was said in our own words. This will further embed it in our mind. Our notebook can be used for all kinds of notes at the meetings or during our personal study, but if we take notes on some objection or a Bible difficulty of some sort, highlight it a particular color. Why? We do this because we will also have another notebook that is specifically for Bible difficulties and Bible objections, so we have prepared and refutations. In this special notebook, leave the first few pages blank, as it will serve as out table of content. We can number our pages, so in the front we can write down a phrase that will tell us what the issue is and the page on which it can be found.

Therefore Christian defenders of God's Word and principles,

2 Timothy 2:15 English Standard Version (ESV)

¹⁵ Do your best to present yourself to God as one approved, a worker who has no need to be ashamed, rightly handling the word of truth.

Let us have the spirit of Paul,

1 Corinthians 9:16-17 English Standard Version (ESV)

¹⁶ For if I preach the gospel, that gives me no ground for boasting. For necessity is laid upon me. Woe to me if I do not preach the gospel! ¹⁷ For if I do this of my own will, I have a reward, but if not of my own will, I am still entrusted with a stewardship.

Exercise

- So that it is easy understand, sequentially explain:

(1) how the fall of man came about and

(2) the nature of sin

(3) and what hope was offered from Genesis 3:15 forward

Review Questions

- When Peter says that we need always to be ready to make a defense of the hope that is in us, to whom does this rule apply?

- What is needed if we are to effectively defend the hope that is in us?

- Why should we use the Bible in proclaiming and defending our hope?

Why should Christians be able to simplify Bible teachings to make them easy to understand?

CHAPTER 6 Effectively Reasoning From the Scriptures

Acts 17:2 Updated American Standard Version (UASV)

² And according to Paul's custom, he went to them, and for three Sabbaths **reasoned with them from the Scriptures**,

The value of God's Word is incomprehensible. With it, we are able to answer some of life's most difficult questions. Why are we here? What is the meaning of life? If there is a God and he is good, why so much suffering? What is the purpose of our existence? What is right and wrong and who should determine it? Will world peace ever be achieved? Will poverty ever end? How can we be happy? What is true freedom and does it exist? What happens after we die? Is there such a thing as **absolute truth**? Moreover, I am certain that each of us could add many more life questions to this list. However, the last question above, is there such a thing as absolute truth, can be answered with an absolute yes and it is found within the Bible alone. In the Bible, we find answers to the above questions and far more. We discover that we have a Creator and why such a loving Creator would allow sickness, old age and death, with much suffering all throughout our limited lives.[33] We also learn the truth about why we are here, what our Creator expects of us, and how his decisions in our behalf have been for our good. – Psalm 19:7-11; Isaiah 48:17.

---

[33] **Suffering & Evil - Why God?**

http://www.christianpublishers.org/suffering-evil-why-god

As true Christians, we accept the Bible as the inspired, fully inerrant Word of God and that it has the power to change lives for the better, so we defend it and share it with others. (Heb. 4:12) When we share these truths with others, we want to help them to realize that it is not our absolute truths, but rather truths that belong to the God of the heavens and the earth, which he has revealed to us within the Scriptures. Thus, we want to use the Bible, as it is the authority, the absolute truth, when we talk with others, literally reading from it. Like Paul, we want to 'reason with them from the Scriptures.' (Ac 17:2) We want to help them accept the Bible for what it is, the inspired Word of God, and accept what it teaches as absolute truth. – 2 Timothy 2:15.

It is highly important that we share what God's Word says rather than what we feel, think, or believe. This can be exemplified in the prophetic book of Jeremiah. The prophets other than Jeremiah were merely saying what the people wanted to hear, pacifying, i.e., seeking to make the people and rulers less angry, upset, or hostile, saying untrue things to please them. In other words, they were not telling the people the Word of God.

Jeremiah 23:25-28 Updated American Standard Version (UASV)

[25] I have heard what the prophets have said who prophesy lies in my name, saying, 'I have dreamed, I have dreamed!' [26] How long will this be in the hearts of the prophets who prophesy lies, even these prophets of the deceit of their own heart, [27] who think to make my people forget my name by their dreams that they tell one another, just as their fathers forgot my name for Baal? [28] The prophet who has a dream may relate his dream, but let him who has My word speak My word in

truth. What does straw have in common with grain?" declares Jehovah.

On the other hand, Jeremiah did speak God's Word truthfully, even if it was not well received, or it meant his life was in danger. The apostle Paul tells the Corinthians and us that the historical events of the Old Testament were recorded to serve as "examples for us." Thus, like Jeremiah, we too want to feel obligated to teach only what the authors meant when they penned their particular books and not water down the Word of God or impose modern day thinking into the text, deliberately avoiding offense. For example, today we have an undertaking called the feminist movement, belief in the need to secure rights and opportunities for women equal to those of men, or a commitment to securing these. While the idea of attain the right to vote, equal pay for equal work, among other modern day rights is perfectly fine, it should not retroactively be applied to the Word of God. Paul clearly states at 2 Timothy 2:12, "I do not permit a woman to teach or to exercise authority over a man; rather, she is to remain quiet." The natural reading of 1 Timothy 2:12 is that Paul in his apostolic authority prohibits women from teaching and exercising authority over a man, which means that women cannot serve as pastors or elders in the Christian congregation. We are not to mold to the pressures of the modern day feminist movement because this position goes back to before the fall, has always been applicable, and will always be applicable. For a detail explanation of this text, see the footnote below.[34]

---

[34] **Women in the Pulpit?**

http://www.christianpublishers.org/women-in-the-pulpit

Even Jesus himself said, "My teaching is not mine, but belongs to him that sent me. If anyone wants to do his will, he will know whether the teaching is from God or whether I am speaking on my own authority. The one who speaks on his own authority seeks his own glory, but the one who seeks the glory of him who sent him, this one is true, and there is no unrighteousness in him." (John 7:16-18) Even the Son of God himself refused to speak of his own authority, but rather the authority of the Father, who had sent him. Therefore, how much more so should we avoid speaking on our own authority? Like, the elders, all Christians want to be "holding fast to the faithful word which is in accordance with the teaching, so that he will be able both to exhort in sound doctrine and to refute those who contradict." (Titus 1:9) Then, there is the counsel from Paul for Timothy to hand off to the congregations, "preach the word; be ready in season and out of season; reprove, rebuke, exhort, with complete patience and teaching." (2 Tim. 4:2) Whether we are answering questions at a Bible study in the congregation, an elder or pastor is giving a lecture, or we are witnessing to someone outside of the congregation, we want to "preach the word."

However, the Bible is a deep, complex book, because it was it was written from 2,000 to 3,500 years ago in many different cultures, the language of biblical Hebrew and Koine (common) Greek, among many other things is it difficult to understand. Therefore, we could never evangelize by just reading the Bible alone, saying no more, especially to this generation that is almost entirely unfamiliar with it. If our listener is to grasp fully what the authors meant and how it applies to us, we are going to have to offer that connection. In the account of the Ethiopian eunuch referred to at Acts 8:26-38, he did not fully understand what was meant in the Book of

Isaiah that he was reading in his travels. This Eunuch was familiar with the Hebrew or Greek translation of the Old Testament, as he had come to Jerusalem to worship and was returning to his homeland, and yet he still did not understand Isaiah 53:7-8. How much more help do the unbelievers of today need? Nevertheless, once this eunuch fully understood the importance of the text, seeing how it applied to him personally, he chose to leave the Judaism of the day and become a Christian.

How Jesus Used the Scriptures

Matthew writes, "And when Jesus finished these sayings, the crowds were astonished at his teaching, for he was teaching them as one who had authority, and not as their scribes." (7:28-29) He later writes of Jesus return to his hometown, "He taught them in their synagogue, so that they were astonished." (13:54) After that, when Jesus is speaking on a number of subjects, but especially who shall be saved, Matthew says the disciples "were greatly astonished." (19:25) Later still when Jesus dealt with the resurrection belief of the Sadducees, "when the crowd heard it, they were astonished at his teaching." (22:33)

Why were the crowds astonished at Jesus' way of teaching? What does it mean that he was teaching them as one who had authority? How is it that they say no one had ever spoken as Jesus had? The Greek verb used by Matthew about how Jesus' teaching affected others was *ekplessomai*, which meant that they were "so amazed as to be practically overwhelmed–'to be greatly astounded.'[35] In 7:28, the verb is in the imperfect tense, which suggested an ongoing effect. Jesus taught with the authority of the Scriptures, unlike the scribes, who were busy quoting Rabbis as their authority. Jesus, on the other hand, quoted over 120 Hebrew verses in the dialog that is given to us in the Gospel accounts, accounts that would amount to about a three-hour lecture.

Bible Background on the Scribes

In ancient times, the scribes were merely officers whose duties included writing of various kinds; but, on the return of the Jews from Babylonian captivity, the sopherim, as the scribes were called, were organized by Ezra into a distinct body. Among other duties, they copied the Pentateuch, the Phylacteries, and the Mezuzoth. So great was their care in copying that they counted and compared all the letters to be sure that none were left out that belonged to the text, or none inserted wrongly. On stated occasions they read the law in the synagogues. They also lectured to their disciples. Because of the knowledge they obtained through their work, they became natural interpreters of God's law as well as copyists.

The lawyers (Matthew 22:35; Luke 7:30; 11:45; 14:3) and the doctors of the law (Luke 2:46; 5:17; Acts 5:34) were substantially the same as the scribes. Efforts have been made to

[35] Johannes P. Louw and Eugene Albert Nida, *Greek-English Lexicon of the New Testament: Based on Semantic Domains* (New York: United Bible Societies, 1996), 311–312.

show that different classes of duties were assigned to lawyers, doctors, and scribes, but without any measurably different results. It may be, as some believe, that the doctors were a higher grade than the ordinary scribes. The scribes were all carefully educated for their work from early life, and at an appropriate age—some say thirty-years-old—they were admitted to office through a solemn ceremony.

The scribes were not only copyists of the law; they were also keepers of the oral traditional comments and additions to the law. Gradually accumulating with the progress of time, these were numerous, and were regarded by many as of equal value with the law itself. To this Jesus alludes in Mark 7:5–13. Paul represents himself as having been, before his conversion, "exceedingly zealous of the traditions" of his fathers (Galatians 1:14). The scribes also adopted forced interpretations of the law, endeavoring to find a special meaning in every word, syllable, and letter. Thus the Savior charges them: "Woe to you experts in the law, because you have taken away the key to knowledge. You yourselves have not entered, and you have hindered those who were entering" (Luke 11:52).

At the time of Christ, the people were increasingly dependent on the scribes for a knowledge of their Scriptures. The language of the Jews was passing into the Aramaic dialect, and the majority of the people, being unable to understand their own sacred books, were obliged to accept the interpretation that the scribes put upon them. Hence, their astonishment, as indicated in our text-verse, at the peculiar style of teaching adopted by Jesus, and especially illustrated in His Sermon on the Mount. The scribes repeated traditions, but Jesus spoke with authority: "I tell you." The scribes had little sympathy with the masses, but Jesus mingled with the people, explaining to them in a simple, practical way the requirements of religion.[36]

Hendriksen and Kistemaker asked the question that concerned us as well, "What were some of the reasons for this feeling of wonder and astonishment? Matt. 13:54, 55 may supply part of the answer. Nevertheless, on the basis of the sermon itself and of 7:28 ("not as their scribes") the following items are worthy of consideration:"

a. He spoke the truth (John 14:6; 18:37). Corrupt and evasive reasoning marked the sermons of many of the scribes (Matt. 5:21 ff.).

b. He presented matters of great significance, matters of life, death, and eternity (see the entire sermon). They often wasted their time on trivialities (Matt. 23:23; Luke 11:42).

c. There was system in his preaching. As their Talmud proves, they often rambled on and on.

d. He excited curiosity by making generous use of illustrations (5:13–16; 6:26–30;

[36] James M. Freeman and Harold J. Chadwick, *Manners & Customs of the Bible* (North Brunswick, NJ: Bridge-Logos Publishers, 1998), 420–421.

7:24–27; etc.) and concrete examples (5:21–6:24; etc.), as the sermon shows from beginning to end. Their speeches were often dry as dust.

e. He spoke as the Lover of men, as One concerned with the everlasting welfare of his listeners, and pointed to the Father and his love (5:44–48). Their lack of love is clear from such passages as 23:4, 13–15; Mark 12:40; etc.

f. Finally, and this is the most important, for it is specifically stated here (verse 28), he spoke "with authority" (Matt. 5:18, 26; etc.), for his message came straight from the very heart and mind of the Father (John 8:26), hence also from his own inner being, and from Scripture (5:17; 7:12; cf. 4:4, 7, 10). They were constantly borrowing from fallible sources, one scribe quoting another scribe. They were trying to draw water from broken cisterns. He drew from himself, being "the Fountain of living waters" (Jer. 2:13).[37]

Clearly, Jesus set the example in how one is to use the Scriptures effectively. Let us examine his use of questions.

Luke 10:25 Holman Christian Standard Bible (HCSB)

[25] Just then an expert in the law stood up to test Him, saying, "Teacher, what must I do to inherit eternal life?"

---

[37] William Hendriksen and Simon J. Kistemaker, Exposition of the Gospel According to Matthew, vol. 9, New Testament Commentary (Grand Rapids: Baker Book House, 1953–2001), 382–383.

A historical note here, "an expert in the law," or "lawyer" as some translations have it, is not a lawyer as we would think of one today. A lawyer was someone that was an expert in the Mosaic Law. However, this person would have the same level of education on the law as a lawyer would today, many years of study and memorization. Thus, this man would certainly know the answer to such an easy question as the one he asked. Now, if a believer is asked a straightforward Bible question, we might be tempted just to offer an answer. Indeed, as the wisest man ever to live, Jesus could have easily answered the question. Instead, Jesus wanted the man to offer his own thoughts, insights or understanding. However, Jesus knew this man was "an expert in the law," and he recognized the man would have had a certain perspective on his question. In other words, the man was not asked because he did not know. Thus, Jesus asked:

Luke 10:26 Holman Christian Standard Bible (HCSB)

26 "What is written in the law?" He asked him. "How do you read it?"

The man answered correctly,

Luke 10:27 Holman Christian Standard Bible (HCSB)

27 He answered: Love the Lord your God with all your heart, with all your soul, with all your strength, and with all your mind; and your neighbor as yourself.

The conversation could have ended there. Again, the man knew the Mosaic Law but seemingly wanted to see if Jesus would agree with what he knew. Jesus gratified him, letting him feel good, by giving the correct answer. Jesus responded:

Luke 10:28-29 Holman Christian Standard Bible (HCSB)

²⁸ "You've answered correctly," He told him. "Do this and you will live."

²⁹ But wanting to justify himself, he asked Jesus, "And who is my neighbor?"

Here again, the man looks to prove himself righteous, and Jesus could have just stated the truth, even the Samaritan. However, Jesus having insight into the setting, the Jews detested the Samaritans; so, while he would give the correct answer it would be disputed in a long, back-and-forth conversation, and the Jews who listened would have sided with the man. Thus, Jesus boxed the man into giving an answer by having him reason on an illustration.

Luke 10:25-37 Holman Christian Standard Bible (HCSB)

The Parable of the Good Samaritan

³⁰ Jesus took up the question and said: "A man was going down from Jerusalem to Jericho and fell into the hands of robbers. They stripped him, beat him up, and fled, leaving him half dead. ³¹ A priest happened to be going down that road. When he saw him, he passed by on the other side. ³² In the same way, a Levite, when he arrived at the place and saw him, passed by on the other side. ³³ But a Samaritan on his journey came up to him, and when he saw the man, he had compassion. ³⁴ He went over to him and bandaged his wounds, pouring on olive oil and wine. Then he put him on his own animal, brought him to an inn, and took care of him. ³⁵ The next day he took out two denarii, gave them to the

innkeeper, and said, 'Take care of him. When I come back I'll reimburse you for whatever extra you spend.'

36 "Which of these three do you think proved to be a neighbor to the man who fell into the hands of the robbers?"

37 "The one who showed mercy to him," he said.

Then Jesus told him, "Go and do the same."

This man had to admit the elite in the Jewish religion, the priest, and the Levite, had not been neighborly, but the Samaritan proved to be a good neighbor. Jesus moved him to reason out a new way of viewing exactly what "neighbor" meant. Instead of letting the man walk him into a long debate, Jesus made the man do all of the reasoning in the conversation, and moved him to admit something no Jew would ever utter,[38] as well as grasp a whole new understanding of what it meant to be a neighbor. Jesus took this approach because the circumstances called for it. However, on another occasion, a scribe, another expert in the law, asked him the same question and on that occasion, he chose to give the direct answer. (Mark 12:28-31) Circumstances vary.

What lessons can we take in from the example that Luke provided us? **(1)** Jesus **used Scriptures** initially to answer the man's question. **(2)** Jesus proved **perceptive** enough to **take notice** of the man's agenda. **(3)** Jesus did not just answer the easy Bible question but **shifted the responsibility** to **a question** of his own, by asking the man how he understood the law, giving him a chance

---

[38] Notice the hatred ran so deep between Jews and Samaritans that when asked by Jesus, who was the neighbor I the illustration, he did not say, the Samaritan, but rather, "the one who ..."

to express himself. **(4)** Jesus **complimented** the man for a discerning with the correct answer. **(5)** Jesus made sure the man, and the listeners **made the connection** between the initial question and the Scriptures. **(6)** Jesus **used an illustration** that was able to **reach the heart and mind**, where the answer was kept to the forefront. **(7)** Jesus moved the man **to reason** beyond his basic understanding of a neighbor.

The apostle Paul, as well, was an excellent teacher, one from whom we can learn. His traveling companion, Luke the physician, went with him, and his account of Paul's activity is significant.

Reasoning Adapted to the Listeners

Acts 17:2-3 Updated American Standard Version (UASV)

² And according to Paul's custom, he went to them, and for three Sabbaths reasoned with them from the Scriptures, ³ **explaining and proving** that it was necessary that the Christ had to suffer and rise again from the dead, and saying, "This Jesus whom I am proclaiming to you is the Christ."

We have already spoken about the fact that Paul reasoned from the Scriptures. However, he did more, as one can see from the above, that he explained, proved, and made application. Many times, we may read a Scripture to someone, and while it seems straightforward, enough to us, yet the listener fails to see the point. We may highlight a word or phrase or a part of the text and then explain the verse. We are doing that with Acts 17:2-3, as we highlight **explaining and proving**. You could also offer to walk them through the context, as we also did previously with Acts 17:2-3, when we backed up to verse 1, to show that Paul reasoned from the Scriptures because he talked with Jews in the Synagogue, people, who would be familiar with the Hebrew Scriptures. Another option is offering them additional texts that support the one the evangelist used. If the listener does not grasp the text and the explanation, add an illustration like Jesus did over forty times. Then again, asking the right questions might get the listener to reason on things further. We can learn much by looking at Paul's method of teaching. He did not merely quote a Scripture. Thus, we need to do more than just read a Scripture. Not only did he reason from the Scriptures, he adapted his reasoning so that it would fit his audience. He did more than share the gospel with the people; he explained it to them, providing them with proof from the Word of God. Let us consider two examples of how effective Paul's teaching was.

At Acts 13:16-41, we find Paul preaching in the Synagogue at Pisidian Antioch. The first thing Paul did was to attempt to find some common ground with his Jewish audience. (Read 13:16-17) Why take that approach? Well, if he could find some common ground, this would draw his listeners in, making them more willing to reason on a subject that they were not going to agree. Notice too that he did not introduce himself as a Christian, nor did he attempt to bring them the good news of Jesus Christ. He was speaking to Jews, who took issue on both accounts, and he being a former Pharisee, he knew their thinking. Rather he referred to them as 'men of Israel, who fear God, asking them to listen.' He also inferred that he too was like them, a Hebrew from birth. After that, he gave them an important part of Israelite history, which they would have been familiar. Now, here is where the skill comes in, as he held to the common ground he had established when he began to speak about Jesus Christ.

Notice the tie in as Paul moved through the Israelite history, saying God "raised up David to be their king, of whom he testified and said, 'I have found in David the son of Jesse a man after my heart, who will do all my will.' Of this man's offspring God has brought to Israel a Savior, Jesus, as he promised." (13:22-23) Then, he pulled in John the Baptizer as a witness to this fact, a person that these Jews viewed as a prophet of God. (13:24-25; Lu 20:4-6) Knowing that his listeners were well aware that the Jewish leaders in Jerusalem had rejected Jesus, Paul beat them to the punch by mentioning it first; then, establishing that this was fulfilled prophecy. (13:27-29) After that, he drew their attention to the fact that God had not abandoned Jesus, by resurrecting him from the dead, to which there were eyewitnesses among the Jews themselves. (13:30-31) Paul brought this complicated matter home, saying, "We preach to you the good news of the promise made to the fathers." (13:32) From there he went to the Hebrew Old Testament as his evidence of this truth. Paul quoted first from Psalm 2:7 ["'You are my Son, today I have begotten you.'], then Isaiah 55:3 ["'I will give you the holy and sure blessings of David.'], and finally Psalm 16:10 ["'You will not let your Holy One see corruption.']. Paul then went on to reason from those scriptures, "For David, after he had served the purpose of God in his own generation, fell asleep and was laid with his fathers and saw corruption, but he whom God raised up did not see corruption." (13:36-37) Now, Paul closed his argument in a motivating conclusion. Many took serious what he had said. "As they went out, the people begged that these things might be told them the next Sabbath." – Acts 13:38-43.

Now, how did Paul do when he approached a non-Jewish audience? When Paul addressed the Areopagus in Athens, Greece, he used a comparable approach; he essentially adjusted his witness to the new environment and thinking of the Athenians. Here again he sought a common ground. So Paul, standing in the midst of the Areopagus, said: "Men of Athens, I perceive that in every way you are very religious. For as I passed along and observed the objects of your worship, I also found an altar with this inscription, 'To the unknown god.' For as I passed along and observed the objects of your worship, I also found an altar with this inscription, 'To the unknown god.' What therefore you worship as unknown, this I proclaim to you." (Ac 17:22-23) Rather than get explicit with the Scriptures as he did with the Jews, who would have been familiar with such, he paraphrased portions of God's Word, from which he reason from them, proving and explaining what he was saying. Moreover, since Paul had some knowledge of Greek literature, he quoted two different Greek poets.[39] He did not quote these Greek poets as though they were an authority as the Scriptures are, but the portion he quoted was in harmony with Scripture, and he wanted them to realize the points he was making could be found in their own literature. Because of this approach, "some men joined him and believed, among whom also were Dionysius the Areopagite and a woman named Damaris and others with them." – Acts 17:24-31, 34.

The good news that Paul preached in both Athens and Antioch was the same. The approach he took was very similar, but adapted specifically for a particular

---

[39] Verse 28 has a possible quote from Epimenides of Crete, or it could be a traditional Greek formula. The verse also contains a quote from Aratus's poem "Phainomena."

audience because he wanted to find a common ground, to reason with them. His love for God and humanity was so deep that Paul took the time to develop his teaching abilities because he cared. Also, such efforts were fruitful because in both cases he found those, who were receptive to the truths he was sharing. It is hoped this book and others by this author will go a long way in helping us to do the same, reasoning from the Scriptures, explaining and proving the points that need to be made, effectively evangelizing our family friends, coworkers, and community.

Exercises

A hypothetical friend loves adventurous sports that are life risking. For example, he likes serious white water rafting, rock climbing up the sides of cliffs and hang-gliding. How would you reason with him that these life-risking sports are unbiblical?

Find someone you know who has strong beliefs that are unbiblical and engage them in a conversation. If you do not know such a person, find them within social media. After the discussion is over, analyze the discussion. What evidence did you present, did you use any illustrations, did you lead him along with questions, and did you evidence concern for his feelings and background.

Review Questions

- When we witness to another, how can we help them to see the importance of the Word of God?

- How did Jesus use the Scriptures?

- What can we learn from the way Paul taught?

- How can we further develop our ability to reason from the Scriptures?

- How can we adapt our reason to our listener?

CHAPTER 7 Effectively Communicating With Others

Whether you are gathering to go out into your community, to share the good news with the locals, or you are just staying at the church to make calls, your frame of mind is important. If you have a negative attitude that day, you must get it right. You need to go to God in prayer before ever leaving the house, asking him for the strength to set aside any mental disposition that may hamper your communication, as well as help endure and overturn any potential negativity from others.

Negative Attitudes

The way you approach others while communicating biblical truths to them will determine if they will be receptive or unreceptive to your message. People love to share their perspective on everything, and so you are bound to hear some whom you will be witnessing to, who will offer incorrect information, irrational thoughts, misconceptions about the Bible, even criticism of the Bible and Christianity as a whole, among other things. We are the ones that must maintain our composure, because "A soft answer turns away wrath, but a harsh word stirs up anger." (Proverbs 15:1)

REVIEW QUESTION: Why is it important that we pray about our mindset before we ever go out to evangelize our community?

Finding Fault

First, you do not want to **find fault** with every incorrect statement that they may make. If you are correct everything they say, you will come across as negative. It is best to choose your battles so to speak. Then, if you **word things thoughtfully**, it will fall on receptive ears. The one you are talking with says, "I have read a few books that claim the Bible has thousands of errors and contradictions, it then listed dozens throughout." First, they are the victim of the Bible critic, so you will need to choose your words carefully.

'Yes, this is a common comment that I hear, and I would add that they are more along the lines of what we call Bible difficulties, not contradictions and errors. A Bible difficulty is something in the Bible that is difficult to understand, because we are thousands of years removed from their culture, because it was written in ancient languages, because the reader has not noticed that two writers are looking at things from two different points of view, among many other things." Then you offer to give an example. "May I give you an example?" He responds with a yes, and you offer an example.

You tell him, "If you were to speak to officers that take accident reports for their police department, you would find that there is cohesion in the accounts, but each person has merely witnessed aspects that have stood out to them. We will see that this is the case as we look at the same account by two different Bible writers." You open your Bible and have him read,

Matthew 8:5: When he entered Capernaum, *a centurion* came forward to him, appealing to him.

Then have him read,

Luke 7:3: When *the centurion* heard about Jesus, he sent to him *elders of the Jews*, asking him to come and heal his servant.

You then say, "Immediately you likely noticed the problem of whether **the centurion** or the **elders of the Jews** spoke with Jesus." He nods his head in agreement. You then say, "The solution is not really hidden from us." You then ask, "Which of the two accounts is the more detailed account?" He responds with, "Luke." "Correct," you respond. Then you explain to him, "The centurion sent the elders of the Jews to represent him to Jesus, so that whatever response Jesus might give, it would be as though he were addressing the centurion; therefore, Matthew gave his readers the basic thought, not seeing the need of mentioning the elders of the Jews aspect. This is how a representative was viewed in the first century, just as some countries see ambassadors today as being the person they represent. Therefore, both Matthew and Luke are correct."

REVIEW QUESTIONS: What balance should someone have if the unbeliever to whom one witnesses to is mistaken on almost everything they believe about the Bible? How might you respond to an unbeliever that has heard that the Bible is full of errors and contradictions?

Respecting the Person

People will have their own view, but you will must come across **respectfully**. You respect the person, not necessarily their view. The person you are talking with may ask, "Why do Christians hate homosexuals?" You

140

would respond with something like, "Christians should not have an irrational hatred for those that struggle with same sex attraction. We are to respect all people. Anyone spewing hatred, he is not truly acting like Jesus. (Matt. 7:12) We are to reject same-sex relationships, the conduct, not the person. For those that are advocates for gay rights, this is their viewpoint, and we **respectfully** disagree, and **respectfully** articulate as to why."

She responds with another question: "Did Jesus not visit sinners and was he not tolerant of others?" You then reply with something like, "Yes, this is partially true, but the inference is mistaken. Jesus spent time with sinners, but he did not ever condone their sin."

"You are right,[40] the Bible does not condone hating those who struggle with same sex attraction, but we are to hate the sin, not the one who may be practicing the sin. However, we are to make a stand against sin that is against the moral code of our Creator, and we are not to cave to public opinion. Our Christian lifestyle is reflective by the moral code within Scripture, and we have a right to our position, by the Creator himself. There is no reason that we should be ashamed of our viewpoint."

REVIEW QUESTIONS: What does it mean to respect the person, but possibly not their view? How might you respond to a person that claims that Christians hate homosexuals? How would you respond to a person who uses Jesus visiting sinners and tolerating others as a means to rationalizing

---

[40] You want to say that they are right at every opportunity where that is the case, which helps them to see that you do not just disagree blindly, because not everything is always bland and white.

	and accepting practicing homosexuals?

Good Communication

Your objective is to share truth, without giving in to popular opinion. However, the truth you want to share will be better received when you afford them the opportunity to share their thoughts and ideas. Then, you express your respectful appreciation for sharing their time with you. You engender trust when they feel that you are listening, and that they are involved in a two-way conversation, as opposed to being on the receiving end of a lecture.

	REVIEW QUESTION: What is one sign of good communication?

Take Notice of Your Surroundings

If you are going to be effective in sharing your Bible beliefs, you will have to be observant to your surroundings. By taking note of what you hear and see, it will help you have far more success. You may be witnessing from house to house, and so you should take note when the person answers the door, or comes from the back yard to greet you. Are there toys, meaning they have children? Is the house immaculately clean? Are there trophies on mantles? Does the house look like it is going through some restoration? Is the newspaper or a magazine laying there with a current affair on the cover? These types of things can be used to generate conversations. However, at the same time, do not come across as being too curious. You should make eye contact, letting them know that you are listening, but not to the point of making them uncomfortable. You may also note body language, as well as the pitch and tone of their words, helping you to know their interest level.

> **REVIEW QUESTION:** What is the benefit of being observant when witnessing to others?

How You Can Be Clear

Do not rush your words, and express them so that the other person can easily understand you. This means that you should be aware of the pace of your speech, and you may want to slow down and pronounce your words more distinctly in private reading. You can practice this in your private Bible reading, where you can read aloud, speaking clearly. However, do not let this become a habit.

In being clear with what you mean to convey, this can be accomplished by not being bogged down in many unnecessary words, but rather being more concise. In other words, if you need to make a point that has multiple parts, it is best that your initial basis of your argument be short and clearly written or stated. Thereafter, you follow it with rational arguments that are mentally clear in their meaning or intention, which your reader or listener is able to easily understand. Jesus was the greatest teacher who ever lived. He on many occasions, took the incredibly complex Mosaic Law, and made it easier to understand for his audience.

In order for you to effectively to teach someone, you must have a solid understanding of the subject yourself, to then help others understand the material. You are ready to teach a subject when you are, in your own words, able to offer reasons as to why it is or is not so. Jesus was able to get his points across by keeping things simple, using indisputable reasoning, stimulating questions, remarkable figures of speech, as well as discernible illustrations that were taken from his listeners everyday life. (Matt. 6:25-30; 7:3-5, 24-27) Jesus was also known for his taking an incident occurring around him and his disciples, which he would then use as an opportunity for teaching a lesson. (John 13:2-16)

Sadly, some Bible scholars have placed their books out of the hands of the common person, as they use language that requires the reader to hold their book in one hand and a Webster's Dictionary in the other. By their nature, these individuals are a polysyllabricator who uses sesquipedalian words. In other words, they use long words with many syllables. Sadly, these individuals spend hundreds, if not thousands of hours researching and writing a book that five people are going to read. In the Sermon on the Mount, Matthew 5:3–7:27, Jesus spoke for a mere half hour, covering such issues as anger toward others, lust, divorce, retaliation, helping the needy, prayer, fasting, anxiety, judging others, materialism. He did not use long words with many syllables here, and could be understood by children, farmers, fishermen and shepherds. (Matt. 7:28)

Jesus expressed word pictures that conveyed the riches of meaning, even today. For example, "No one can serve two masters ... You cannot serve God and money." (Matt. 6:24) "You will recognize them by their fruits." (Matt. 7:20) "Judge not, that you be not judged." (Matt. 7:21) But when he heard it, he said, "Those who

144

are well have no need of a physician, but those who are sick." (Matt. 9:12) Then Jesus said to him, "Put your sword back into its place. For all who take the sword will perish by the sword. (Matt. 26:52) Jesus said to them, "Render to Caesar the things that are Caesar's, and to God the things that are God's." (Mark 12:17)

REVIEW QUESTIONS: Why is clear pronunciation important? What should you do if an unbeliever asks you a Bible question that requires a complex answer? Why have some Bible scholars found themselves out of touch with most people? How did Jesus usually express himself?

Effective Use of Questions

On many occasions, Jesus could have simply told his listeners the point that he wanted to get across, but instead, he chose to ask them questions. For those that were looking to make him look the fool, Jesus asked questions to expose these people. (Matt. 12:24-30; 21:23-27; 22:41-46) However, far more often, he used his questions to convey the point he wanted to make, and he wanted them to remember.

Matthew 17:24-27 English Standard Version (ESV)

24 When they came to Capernaum, the collectors of the two-drachma tax went up to Peter and said, "Does your teacher not pay the tax?" 25 He said, "Yes." And when he came into the house, Jesus spoke to him first, saying, "What do you think, Simon? From whom do kings of the earth take toll or tax? From their sons or from others?" 26 And when he said, "From others," Jesus said to him, "Then the sons are free. 27 However, not to

give offense to them, go to the sea and cast a hook and take the first fish that comes up, and when you open its mouth you will find a shekel. Take that and give it to them for me and for yourself."

 **REVIEW QUESTION:** Who set the example of effective use of questions? Give an example.

Effective Use of Hyperbole

Again, Jesus is by far the most effective teacher of all time, and hyperbole is one method that he used quite often. Hyperbole is a deliberate and obvious exaggeration used for effect, e.g., "I could eat a million of these." The objective is to add emphasis and importance to what is being said. Moreover, like other special literary forms, hyperbole imprints a mental picture in your mind, one that is hard to forget.

There are actually two different types of exaggerations: **(1)** the first being an overstatement, but possible and **(2)** hyperbole, which is a statement that is impossible. Our concern is having the ability to recognize either of these when we see them. Let us take a look at a few examples.

Matthew 7:1-3 English Standard Version (ESV)

[1] "Judge not, that you be not judged. [2] For with the judgment you pronounce you will be judged, and with the measure you use it will be measured to you. [3]Why do you see the speck that is in your brother's eye, but do not notice **the log** that is in your own eye?

146

Try to picture what is being emphasized. You have a person who is continuously, and aggressively judging others, who goes up to a brother that is seldom critical, to offer advice on not being critical. A brother that has a log's worth of being judgmental to him is advising the brother that has a mere straw of judgmentalism to him. Is this not a beautiful way to illustrate how a brother, who has immense problems in a particular area, should be slow to offer advice to another brother, who seldom offends in this area? Below Jesus is rebuking some Pharisees, Jewish religious leaders.

Matthew 23:24 English Standard Version (ESV)

[24]You blind guides, straining out a gnat and swallowing a camel!

This was a foremost way to use hyperbole. Take note of the fact that he is contrasting a small gnat with a huge camel, which represents the largest animal known to his audience. One religious magazine stated, "It is estimated that it would take up to 70 million gnats to equal the weight of an average camel!" Jesus was also very much aware that the Pharisees strained their wine through a cloth sieve to avoid ceremonial uncleanness by accidently drinking a gnat. However, they were quite eager to gulp down the figurative camel, it also being unclean. (Lev. 11:4, 21-24) How? The Pharisees were very quick to follow the minor points of the Mosaic Law, but set aside the weightier laws, like "justice and mercy and faithfulness." (Matt. 23:23) This one point makes using hyperbole all too clear, and exposed them for the hypocrites they were.

Matthew 17:20 English Standard Version (ESV)

[20]He said to them, "Because of your little faith. For truly, I say to you, if you have faith like a grain of

mustard seed, you will say to this mountain, 'Move from here to there,' and it will move, and nothing will be impossible for you."

Jesus could have simply said that they need more faith, but that would have not made the impact this figurative comment did. He only stressed the need for a little faith in an effective manner, making the point that a small amount of faith can move mountain-like objects.

Matthew 19:24 English Standard Version (ESV)

24 Again I tell you, it is easier for a camel to go through the eye of a needle than for a rich person to enter the kingdom of God."

Try if you will to picture a camel fitting through the eye of a sewing needle. It is impossible, not difficult! Of course, this does not mean that rich people are excluded from the kingdom of God. The context is about people, who have a greater love for money than their love of the kingdom. It is their love of money, which makes them ineligible. Jesus' colorful, vivid idioms have an effect so powerful that literally hundreds of millions of people have used them over the last 2,000 years.

Throughout his three and a half years of ministry, Jesus masterfully used hyperbole. Are you not in awe of Jesus' exciting figures of speech and his skill of accomplishing a supreme effect without long words with many syllables?

REVIEW QUESTIONS: What is hyperbole? What two different types of exaggerations are there? How effective was Jesus in his use of hyperbole? Give an example.

Overcoming Dismissive Comments

Many today are just not interested in your desire to share the Good News with them. They will attempt to shut you down with one good dismissive comment in the beginning. Your objective is to become effective in your ability to overcome or get around these walls of disinterest. They may hold up their hand, which is a dismissive gesture, and say in a dismissive tone,

- "I am not interested."
- "I am not interested in religion."
- "I am busy."
- "Why do Christians feel the need to share?"
- "I am a Buddhist, a Hindu, a Muslim, or a Jew."
- "I don't believe the Bible."
- "Everyone interprets the Bible differently."
- "The Bible is not practical in today's scientific world."
- "The Bible contradicts itself."
- "The Bible is a good book by man, but there is no such thing as absolute truth."

These quick comments are meant to stop us in our tracks. These dismissive comments can be general, "I am

---

[41] The Evangelism Program Director or Assistant Director will select the topic.

not interested," or they could be based on the subject you start the conversation with. People have many reasons as to why they do not want to talk. Most are misconceptions.

- They had a bad experience in a congregation they attended before.
- They have taken many liberal classes throughout their high school and college years.
- They are aware of Christian history, like crusades, inquisitions, or immoral Popes in church history.
- They are aware of major church scandals.
- They have read popular books that tear down the Bible as being full of historical, geographical and scientific errors, and contradictions. To them the book is by imperfect men, not inspired of God.
- Maybe their life has been filled with one tragedy after another, and they cannot grasp how a loving God would allow such suffering.

These are some of the reasons, why they use dismissive comments. They have issues that are not well founded, and need to be reasoned on further. That is why, many times, if you can get beyond the comment, you can get at what really troubles them, and help them reason through it. Below is an example of one trying to be dismissive, using the Bible as a means of shutting down the conversation.

REVIEW QUESTIONS: What are some dismissive comments that the unbeliever might make, and what is his purpose for making such comments? What are some legitimate reasons the Bible critic might not be interested in talking about

'The Bible contains contradictions, mistakes, and errors'

Whoever makes a claim carries the responsibility, so tactfully inquire, "Yes, this is a common claim, could you take my Bible, and point to an example?" Most will not take the Bible, because they are just repeating a common complaint about the Bible. However, for the sake of those few, who will, he takes your Bible, and turns to Matthew 27:5 and says, "It states that Judas hanged himself," whereas Acts 1:18 says that "falling headlong he burst open in the middle and all his bowels gushed out."

Matthew 27:5: And throwing down the pieces of silver into the temple, he departed, and **he went and hanged himself**.

Acts 1:18: Now this man acquired a field with the reward of his wickedness, and **falling headlong he burst open in the middle and all his bowels gushed out**.

You Respond: "Neither Matthew, nor Luke made a mistake. What you have is Matthew giving the reader the manner in which Judas committed suicide. On the other hand, Luke is giving the reader of Acts, the result of that suicide. Therefore, instead of a mistake, we have two texts that complement each other, really giving the reader the full picture. Judas came to a tree alongside a cliff that had rocks below. He tied the rope to a branch and the other end around his neck, and jumped over the edge of the cliff in an attempt at hanging himself. One of two things could have happened: (1) the limb broke plunging him to the rocks below, or (2) the rope broke

151

with the same result, and he burst open onto the rocks below."

Then you could add, "Generally, what it comes down to is that many books that criticize the Bible, pointing to Scriptures, showing what they call errors, contradictions, and mistakes. However, what they do not show the reader is that there are reasonable answers for ninety-nine percent of these complaints.'

A longer response might be, "Considering that there are 31,000 plus verses in the Bible, encompassing 66 books written by about 40 writers, ranging from shepherds, to kings, an army general, fishermen, tax collector, a physician and on and on, and being penned over a 1,600 year period, one does find a few hundred *Bible difficulties* (about one percent). However, 99 percent of those are explainable. Yet no one wants to be so arrogant to say that he can explain them all. It has nothing to do with the inadequacy of God's Word, but is based on human understanding. In many cases, science or archaeology and the field of custom and culture of ancient peoples has helped explain difficulties in hundreds of passages. Therefore, there may be less than one percent left to be answered, yet our knowledge of God's Word continues to grow. R. A. Torrey said about 100 years ago, "Some people are surprised and staggered because there are difficulties in the Bible. For my part, I would be more surprised and staggered if there were not."

You explain that these are not contradictions, errors, or mistakes, but are Bible difficulties, which are difficult because the Bible was written in dozens of different cultures and times that range from 2,000 to 3,500 years ago. In addition, the Bible was written in three different ancient languages. Moreover, the Bible

152

was written from the intention of human author back then, and we should not impose our modern world on that author. Today, we say in our news reports that the sun rises and sets at certain times, even though we know this is scientifically inaccurate. However, it is a human observation. Today, we round numbers because it is a way of simplifying things, if we are trying to make a point, like how many people living in America. We would just say 316 million, not, 315,940,341 unless we were doing a census. Jesus spoke of mustard seeds as the smallest of all seeds. This is not accurate. However, was Jesus giving a lesson on botany? No, he was making a point to a people, who knew this seed as being the smallest. Therefore, considering Jesus' audience, the point that he was making, and how the mustard seed was commonly used as a figure of speech, this was the tiniest seed in that setting and circumstance.

Either this person raising issues about the Bible is going to be more receptive to the conversation, or he will ignore your insight as though you never made it, moving on to the next criticism that he has memorized. His response is a way for you to read his heart-attitude. You will not want to throw your pearls before the swine of Bible criticism, so move on, if it is evident that no answer will satisfy this one. However, far more right-hearted ones are going to be receptive to your insightful words. This brings us to our next point, how they listen to you.

REVIEW QUESTION: How might you respond to someone that claims the Bible contains contradictions, mistakes, and errors? How might you explain why there are no contradictions, errors, or mistakes in

	the Bible, just Bible difficulties?

How the Unbeliever Listens to Us

Getting a sense of how one is listening to us, will enable us to determine if more time should be given to this one. The person we are talking with may very well be what is known as a **judgmental listener**. They are listening to us to ascertain whether we are right or wrong, and are labeling us in their mind ('that was foolish'), as opposed to hearing what we are saying. Then, there is what is known as the **distorted listener**. In other words, this one does not hear us clearly, because he is viewing us in a biased and prejudiced way ('Christians are such fools!'). There is the **stereotype listener**, who also fails to hear our real message, because they are labeling us in their mind, as "just a woman," "Bible thumper," "so naïve," and so on.

Then, there is the **resistive listener**, who will not be receptive to anything that is not a part of his worldview. Moreover, anyone in opposition to their worldview is viewed as the enemy, and they resist anything they say, no matter how reasonable it may be. They think things like, 'Why do these people not see that science has displaced the Bible as a book by man." We also have the **interpretive listener**. These view everything through their preconceptions, ideas based on little or no information, just personal bias. They incorporate their life experience into what they are hearing, making snap interpretations of our every word. They filter everything through their worldview, their knowledge and understanding.

Then, there is the **association listener**, who evaluates our Christian visit with everything bad they have ever heard about Christianity and the Bible, and we are guilty by association. No matter what we say, it is ignored, because they see us as a member of a group that they perceive a certain way. Of course, this could go the other way if they have a favorable view of Christianity. While these are the negative side of listening, it can give us an idea of why and how we could be shut out, before we ever get started. If we feel that we are unfairly dismissed, we could ask some open-ended questions such as 'how do you feel,' 'what do you think,' 'what do you believe,' or 'how do you see these questions.' Open-ended questions enable us to get at their heart condition, enabling us to better formulate our arguments.

Lastly, there are the persons that all Christian evangelizers are looking for, which is the **receptive heart listener**. One who has a receptive heart, will let reasoning from the Scriptures in receptively, which will build confidence in what we are saying is true. We will be able to plant seeds of truth within this person's heart, which God will make grow. In writing to the Corinthians, who were caught up in arguing over who was greater (Paul or Apollos); Paul made the comparison of a Christian evangelist with that of a farmer. The Apostle Paul planted the Corinthian congregation. Apollos came later on the scene, and watered the Bible truths that Paul had already planted. Apollos with his passion and force, as well as his authoritative Scriptural refutations of the arguments that had been raised by the unbelieving Jews was very beneficial to the Corinthian Christians. However, it was God, who made those truths grow.

1 Corinthians 3:1-9 English Standard Version (ESV)

[1] But I, brothers, could not address you as spiritual people, but as people of the flesh, as infants in Christ. [2] I fed you with milk, not solid food, for you were not

ready for it. And even now you are not yet ready,[3] for you are still of the flesh. For while there is jealousy and strife among you, are you not of the flesh and behaving only in a human way? [4] For when one says, "I follow Paul," and another, "I follow Apollos," are you not being merely human?

[5] What then is Apollos? What is Paul? Servants through whom you believed, as the Lord assigned to each. [6] I planted, Apollos watered, but God gave the growth. [7] So neither he who plants nor he who waters is anything, but only God who gives the growth. [8] He who plants and he who waters are one, and each will receive his wages according to his labor. [9] For we are God's fellow workers. You are God's field, God's building.

Keep in mind, that the receptive heart listener is not just the person, who shakes his head yes, as he agrees with your every word. Peter was sent to the Ethiopian Eunuch (Acts 8:26-38), who had rapid spiritual progress, while the Apostle Paul was sent to the Greek philosophers on Mars Hill.

Mars Hill (Areopagus) was a "prominent rise overlooking the city of Athens where the philosophers of the city gathered to discuss their ideas, some of which revolutionized modern thought. Paul discussed religion with the leading minds of Athens on Mars Hill. He used the altar to an 'unknown god' to present Jesus to them (Acts 17:22)."[42]

The point is that the Apostle Paul was sent to people who were very knowledgeable, intelligent, and wise,

---

[42] "Mars Hill", in Holman Illustrated Bible Dictionary, ed. Chad Brand, Charles Draper, Archie England et al., 1084 (Nashville, TN: Holman Bible Publishers, 2003).

people who only lacked the light to see where the real truth lie. This was no easy assignment, but in the end, "some men joined [Paul] and believed, among whom also were Dionysius the Areopagite and a woman named Damaris and others with them." (Acts 17:34) Yes, Paul reasoned from the Scriptures in the synagogue with the Jews, and he reasoned with Epicurean and Stoic philosophers, who also conversed with him. It says that he was "explaining and proving." This illustrates that a receptive heart listener also includes those who require us to reason from the Scriptures; therefore, we have to have the ability to reason from the Scriptures. (Acts 17: 2-3, 17-18)

REVIEW QUESTIONS: What type of listeners is there, and which one is the evangelist seeking? Are Christians expected to only evangelize those who are easy to convince?

Effective Listening and Responding

In trying to communication with strangers, it can be quite a challenge at times. We may deal with biases, prejudices, a person in the middle of life trauma, someone who has had bad experiences, someone who just lost a loved one, and many more communication challenges. We will be able to overcome some of the anxieties of starting conversation, by taking a moment to consider some of these challenges.

One of the ways to deal with a challenge is empathy. We in our hearts must place ourselves in their shoes, getting their mindset. Just because a person comes across abrasively about talking about the Bible, this does not mean that we let them go. There may very well be a reason as to why they are not open to a Bible conversation. This is where insightful, thought-provoking questions, can get at the significant part that has closed them down.

By employing active listening, allowing them to vent, we will understand whatever issues we need to overcome. We might ask, 'tell me, what has you to where you are unable to talk about the Bible.' This will let them know that we are open to listening. While they are expressing themselves, do not be tempted to resolve their issue, just listen as they fully explain. First, make sure we respond in a calm voice. Then reiterate what they said in a summary point, which will let them know we were listening, and it helps us to know we understand what it is. In the end, we may not agree, but we can empathetically understand in some way.

Now, if we have a solution to what was mention, offer it at this time. If we do not have a biblical answer, be honest, saying something like, "I can understand, and while I do not have a ready answer for you at this time, I will research it at home, and we can talk again." This lets them know that we are going beyond what one would expect and that we are very concerned about them.

REVIEW QUESTION: What are some communication challenges that you may face, and how may you overcome these?

Course Project D	**Reasoning From The Scriptures**: Using several Scriptures, effectively

communicate why _____ is not biblical or is biblical. The director or assistant direct will assign a subject.[43]

---

[43] The Evangelism Program Director or Assistant Director will select the topic.

CHAPTER 8 Using Persuasion to Reach the Heart of Our Listeners

In some ways, many might think that the word "persuasion" seems like a sneaky or devious kind of word. Some might think of the salesperson that sells cars, who comes across as pushy or those using deceptive language in a contract that someone wants us to sign. Maybe the word "persuasion" hits us as if it is simply manipulation. It is used in a similar vein by the apostle Paul when he writes of Christians in Galatia, "You were running well. Who hindered you from obeying the truth? This **persuasion** is not from him who calls you." (Gal. 5:7-8) The Greek word used here *peismone* has the sense of 'persuasion, i.e., communication intended to induce belief or action.'[44] Paul also told the Colossians, "I say this so that no one will delude you with **persuasive** argument." (Col 2:4) The Greek word use here *pithanologia* has the sense of 'persuasive speech, namely, using language effectively to please or persuade.'[45] When persuasion is used in this way, it does have somewhat of a negative connotation, as it hinges on crafty arguments built on false details. However, the sense of the two words is very similar.

Nevertheless, we have the apostle Paul using the art of persuasion or convincing with a different implication. In his second letter to Timothy Paul writes, "You, however, continue in the things you have learned and were **persuaded** to believe, knowing from whom you

---

[44] Bible sense Lexicon by Logos Bible Software

[45] IBID

have learned them." (2 Tim. 3:14, UASV) The NASB renders the verse this way, "Continue in the things you have learned and become **convinced** of." (The ESV, HCSB and LEB render it similarly.) The Greek word here Pistoo[46] has the sense of 'being convinced, or being persuaded or sure of the truthfulness or validity of something.'[47] When Paul was speaking of what Timothy had been persuaded or convinced to believe, it was used in a different connotation from the above Greek words, while still having the same sense as the other two Greek words. In the above verses to the Galatians and Colossians it was a manipulation of the truth that was being used to persuade, while here Timothy's mother and his grandmother were persuading or convincing Timothy to believe based on the truth itself.– 2 Timothy 1:5.

When Paul was under house arrest in Rome, he effectively witnessed to many. The account reads, "When they had appointed a day for him, they came to him at his lodging in greater numbers; and he expounded to them, testifying about the kingdom of God and trying to **persuade** them concerning Jesus both from the Law of Moses and from the Prophets, from morning till evening." The Greek word *peitho* has the sense persuading, causing someone to adopt a certain position, belief, or course of action.'[48] Was the apostle Paul manipulating truth to deceive those to whom he was witnessing? No, he was persuading them to believe about

---

[46] The Greek word e**pisto**thes in the New Testament is identified as a New Testament hapax legomenon, a word of which there is only one recorded use.

[47] Bible sense Lexicon by Logos Bible Software

[48] IBID

Jesus Christ based on truth. Therefore, the art of persuasion can be used for good or for bad. Christians use persuasion to help others adopt a certain position, belief about the Father and the Son, and the Word of God. As teachers, evangelists, proclaimers we can use sound logical reasoning, as we explain, persuade and convince, convicting others of Bible truth. (2 Tim. 2:15) Clearly, one of the most skilled persuaders in the history of Christianity was the apostle Paul. Demetrius, the "silversmith in Ephesus who incited a riot directed against Paul because he feared that the apostle's preaching would threaten the sale of silver shrines of Diana, the patron goddess of Ephesus." He said of Paul, "And you see and hear that not only in Ephesus but in almost all of Asia this Paul has persuaded and turned away a great many people, saying that gods made with hands are not gods."–Acts 19:26

Using Persuasion in Our Evangelism

Jesus commanded all Christians, "Go therefore and make disciples of all nations, baptizing them in the name of the Father and of the Son and of the Holy Spirit, teaching them to observe all that I have commanded you. And behold, I am with you always, to the end of the age." Christianity has been sending missionaries for centuries and it has been very productive in that Christian congregations are now found throughout the entire world. The last forty years or so, many missionaries have come to believe that evangelism is needed to enter a new era of all Christians effective evangelizing in their own communities.

A *Part-Time or Full-Time Evangelist* is one who sees this as their calling and chooses to be very involved as an evangelist in their local church and community. They may work part-time to supplement their work as an evangelist. They may be married with children, but they realize their gift is in the field of evangelism. If it were the wife, the husband would work toward supporting her work as an evangelist and vice-versa. If it were a single person, he or she would supplement their work by being employed part-time, but also the church would help as well. This person is well trained in every aspect of bringing one to Christ. *Congregation Evangelists* should be very involved in evangelizing their communities and helping the church members play their role at the basic levels of evangelism. There is nothing to say that one church could not have many within, who have the calling of an evangelist, which would and should be cultivated. What are some tools that can use in our effort to persuade others of the truth of God's Word?

Listening Carefully will enable us to understand fully what the unbeliever knows about any subject that we may be discussing with him. For example, if he says that he does not believe in the Bible, it may seem natural to launch into a solid explanation as to why he should believe in the Bible. However, we need to know specifically what it is that has him rejecting the Bible. Is it because he thinks it is just a man's book or does he feel it is full of contradictions and errors, or that it is an ancient book and not practical for today. Therefore, we need to listen carefully to the why of a stated position and not just assume we know what he means.–Proverbs 18:13.

Asking Questions goes right along with listening. Questions can be used to reiterate, making sure we understand what they meant. Questions can be used to get them to explain exactly what it they meant by a statement or a position. Questions can be used to lead a person to the right answer. We might ask the above person that does not believe in the Bible, "have you always felt that way and what is it that contributed to your not believing in the Bible?" After they give us the specifics of why, we can use questions to dig deeper or lead. Suppose they said, 'it is because the Bible is full of contradictions and errors.' We can ask, "Have you ever considered what the difference between errors and contradictions and Bible difficulties is? "Have you ever studied the subject of errors or contradictions within the Scriptures?" After those questions, we might ask, "Do you have a couple examples of those errors and contradictions?" There are literally thousands of Bible difficulties between Genesis 1:1 and Revelation 22:21, which the Bible critic labels as errors and contradictions. Everyone uses common ones as their examples, if we recognize one and know that there is a reasonable explanation, we might offer a brief explanation of what a Bible difficulty is. Then we can demonstrate how that helps us better understand these are not errors and contradictions at all, as we also give him a reasonable explanation of his supposed error or contradiction. Then, we can ask, "would you agree with this explanation?" When we use questions and listen, we are involving the unbeliever to join us in a respectful conversation, giving them a chance to be heard, as opposed to him just hearing us go on and on about a subject.

Using Sound Reasoning will help us reach the heart and mind of our listeners. For example, the above listener said he did not believe in the Bible and we asked why, got the specifics that he was hung up on perceived errors and contradictions, and gave him reasonable and logical answers that they were actually Bible difficulties, followed by a reasonable and logical explanation of his specific error or contradiction. Thus, we close out with the following, "The authors of Bible claim that what they wrote was inspired of God and they were moved along

164

by Holy Spirit as they penned God's Words. (2 Tim 3:16-17; 2 Pet. 1:20-21) Those inspired authors tell us of an opportunity at eternal life, if we trust in the Son of God. (John 3:16) Would you not agree that while this is not evidence that it is, in fact, the Word of God and those things are true, but that it would be sensible nonetheless to investigate it objectively and find out if such claims are true or not?

The person above, who claimed he did not believe in the Bible, gave his reason, saying it is full of errors and contradictions. In our listening and asking questions, he gave us an example, when he says, "If God hardened the Pharaoh's heart, what exactly makes Pharaoh responsible for the decisions he makes?" When we look at the verse below, it does seem to say what our listener has claimed. How can God harden the heart of Pharaoh, so that he says no to all requests from Moses and Aaron and then punish him and his people for his saying no?

Exodus 4:21 Updated American Standard Version (UASV)	**Exodus 4:21** Revised Standard Version (RSV)
21 Jehovah said to Moses, "When you go and return to Egypt see that you perform before Pharaoh all the wonders which I have put in your hand; but I will harden his heart so that he will not let the people go.	21 And the Lord said to Moses, "When you go back to Egypt, see that you do before Pharaoh all the miracles which I have put in your power; but I will harden his heart, so that he will not let the people go.

Answer: This is actually a prophecy. God knew that what he was about to do would contribute to a stubborn and obstinate Pharaoh, who was going to be unwilling to change or give up the Israelites so they could go off to worship their God. Therefore, this is not stating what God is going to do; it is prophesying that Pharaoh's heart will harden because of the actions of God. The fact is, Pharaoh allowed his own heart to harden because he was determined not to agree with Moses' wishes or accept Jehovah's request to let the people go. Moses tells us at Exodus 7:13 that "Pharaoh's heart was hardened,[49] and he would not listen to them, as Jehovah had said." Again, at 8:15, we read, "But when Pharaoh saw that there was a relief, he hardened[50] his heart and would not listen to them, as Jehovah had said."

Dealing With the Emotional Beliefs of Others

Everyone has deeply held beliefs that if jabbed emotions may flare. We may be in a conversation with a devout Catholic, who believes that it is proper to address prayers to Mary as intercessor. Even if we were to show Scriptures and respectfully reason with him, he may come back sternly, "I still believe it proper to address prayers to Mary as intercessor." Whether we are witnessing to a Catholic, an atheist, and agnostic, a Muslim, a Hindus, a Buddhist, a Jehovah's Witness, a Mormon and so on, emotions are involved. In some cases, like the Witnesses, it is against their beliefs to be witnessed to, but they can witness to others. If you are aware of their teachings, their background and begin to question these things, even in a respectful manner, they will abandon the conversation quickly.

---

[49] Lit *strong*

[50] Lit *made heavy*

Many view their beliefs as absolute truths, even relativism,[51] which claims there is no such thing as absolute truth. When relativist's state there is no such thing as absolute truth, this is self-defeating within itself, as they are defeating the very absolute truth claim that they are trying to make, i.e., "all truth is relative." If there is no absolute truth; then, their belief that there are no absolutes cannot be true.[52] However, they would argue their belief vigorously as though it were absolutely true, even get emotional over it. Our beliefs are our worldview. A worldview is "the sum total of answers that a person gives to the most important questions in life." (Dr. Ronald Nash) Dr. Nash goes on to say, "Many people remain blissfully unaware that they have a worldview, even though the sudden change in their life and thought resulted from their exchanging their old worldview for their new one."[53] If we are going to overturn any false reasoning within one's worldview, say that of an atheist, it will take more than simple logic or even Scriptures that would demonstrate their view is erroneous.

---

[51] Relativism is the belief that concepts such as right and wrong, goodness and badness, or truth and falsehood are not absolute but change from culture to culture and situation to situation.

[52] "To claim that all moral truths are relative is self-defeating. A statement is self-defeating when what is being affirmed fails to meet its own requirements. An example is the statement, "I can't speak a word in English," to which one might respond, "You just did." The moral relativists' claim commits the same error, since the statement 'All truth is relative' is itself an absolute claim for truth. It is impossible to consistently hold the claims of moral relativism because it denies what it tries to affirm in its very statements."—Hindson, Ed (2008-05-01). The Popular Encyclopedia of Apologetics (p. 354). Harvest House Publishers.

[53] Zondervan (2010-06-19). Life's Ultimate Questions: An Introduction to Philosophy (p. 32). Zondervan.

We will have to be empathetic and have compassionate hearts, kindness, humility, meekness, and patience, as we use the art of persuasion. (Rom. 12:15; Col. 3:12) We as a teacher, an evangelist, a proclaimer of God's Word, never water down the truth. Moreover, we have strong convictions in what we hold to be true, i.e., our biblical or Christian worldview. For example, Paul stated it this way, "I am convinced that ..." and "I know and am convinced ..." (Rom. 8:38; 14:14, NASB) Even though we know we possess absolute truth, this does not mean we are free to be dogmatic or self-righteous about it, which can come across in our tone. Moreover, we would never use sarcasm or talk down to another when we are sharing our biblical truths, even if this is the way we are being treated in the conversation. We would never want to cause offense or even insult our listener.— Proverbs 12:18.

The apostle Peter tells us that we are to "sanctify Christ as Lord in your hearts, always being ready to make a defense to everyone who asks you to give an account for the hope that is in you, yet with gentleness and reverence." (1 Pet. 3:15, NASB) We will reach far deeper into their mind and heart if we respect their beliefs acknowledging that they have a right to possess them, even though we do not agree with them. This will require humility on our part, for which Paul makes the point that we should "do nothing from selfish ambition or conceit, but in humility count others more significant than yourselves." (Phil 2:3-4, ESV) Jesus in one of his parables said, "For everyone who exalts himself will be humbled, but the one who humbles himself will be exalted." (Luke 18:9-14, ESV) Yes, if we are to persuade others, it will come through our humility, as we truly appreciate God for his helping us to see the truth, and our greatest desire it to share that same truth with others.

168

Paul wrote to the Corinthians, "For the weapons of our warfare are not of the flesh but have divine power to destroy strongholds. We destroy arguments and every lofty opinion raised against the knowledge of God, and take every thought captive to obey Christ." (2 Cor. 10:4-5) "Paul was certain that he was on a course **to demolish** the **strongholds** or fortifications of **arguments and every pretension** that anyone set up **against the knowledge of God**. As Paul traveled the world proclaiming the gospel of Christ, he encountered pretentious disbelief supported by clever arguments and powerful personalities. But through the "weakness" of preaching Christ, Paul went about taking **captive every thought to make it obedient to Christ**." (Pratt Jr 2000, p. 417) We as Christians seek to use the Word of God, logic,[54] reason,[55] in our art of persuasion to

---

[54] What is logic? And why in the world would anyone want to study it? Isn't it just a bunch of incomprehensible and arbitrary rules that no one really follows anyway? What good does it do? To most people, logic is an unknown language about an unknown realm, where everything is turned upside down and no one with an IQ below 300 is allowed. You can see it in the panic on their faces when you just mention the word-LOGIC!

Despite all the bad press, logic is not so tough. In fact, it is one of the simplest things to use because you use it all the time, though you may not realize it. We don't mean that you put all of your thoughts into logical form and do a formal analysis of each thought. But when you are at the supermarket and one brand of sugar is 3 cents per ounce but another is 39 cents per pound, it doesn't take long for you to pull out your calculator and settle the issue. Why do you do that? Because you recognize nize that those ounces and pounds have to be put in the same category to be compared. That's logic. You use logic to do most everything. When you decide to take your shower after you work out instead of before, you don't necessarily go through all the formal steps it takes to reach that conclusion validly, but your decision rests on logic nonetheless. Logic really means putting your thoughts in order.–Ronald M. Brooks; Norman L. Geisler. Come, Let Us Reason: An Introduction to Logical Thinking (p. 11) "destroy arguments and every lofty opinion." We must remember that God has shown us much patience in our early walk in coming to know him. We are over joyed that we have the Word of God, this powerful tool (Heb. 4:12), which will enable us to overturn false reasoning, reaching hearts and minds with the art of persuasion.

Exercise

- Someone just said to you, "I don't believe the Bible, as it is full of errors and contradictions." How would you persuade him that this is not the case?

Review Questions

- What does it mean to persuade?

- How can we use persuasion in our evangelism?

- How can we deal with the emotional beliefs others?

---

[55] "God is rational, and the principles of good reason do flow from his very nature. Consequently, learning the rules of clear and correct reasoning is more than an academic exercise. For the Christian, it is also a means of spiritual service."—IBID p. 7

CHAPTER 9 Skillfully Using the Word of God

Ephesians 6:17 Updated American Standard Version (UASV)

[17] And take the **helmet of salvation**, and **the sword of the Spirit**, which is the word of God.

Not long ago, those trying to curb the use of drugs within the American youth had the saying, "the mind is a terrible thing to waste." Our next piece of the armor of God would be a very useful tool for protecting the Christian mind, **the helmet of salvation**. The Apostle Paul said to the Thessalonians, "we must stay sober and let our faith and love be like a suit of armor. Our firm hope that we will be saved is our helmet," because it protects our Christian mind. (1 Thessalonians 5:8) Even though we may have accepted Christ, and have entered onto the path of salvation, we still suffer from imperfect human weaknesses. Even though our foremost desire is to do good, our thinking can be corrupted by this fleshly world that surrounds us. We need to **not** be like this world, but rather openly allow God to alter the way we think, through his Word the Bible, which will help us fully to grasp everything that is good and pleasing to him. (Romans 7:18; 12:2) You likely recall the test that Jesus faced, where Satan offered him "all the kingdoms of the world and their glory." (Matthew 4:8-10) Jesus response was to refer to Scripture, "Be gone, Satan! For it is written, 'you shall worship the Lord your God and him only shall you serve.'" Paul had this to say about Jesus, "looking to Jesus, the founder and perfecter of our faith, who for the joy that was set before him endured the cross, despising the shame and is seated at the right hand of the throne of God."–Hebrews 12:2.

We need to understand that the examples of faith within Scripture do not come to us automatically. If we are focusing on what this current satanic world that caters to the fallen human flesh and what it has to offer, as opposed to focusing on the hopes that are plainly laid out in Scripture, we will be weak in the face of any severe trial. After a few stumbles, it may be that we suffer spiritual shipwreck, and lose our hope altogether. Then again, if we frequently feed our minds or concentrate the mind on the promises of God, we will carry on delighting in the hope that has been offered us.–Romans 12:12.

If we are to keep our Christian mind on the hope that lies ahead, we need to possess the **Sword of the Spirit**. The book that reveals heavenly Father, his will and purposes, i.e., the Bible is stated to be "living and active, sharper than any two-edged sword, piercing to the division of soul and of spirit, of joints and of marrow, and discerning the thoughts and intentions of the heart." This Word, if understood correctly, applied in a balanced manner, can transform our lives, and help us avoid or minimalize the pitfalls of this imperfect life. We can depend on that Word when we are overwhelmed, or temple to give way to the flesh, and when the Bible critics of this world attempt to do away with our faith. (2 Corinthians 10:4-5) We need to heed the words of the Apostle Paul to his spiritual son, Timothy:

2 Timothy 3:15-17 Updated American Standard Version (UASV)

[14] You **[Timothy]**, however, continue in the things you have learned and were persuaded to believe, knowing from whom you have learned them **[Paul, who Timothy traveled with and studied under for**

15 years], **15** and that from infancy[56] you have known the sacred writings **[the whole Old Testament]**, which are able to make you wise for salvation through trust[57] in Christ Jesus. **16** All Scripture is inspired by God and profitable for teaching, for reproof, for correction, for training in righteousness; **17** so that the man of God may be fully competent, equipped for every good work.

The goal of all this instruction, discipline, and training is not to keep us busy. God intends **that the man of God may be thoroughly equipped for every good work**. We study the Bible, we rely upon God's Spirit, his revelation, and the community of the faithful to keep us on track—obedient and maturing in faith. Continuing in this commitment will enable us to do whatever God calls us to do. Timothy could withstand the attacks of false teachers, the abandonment of professing believers, and the persecution that surrounded him because God had equipped him for the task. God never calls us to do something without first enabling us through his Spirit and the power of his truth to accomplish the task.

We neglect the Scriptures at our own peril. Through them we gain the ability to serve God and others. The Scriptures not only point the way; through the mysterious union of God's

---

[56] *Brephos* is "the period of time when one is very young—'childhood (probably implying a time when a child is still nursing), infancy." – GELNTBSD

[57] *Pisteuo* is "to believe to the extent of complete trust and reliance—'to believe in, to have confidence in, to have faith in, to trust, faith, and trust.' – GELNTBSD

Word and faith, they give us the ability to serve. (Larson 2000, 307)

After two years of proclaiming the good news, Jesus entered into another campaign throughout Galilee. "Jesus went throughout all the cities and villages, teaching in their synagogues and proclaiming the gospel of the kingdom and healing every disease and every affliction." Jesus had compassion for the lost sheep of Israel,

Matthew 9:36-38 American Standard Version (ASV)

[36] When he saw the crowds, he had compassion for them, because they were harassed and scattered, like sheep without a shepherd. [37] Then he said to his disciples, "The harvest is plentiful, but the workers are few. [38] Therefore, beg the Master of the harvest to send out workers into his harvest."

After stating the above, Jesus "called to him his twelve disciples" and "sent out after instructing them." (Matt. 9:35-38; 10:1, 5) Later, Jesus "appointed seventy[58] others and sent them on ahead of him, two by two, into every town and place where he himself was about to go. Then he was saying to them: 'The harvest, indeed, is great, but the workers are few; therefore beg the Master of the harvest to send out workers into his harvest.'"– Luke 10:1-2

This was true in Jesus' day when there were but about one hundred million people on the planet, how much more true it is today with over seven billion. Moreover, the need for workers is far graver today, as the churches are not sending workers out into their communities to share the good news.

---

[58] Some mss read *seventy-two*

John 4:34-35 Updated American Standard Version (UASV)

[34] Jesus said to them, "My food is that I do the will of the one who sent me and complete his work. [35] Do you not say, 'There are yet four months and the harvest comes'? Behold, I say to you, lift up your eyes and look at the fields, that they are white for harvest already.

The fields of humankind alienated from God are, indeed, white for harvesting. Therefore, all should pray that God gather together workers, preparing them, to go out into the communities of their churches, to sow the good news. When we pray such things, we need to act in harmony with our prayers. One way we can do this is by reading such books as CONVERSATIONAL EVANGELISM, THE EVANGELISM HANDBOOK and THE CHRISTIAN APOLOGIST, all by Edward D. Andrews. These books will prepare all Christians to share God's Word effectively in their community, in their family, in the workplace or school, and informally.—Matthew 28:19-20; Mark 13:10.

The Word of God Is Living and Active

Hebrews 4:12 English Standard Version (ESV)

[12] For the word of God is living and active, sharper than any two-edged sword, piercing to the division of soul and of spirit, of joints and of marrow, and discerning the thoughts and intentions of the heart.

What power the message within the Word of God has! It is so powerful that it can change the entire makeup of anyone's inner person, if he are receptive to the truth.

Colossians 3:9-10 English Standard Version (ESV)

⁹ Do not lie to one another, seeing that you have put off the old self with its practices¹⁰ and have put on the new self, which is being renewed in knowledge after the image of its creator.

The Bible contains so much wisdom; it is almost unfathomable to contemplate it. There are endless amounts of life principles, do's and don'ts, commands, counsel, which can help its reader to have far more success in this wicked world than those who refuse to consider its unrivaled wisdom. Psalm 119:105 makes the point perfectly, 'the Word of God is a lamp to my feet [immediate concerns] and a light to my path [what lies ahead].' The Bible will lead us in the way we ought to go in making everyday decisions, or choosing friends, deciding entertainment, employment choices, just how revealing our clothes will be, and so on. (Ps. 37:25; Prov. 13:20; John 15:14; 1 Tim. 2:9) Living by the principles and counsel of the Word, will help us to have better relationships with others. (Matt. 7:12; Phil. 2:3-4) We can make a decision for the day, but we can also plan a life, based on what the future hold, as we have our roadway lit with the Word. (1 Tim. 6:9) Our objective is to live under the umbrella of God's sovereignty, to live according to his will and purposes. (Matt. 6:33; 1 John 2:17-18) Life need not be meaningless to the one living by the Word of God.

Then, there is the fact that the Bible is also a weapon in spiritual warfare. The apostle Paul referred to the Word of God as "the sword of the Spirit." (Eph. 6:12, 17) **"The sword of the Spirit** pictures the soldier's weapon sheathed to his belt and used both for offensive and defensive purposes. Taking the sword of the Spirit—defined for us as the Word of God—can be understood as using Scripture specifically in life's situations to fend off attacks of the enemy and put him to flight. We see the example of Jesus using the Scripture this way in Matthew 4:1–11."[59] If we are effective in our evangelism, we can be used by God as his ambassador, helping those within Satan's world to be set free from spiritual bondage. Unlike imperfect man sword of carnal warfare, "the sword of the Spirit, which is the word of God," saves lives rather than destroy them. However, this is dependent on just how effective we are at wielding this sword.

Teach the Word of Truth Correctly

Can we imagine the ancient soldier who dared enter into warfare without practicing with his sword? How effective would he be with his weapon? He would likely be killed within minutes. The same holds true with our use of "the sword of the spirit," namely, God's Word, in our spiritual warfare, i.e., we would be beaten down by the critic or opponent in short order. If our faith is genuine, we will be like the prophet Jeremiah. In the beginning, he was hesitant to speak out, saying to God, who had just commissioned him to be his prophet to the nations, "I do not know how to speak, for I am only a youth." However, in time Jeremiah became a force to be reckoned with, so effective a communicator that his enemies viewed him as one that makes dismal predictions of impending disaster. (Jer. 38:4) After that day of saying, but "I am only a youth," Jeremiah would go on to serve as God's prophet for 65 years, becoming one of

---

[59] (Anders, Holman New Testament Commentary: vol. 8, Galatians, Ephesians, Philippians, Colossians 1999, p. 192)

the best-known prophets in the history of God's Word. So much so, when Jesus came, the people were discussing who the Son of Man might be, and some thought he was Jeremiah the prophet returned. Thus, we must ask, how did the young, she boy overcome his reluctance to proclaim God's Word? Jeremiah tells us,

Jeremiah 20:9 English Standard Version (ESV)

⁹ If I say, "I will not mention [God],
   or speak any more in his name,"
there is in my heart as it were a burning fire
   shut up in my bones,
and I am weary with holding it in,
   and I cannot.

Yes, the truth of God's Word on the heart of man is so very powerful; it will, compel, provoke, and encourage him to speak. While we may be shy or reluctant to proclaim God's Word to others, it will become a burning fire within us, to the point we will eventually share it. However, if we have not prepared ourselves to use "the sword of the spirit," namely, God's Word, in our spiritual warfare, we will be beat down by the critic or opponent quickly. Do not believe that every critic is one with a closed heart and mind. Many are critics because they had begun to doubt and started to read books or listen to talks by Bible critics, which only served to reinforce their doubts, and they have never heard anyone overturn these Bible difficulties floating around in their mind and heart. We may recall that the apostle Paul 'reasoned with the unbelievers from the Scriptures, explaining and proving' the truth to those he came across. We may be thinking, "yes, but I am no Jeremiah the prophet nor the apostle Paul." Well, neither were they at one time, and we cannot know who new are until we allow ourselves to be used by God. Paul told young Timothy, "Do your best to present yourself to God as one approved, a worker who has no need to be ashamed, rightly handling the word of truth." (2 Tim. 2:15, ESV) On this, New Testament Bible scholar Knute Larson writes,

> Timothy, by contrast, must do his best to **present [himself] to God as one approved, a workman who does not need to be ashamed.** Timothy, and all who follow Christ, are to consecrate themselves to God, working diligently for his approval. The teacher whom God approves has no need of shame in his presence.
>
> God bestows his approval on the one who exhibits truth, love, and godliness in daily living, and who **correctly handles the word of truth.** The false teachers were mishandling God's words, using them for their own benefit. Timothy was commissioned to handle the words of God correctly. All preaching should present the truth clearly, cutting through erroneous ideas or inaccurate opinions. (Larson 2000, p. 286)

The English Standard Version renders the participial clause of 2:15 "rightly handling the word of truth," while the Holman Christian Standard Bible renders it "correctly teaching the word of truth," and the New American Standard Bible, "accurately handling the word of truth." The Greek word, *orthotomeo*, means "to give accurate instruction—'to teach correctly, to expound rightly.' ... 'do your best ... to teach the word of truth correctly' 2

Tm 2:15."[60] This is all that can be asked of any Christian, that 'we do our best to teach the word of truth correctly.'

What can help us to teach the word of truth correctly? If we are to teach another, we must correctly and clearly understand the Word ourselves. When we clearly understand something, we are able to give reasons as to why it is so. Moreover, we are able to express it in our own words. If we are to understand the Bible correctly, we must read it within the context of the verses that surround it, the chapter it is within, the Bible book it is within, the Testament that it is in, and the Bible as a whole. According to the Merriam-Webster Dictionary, immediate context (i.e., of a word, phrase, clause or sentence) is "the words that are used with a certain word or phrase and that help to explain its meaning."[61] The meaning of a text is what the author meant by the words that he used. On this Robert H. Stein writes,

> Great confusion can result if we do not pay careful attention to context. For instance, both Paul (Rom. 4:1–25) and James (2:14–26) use the term "faith" (pistis). Yet we will misunderstand both if we assume that by faith they mean "a body of beliefs." We will misunderstand Paul if we assume that he means "a mere mental assent to a fact," and we will misunderstand James if we assume that he means "a wholehearted trust." It is evident from the context that Paul means the latter (cf.

---

[60] Louw, Johannes P.; Nida, Eugene A. (**Greek-English Lexicon of the New Testament based on Semantic Domains**)

[61] http://www.merriam-webster.com/dictionary/context

Rom. 4:3, 5) and that James means the former (cf. 2:14, 19). (Stein 1994, p. 59)

Stein also wrote, "A context is valuable because it assists the reader in understanding the meaning the author has given the text." Another example would be Paul's statement at Galatians 5:13 (ESV), "For you were called to freedom, brothers. Only do not use your freedom as an opportunity for the flesh, but through love serve one another." If we were looking at this verse alone, not considering what is before and after, we would be asking, what does Paul mean by "freedom"? Was he speaking of freedom from sin and death, freedom from being enslaved to false beliefs, freedom from corruption, or was it something entirely different? If we consider the context, we get our answer. The context tells us the "freedom" that Paul spoke of was our being freed from "the curse of the law," as Christ became the curse for us. (Gal. 3:13, 19-24; 4:1-5) If we look at Galatians 3:10, "Paul quotes Deuteronomy 27:26 to prove that, contrary to what the Judaizers claimed, the law cannot justify and save. It can only condemn. The breaking of any aspect of the law brought a curse on the person who broke the law. Since no one can keep the law perfectly, we are all cursed. Paul, with this argument, destroys the Judaizers' belief that a person is saved through the law." [62] Thus, Paul was referring to the freedom that Christians possess. Just because we are not under the Mosaic Law, a law that imperfect man cannot keep perfectly, this is no excuse to use our "freedom as an opportunity for the flesh." Rather, if we truly understand and value our freedom, we will slave for one another because of our love for one another. However,

---

[62] (Anders, Holman New Testament Commentary: vol. 8, Galatians, Ephesians, Philippians, Colossians 1999, p. 37)

those in the Galatian congregation who lacked that love were engaged in vicious infighting and quarreling.– Galatians 5:15.

There is another meaning for the word "context," i.e., background, conditions, historical setting, and situation. Some call the surrounding text cotext and the historical setting context. Either way, the second meaning here is just as important. The background information that must be considered is, who penned the book, when and where was it written and under what historical setting. Why was the author moved to pen the book, or more realistically, why did God move him to write the book? Within any book on Bible backgrounds, the author will discuss the social, moral, and religious practices of the time Bible book was written. [63]

Correctly handling the word of truth goes deeper than simply explaining a biblical truth accurately. We do not want to use our knowledge of god's Word in an intimidating way. Of course, we want to defend the truth offensively and defensively, following the example of Jesus, who used Scripture to defeat Satan the Devil when under temptation. Nevertheless, figuratively speaking, we do not use the Bible to club others over the head. (Deut. 6:16; 8:3; 10:20; Matt. 4:4, 7, 10) Rather, we want to follow the counsel Peter gave, "in your hearts honor Christ the Lord as holy, **always being prepared to make a defense** to anyone who asks you for a reason

---

[63] An outstanding study tool in getting background information about the New Testament is:

BIBLE BACKGROUNDS OF THE NEW TESTAMENT

Parables, Metaphors, Similes, Gestures and Attitudes

http://www.christianpublishers.org/apps/webstore/products/show/5904404

for the hope that is in you; **yet do it with gentleness and respect**."–1 Peter 3:15.

New Testament Bible scholar Richard L. Pratt Jr. offered the following on 2 Corinthians 10:3-5,

> Paul responded by reminding the Corinthians that his ministry was successful warfare. He had previously described his gospel ministry as a parade of victory in war, and he used similar military analogies elsewhere as well. His apostolic effort was a war he was sure to win.
>
> Paul admitted that he and his company **live[d] in the world**, but insisted that they did not **wage war as the world does**. They did not employ the intimidation, coercion, and violence normally associated with worldly authorities. Instead of employing **the weapons of the world**, Paul relied on **divine power**. These **weapons** appeared weak by worldly standards, but they were actually very powerful. The preaching of the cross brought great displays of God's power in the lives of believers everywhere, including Corinth.
>
> Consequently, Paul was certain that he was on a course **to demolish** the **strongholds** or fortifications of **arguments and every pretension** that anyone set up **against the knowledge of God**. As Paul traveled the world proclaiming the gospel of Christ, he encountered pretentious disbelief supported by clever arguments and powerful personalities. But through the "weakness" of preaching Christ,

Paul went about taking **captive every thought to make it obedient to Christ**. (Pratt Jr 2000, p. 417)

2 Corinthians 10:3-5 English Standard Version (ESV)

[3] For though we walk in the flesh, we are not waging war according to the flesh. [4] For the weapons of our warfare are not of the flesh but have divine power to destroy strongholds. [5] We destroy arguments and every lofty opinion raised against the knowledge of God, and take every thought captive to obey Christ,

If we have a good knowledge of the Scriptures and are always working toward growing it, we can accomplish much. Our use of God's Word can "destroy strongholds," namely, expose the false or mistaken beliefs of others, any irreligious practices, as well as all worldviews that are not biblical, but rather are fleshly. In Addition, we will be able to remove "every lofty opinion raised against the knowledge of God." Moreover, we can use our knowledge of Scripture to help unbelievers to bring their thinking in line with a biblical worldview, as we make disciples.

We must keep in mind that our obligation is not just toward the unbeliever, but toward the others who claim to be Christians, who are on a false path. No true conservative, evangelical Christian would consider Catholicism to be the true way to pure worship of God, and the same would hold true of Pentecostalism, among many other so-called Christian denominations. Both the unbeliever and those claiming to be Christian are holding onto unbiblical beliefs that are deeply embedded in their mind and heart. If we are able to use the Scriptures, logic and reason effectively, we will be able to remove "every lofty opinion raised against the knowledge of God." In

184

the end, then they will understand and find the knowledge of God.

Using Questions Effectively

Why is it important that we use question effectively when we are witnessing to others about the Word of God? Imagine that you just took your car into the garage because it has been having many different problems. In the first scenario, the mechanic says to throw your keys over on the desk; he can have it fixed as good as new for you, come back Saturday to pick it up. Would you feel comfortable with the mechanic, or would alarms be going off. In a second scenario, you take the car to another garage and the mechanic stops what he is doing; he comes over and asks you some probing questions, like 'what is it doing, what sounds is it making,' and the like. He has you start it; he revs the engine and listens. He asks if he can take it around the block. After that, he asks you some more leading questions based on what he has thus learned. Now, he gives you a preliminary diagnosis but says it would be best to put it on the diagnostics machine to verify his findings. He comforts you with the words; we can get such and such parts in here and have it fixed for you by this Saturday. Why does the second scenario give you much more confidence in the competency of the mechanic? In any field, a person must ask probing and leading questions, to discover symptoms or evidence that can lead them to helping find the 'why' or the 'what.' If we are to help an unbeliever, find the truth we must ask effective questions. If we are to help a "Christian" on a false path, find the correct path, we must ask effective questions. Just like the second mechanic, we are trying to discover the cause of what is contributing to the unbelief or the wrong belief. After that, we can use the Word of God to lead them in the way they ought to go.

Jesus was the master teacher, who used questions as he learned more about the student, but also allowed the one listening to feel involved in the discussion. For example, when the disciples were in need of a lesson on humility, Jesus started with a question, not a lecture. (Mark 9:33) To teach Peter how to find the principle behind the black and white, Jesus offered him a multiple-choice question. (Matt. 17:24-26) When Jesus sought the disciples understanding of who he was, he asked them viewpoint questions. (Matt 16:13-17) Jesus was about imparting knowledge and understanding, but he did not do this with sermons alone. He also used questions combined with statements, which got down into the hearts of his listeners, moving them to act in harmony with the gospel message he was sent by the Father to deliver to the lost sheep of Israel. We use questions in our ministering to other, because we want to help them to act in harmony with the Word of God. We also want to use questions to overcome their objections that are designed to dismiss us. Moreover, we want to find those with receptive hearts.

What would we do as parent, if our child came to us, saying, 'I am constantly being challenged about my belief in creation as opposed to evolution?' Certainly, we want our children to be able to have faith in the Word of God as absolute truth, and to be able to defend that truth with fellow classmates, even teachers. Rather than stressing the importance of defending God's Word, which may come across as being critical, or offering advice, why not show him how effective viewpoint questions can be.

FIRST EXAMPLE

Father: Say you were to ask your science teacher how DNA is packed with the chromosomes, what would she say?

Son: She would go on and on about it, talking about how efficient that it is. She would say something like, "The most striking property of every chromosome within the eukaryotic cell nucleus is the length of each molecule of DNA incorporated and folded into it. The human genome of 3×10^9 bp would extend over a meter if unraveled and straightened, yet it is compacted into a nucleus only 10^{-5} m in diameter. **It is an astonishing feat of engineering** to organize such a long linear DNA molecule within ordered structures that can reversibly fold and unfold within the chromosome."[64]

Father: What if you were to ask her, "How do we explain that such an astonishing feat of engineering rose by an undirected chance of events; does not a feat of engineering suggest an engineer?

SECOND EXAMPLE

Father: Say you were to ask your science teacher, 'Can you please explain to me about DNA's capacity for stored information,' what would she say?

Son: She would say something like; "The information stored in DNA must by no means be underestimated. So much so, that one human DNA molecule contains enough information to fill a million-page encyclopedia, or to fill about 1,000 books. Note this fact well: one million encyclopedia pages, or 1,000

---

[64] http://what-when-how.com/molecular-biology/chromosomes-molecular-biology/

books. This is to say that the nucleus of each cell contains as much information as would fill a one-million-page encyclopedia, which is used to control the functions of the human body. To draw an analogy, we can state that even the 23-volume-Encyclopaedia Britannica, one of the greatest mines of information in the world, has 25,000 pages. Therefore, before us lies an incredible picture. In a molecule found in a nucleus, which is far smaller than the microscopic cell wherein it is located, there exists a data warehouse 40 times bigger than the biggest encyclopedia of the world that includes millions of items of information. This means a huge 1000-volume encyclopedia which is unique and has no equal in the world."

"Computers are currently the most advanced form of technology for storing information. A body of information, which, 30 years ago, was routinely stored in a computer the size of a room, can today be stored in small "discs," yet even the latest technology invented by human intelligence, after centuries of accumulated knowledge and years of hard work, is far from reaching the information storage capacity of a single cell nucleus. The following comparison made by the well-known professor of microbiology Michael Denton, will probably suffice to highlight the contrast between the tiny size of DNA and the great amount of information it contains:"

> The information necessary to specify the design of all the species of organisms which have ever existed on the planet, a number according to G.G. Simpson of approximately one thousand million, could be held in a teaspoon and there would still be room left for all the information in every book ever written.

(Michael Denton. Evolution: A Theory in Crisis. London: Burnett Books, 1985, p. 334)[65]

Father: What if you were to ask her, "How is it that human computer technicians are unable to accomplish these types of results, yet we are to believe that mindless matter can do so alone?"

From a few more examples like this, the son can begin to see how effective viewpoint questions are. Many great publications out there offer strong apologetic reasoning for intelligent design. Some leading authors would be John C. Lennox, William A. Dembski, Jonathan Witt, Stephen C. Meyer, David Klinghoffer, Michael J. Behe, Michael Denton, among many others. How else can we become more effective in our evangelism of others?

Using God's Word with Persuasion

A confusion that arises over using the Bible effectively when witnessing to others is the belief that is simply boils down to knowing and quoting Scripture. What do we read of the way the apostle Paul went about witnessing to others. It says, "He entered the synagogue and for three months **spoke boldly**, **reasoning** and **persuading** them." (Ac 19:8-9) On another occasion, "when some became stubborn and continued in unbelief, speaking evil of the Way before the congregation, he withdrew from them and took the disciples with him, **reasoning** daily in the hall of Tyrannus." Persuasion is "attempting to win others over to one's own point of view. It can be either positive, as with preaching the gospel, or it can spring from a malign

---

[65] http://www.dnarefutesevolution.com/human_celli.html

intent to seduce people from the truth." (Manser 2009) When one is persuaded, he is won over by the ability of the persuader's reasoning, arguments (reasons put forward in support), explaining of the Scriptures, i.e., he is so convinced that he gains confidence in God's Word. When Christians persuade a person to accept the Bible as the inspired, inerrant Word of God, we are winning him over, so that he will place his trust in the Bible. If we are to accomplish this in the skeptical, atheistic, agnostic, humanistic, liberal, progressive world that we live in, we must possess the skills to teach our listeners of the truthfulness of our reasons we put forward in support of the biblical worldview, or rather in opposition to the fleshly worldview of todays' hedonistic society.

We do not want to shy away from using God's Word; because that just demonstrates that, we have a lack of respect for it. The modern day critic of the 20th and 21st centuries has taken over in the driving of the conversation, and it is he who decides what is evidence and what is not. The critic's conclusion is that Bible manuscripts that date back 2,300 years are not historical, archaeological evidence, but rather are biased material and if we cannot offer up secular evidence for what we say; well then, we have no evidence at all. The modern day Bible scholar has chosen to play by the critic's rules of engagement, so they actually run around looking for ways to prove things with secular history alone. First, we do not cower before Satan and his people, leaving them to determine whether we can draw attention to God's Word. It is certainly beneficial and appropriate that our great apologetic arguers, like Norman L. Geisler, William Lane Craig, or Craig Evans defend the truth against the lies of the great minds of Satan's side. However, our primary commission is winning the hearts and minds of those receptive to the truth, not winning arguments against those who will never accept the truth, regardless of the evidence.[66]

Therefore, we need to be quite familiar with the Word of God and know what the authors meant by the words that they used. Whether we open our Bible to share a Scripture or reference it aloud, draw attention to the importance of what God's thinking is on the subject that we may be discussing. After a very brief introduction and our mission of sharing God's Word, we might open with an open-ended question. We might say, fifty percent of marriages in America fail, and then ask, "Why do you think that is?" [Allow for an answer] How do you think this principle from God's Word would help, Paul said, "Let no one seek his own good, but the good of his neighbor." (1 Cor. 10.24, ESV) If both mates were to seek the good of the other, how might we see that playing out, can you think of any examples? [Allow for an answer] If the person is receptive, offer a couple more Bible principles that deal with spouses that seem to be growing apart (Phil 1:10), mates that fail to fulfill their responsibilities (Rom 14:12), the husband that seems to not care where the family is heading (Pro. 14:1) habits that annoy one another (Col. 3:13), and so on.

We need to reason from the Scripture where we leave our listeners with no doubt whatsoever that what they are hearing is the truth. Therefore, we need to use genuine, warm, earnest, profound and honest entreaty, with sound logic. As Jesus and Paul, our objective is to

---

[66] Keep in mind that when Geisler, Craig and Evans are debating to on stage against a atheist scientist or the like; they are talking past him, if he is unreceptive to any in the audience that may be receptive. It is evidence that we have answers in the conversation, whether they want to hear them or not, so that unbelievers can see that we do have reasonable, logical answers to the deep questions that plague humanity.

reach the heart of those to whom we witness. This is realized in the words of wise King Solomon, "The purpose in a man's heart is like deep water, but a man of understanding will draw it out." (Pro. 20:5) Yes, we need to draw out what is in the heart of our listener, by using kind, loving and respectful questions that evidence we are personally interested in them. We must avoid being too direct and frank. In other words, we do not want to have a cutting edge to our questions, nor do we want to be too frank or straightforward and showing no delicacy or consideration when using questions. When we are making arguments to substantiate a point, make them clear and logical. We want to offer evidence that will satisfy the listener. Moreover, we want to share what the Bible author meant by the use of his words, not what we think he meant. Time is critical and should be used judiciously. Rather than rush through reading three or four verses that make our point, we should choose the clearest one, use it well by explain, reasoning and illustrating. When we think of using corroborative evidence, again, we turn to Solomon, "From a wise mind comes wise speech; the words of the wise are persuasive." (Pro. 16:23, NLT) If there is a need for more research on our part, say so, by stating that we will look into this further and get back to them another time.

Carry on Using God's Word Skillfully

The world is ever changing toward being more wicked each and every day. In fact, Paul told Timothy, "Evil people and impostors will go on from bad to worse, deceiving and being deceived." (2 Tim. 3:13) Thus, 2,000 years later this is even truer. Therefore, it is highly significant that "we destroy arguments and every lofty opinion raised against the knowledge of God, and

192

take every thought captive to obey Christ." We do this by using "the sword of the Spirit, which is the word of God."–Ephesians 6:17.

Exercise

- Someone just said to you, "I don't believe the Bible, as it is just a book by men, not the Word of God." How would you persuade him that this is not the case?

Review Questions

- How powerful is the Word of God?

- How is the Word of God living and active?

- How can we handle the Word of truth aright when we evangelize?

- How can we use the Word of God with persuasion?

How can we carry on in our skillful use of the Bible?

CHAPTER 10 Giving Good Answers When We Share God's Word

Colossians 4:6 Updated American Standard Version (UASV)

⁶ Let your speech always be gracious, seasoned with salt, so that you may know how you ought to answer each person.

On this New Testament scholar, Max Anders writes, "For the sharing of the message of Christ to be effective, the wise walk must be accompanied with flavorful talk. The believer's talk is to be gracious, rather than gruff, and charming, rather than coarse. The believer's talk is to be **seasoned with salt**. Salt was used for two purposes in Paul's time. It was used as a preservative to keep food from spoiling. This would mean the believer's speech is to be free from corruption, wholesome. Salt was also used as an additive to give flavor to food. If this meaning lies behind the figure, then the believer's speech is to be interesting, witty, tactful, and appealing. Perhaps the best understanding of the reference to **salt** is that the believer's speech is to be both wholesome and appealing. Paul wants believers to **know how to answer everyone**. He tells them to answer with speech which is gracious, wholesome, and appealing." (Anders, Holman New Testament Commentary: vol. 8, Galatians, Ephesians, Philippians, Colossians 1999, p. 346)

Improving Our Answers at Church Bible Studies

As sharers and defenders of God's Word, we need to cultivate our ability to give good answers continuously. Paul wrote that we should "know how [we] ought to answer each person." Certainly, all of us can see the logic in our wanting to endeavor to develop our responses. We can only imagine the heartfelt appreciation that God Himself must feel when we offer a listener a good answer. On this wise King Solomon wrote, "A man has joy in an apt answer, and how delightful is a timely word!" – Proverbs 15:23.

Let us reflect on ourselves for a moment, ask those tough questions, which make us feel uncomfortable. How do we feel about our ability to answer Bible questions? Is our speech "gracious, wholesome, and appealing"? Do we prepare for Christian meetings, so that, we can offer better answers at the meetings? Do we see room for improvement in the answers that we give? Has there ever been a time when talking to a relative, a friend, or a stranger about God's Word that, afterward, we felt that we could have handled that better? This author was engaged in a conversation with four people over 20 years ago, and I was beaten up so bad in that conversation, it caused me to offer the greatest prayer/crying session I had ever had when I got home that night. In short, I prayed that I was very sorry that I let God down that day, and if God could help me afford the books in the years to come, I would make sure this never happened again. It was that night that I became an apologist. Of course, I have been beaten up in conversations since, but when knocked down, I get back up off the mat and continue to fight earnestly for the faith. Therefore, it is true of all of us, we need to continue to grow in our abilities as a communicator, so let us consider what follows.

Giving Answers at Christian Meetings

In most conservative churches across America, all who attend their particular Bible study class know that there are always ones that are ready to give an answer in participation, while the vast majority seldom if ever participate. However, even those who are eager and willing to participate, rarely if at all prepare before the Bible study. We all know what material is going to be covered. We have the book that we are studying through; we have a Bible, and maybe we even have a Bible word dictionary and some other study tools in our home. However, do we ever sit down for an hour and read through the material paragraph by paragraph, looking all the Scriptures up, answering any questions that might be in the book, writing responses in the margins? Even if there are no questions in the book, can we see the important points that we would want to make? It does not matter if we have been going to church for six months on thirty years, we all can give good answers if we prepare beforehand. Wise King Solomon tells us,

Proverbs 15:28 English Standard Version (ESV)

[28] The heart of the righteous ponders how to answer,
   but the mouth of the wicked pours out evil things.

Two benefits that comes from answering at the Bible study meeting at our church is that we are sinking answers deeper into our long-term memory and it enables us to improve our ability to give good answers when sharing or defending Bible truths. Being the first person to answer the night of the Bible study class can be a bit intimidating for some. However, just prepare well before the evening of the class. When the person reads the paragraph, listen well, thinking of the answer you have written in the margin of your book. When he asks the question, put your hand up and read your answer as clearly as possible. If your nerves are high, you will feel like you are outside of yourself, not even remembering what you said. However, in time you will be able to offer the answer extemporaneously, namely, done unrehearsed, that is, prepared in advance but delivered without notes. If someone has gotten a response that you really wanted to give before you, do not lose heart, simply expand on the answer, refer to the Scripture in the paragraph supports the answer, or make a personal application to it.

While this author is certainly more longwinded than most when answering, and this is not the best approach. Long answers are not the best. Rather, short answers, say 30-60 seconds, are actually more weightier and will stay with those listening a lot longer. You see, picking one aspect of the paragraph and making a good point about it is best, instead of rambling through all the points in the paragraph where nothing stands out, and the listeners are more lost than ever as to the appropriate answer. Also, answers that are I our own words are best. We can just reiterate or paraphrase what was within the paragraph, even expanding on it a little. When we put it in our own words, we are making the answer our own, and our way of wording things should be common to those in the church, making it easier to understand. This will help us to improve our ability at being a more effective communicator.

If we do not prepare before the Bible study class, we will be sitting there trying to prepare while someone is reading the paragraph and another is offering an answer on the question. We will not comprehend the totality of the paragraph, but will also miss what the other person was saying. We sometimes hear a person give almost the same identical answer as the previous person, and this is likely because they were not fully paying attention to the response that person gave. We need to build a habit of prepare for the meeting prior to, by reading the paragraph, looking up the Scriptures and writing answers in the margins. We can also use a highlighter to mark the books answer within the paragraph. Remember, when highlighting, do not highlight the whole paragraph, just a few keywords that focus in on the answer, bringing it back to mind. If the book does not have review questions at the end of the chapter, we can still highlight the key points that will help us participate better. We will be able to give spontaneous answers, namely answers that arise from natural impulse or inclination, rather than from planning or in response to prepared questions. This will make the discussion even livelier. It might be our goal at least to give one answer each Bible study meeting, to have something to build on, but we should not hold it at that for too long, or it will become a pattern. We need to feel able to comment freely.

If we are timid at the idea of answering, do not feel alone, as this is common and, in some cases, this stays with us on a small level our entire life. Maybe we have convinced ourselves that other offer better answers than we ever could, so we will just leave it up to them. However, the Bible exhorts us to share, saying, "let us hold fast the confession of our hope without wavering ... and let us consider how to stir up one another to love and good works, not neglecting to meet together, as is the habit of some, but encouraging one another." (Heb. 10:23-25) When we participate in the Bible study, we are 'stirring up one another to love and good works, which encourages them to participate as well. Moreover, there may be times that we come into the Bible study class beat up and worn down by life and after a time of interchange, we leave fully refreshed.

Bible studies classes are usually an atmosphere that is friendly and relaxed. Therefore, if there were an aspect of the study that we did not fully understand, it not being clear in our mind, it would be best to consider the responses to that point and ask some qualifying questions after the meeting of those that may be more qualified at offering a more in-depth, but easy to understand answer. If this is something that is troubling to us, like what the Bible actually says about hellfire. Is eternal torment biblical? Is Hellfire just? Such concerns can be like a burr under a saddle on a horse, over time, it can dig deeper and deeper into us, cause us emotional turmoil. Even after we have discussed it at length with the pastor or elder, we may want to investigate further on our own.

Answering Critics Objections

If we have had

(1) a personal Bible study every day (say 30 minutes),

(2) if we have prepared for all of our meetings

(3) (by reading, looking up Scriptures and highlighting main points, noting how Scriptures apply),

(4) if we have participated in our Bible study classes,

We will find that it is no longer difficult to answer questions of those who are sincerely interested a Biblical response. However, we cannot know everything, so there will be times when the question will be one that we have not addressed before. In that case, we simply say, 'you have raised an excellent point, let me do more research on this, and I will get back with you.' If they actually wanted to know, they will give us this opportunity to investigate it.

While some have questions, others have objections. How are we to deal with complaints? We would not just jump into the answer, as it would be prudent to find out how this objection came about; asking them 'what gave rise to this concern?' For example, a person may misunderstand why God has allowed wickedness, pain, suffering, old age and death for a time. This is because he is confused by those who say everything that has happened and is to happen is how God willed it to be, meaning that free will is not really a reality, and the wicked act of a terrorist cutting the heads off of little children publicly is a part of God's will. This is very unbiblical, and we should empathize with why he is upset and has built up objections. Many objections are the result of a lack of understanding, an unbiblical viewpoint. It is best if we clarify what he has heard, how he understands what he has heard, and then go about rightly explaining what the Bible actually says on the matter.

Another approach is to prevent objections from putting us at odds with each other, as though we were opponents. We can evidence that his objection is of mutual interest. In other words, when we hear an objection, we should not be put off by it, but rather express it as a point the other should be concerned about. For instance, we could say, 'it is good that you brought up wickedness and suffering, it is something that should concern all of us, and we should expect a reasoned answer to such an important issue.' By such an approach, this one may gain a measure of trust and respect for us, opening his mind, where it was closed before, hoping for answers from the Bible.

There will come a time when we are sharing Bible truths with more than one person at a time. At times, the others may not want their friend or family to take an interest in God or what they perceive to be some outdated book that was written by men, so they begin to interrupt. We should not always back away because the newly interested one may perceive his friend or family is correct. If the antagonist raises an objection, he is the one who is really obligated to offer evidence for his remarks, so we can shift the burden of proof back onto the objector. Jesus Christ himself used counter-questions to quiet opposers who tried to hinder with his preaching. Jesus' counter-questions were so effective that Matthew tells us, "And no one was able to answer him a word, nor from that day did anyone dare to ask him any more questions." (Matt. 22:41-46) Therefore, keep in mind that the burden of proof is on the one who is raising the objection, not us. For example, if someone, in a tone that implies disdain, says, "the Bible is a man's book and is full of contradictions and errors." We might respond, "I believe the Bible is written by men, who were inspired by God, moved along by Holy Spirit and the Bible is fully inerrant. Will you please give me a few examples of errors and contradictions in the Bible?" Now, we have placed the burden of proof back on the objector.

The best tool in sharing what the Bible says is the Bible itself. Paul writes, "For the word of God is living and active, sharper than any two-edged sword, piercing to the division of soul and of spirit, of joints and of marrow, and discerning the thoughts and intentions of the heart." (Heb. 4:12) God's word is far more persuasive than we ever could be. Also, when responding to the objection, we need to remain calm and be respectful of other to their beliefs, regardless of whether the objector has a bad attitude or not. Many times, a good answer will turn away his anger or frustration.

After we have had much success in preparing for our Christian meetings and participating in the Bible study class, we will find numerous opportunities to defend and share biblical truths. At work, we may stand out because we do not involve ourselves in their degrading talk, nor do we take smoke breaks, or extra time for breaks and lunch, so they may be curious about why. At school, the same holds true, as students and teachers do not see us as aloof, but rather as being no part of their worldly behaviors. Our neighbors may notice that we never miss our Christian meetings, so they may wonder why such dedication. These are all opportunities to share our faith with others. We can return to the words of Peter from our previous chapter, "but sanctify Christ as Lord in your hearts, always being prepared to make a defense to anyone who asks you for a reason for the hope that is in you; yet do it with gentleness and respect."

Exercise

- Someone just said to you, "You Christians claim that Christianity is the only true religion, I find that arrogant when there so many major religions. Why can they not all simply be different roads leading to the same place?" How would you persuade him that it is not arrogant and that all religions are not different roads leading to the same place?

Review Questions

- How do you personally feel about your ability to answer Bible questions?

- Why is it important to give answers at Christian meetings?

- What must we do if we are to be effective in answering critic's objections?

- Why might it be best to begin giving at answers at church Bible study groups?

- Why is it important to be prepared to give reasons for the hope that lies within us?

Why is important to reach the heart of our listeners?

CHAPTER 11 How Can We Improve Our Evangelism Skills?

1 Corinthians 4:17 Updated American Standard Version (UASV)

¹⁷ That is why I sent you Timothy, who is my beloved and faithful child in the Lord, and he will remind you of my ways which are in Christ, just as I teach everywhere in every congregation.

Develop our Evangelism Skills?

We are all aware of the outpouring of the Holy Spirit at Pentecost 33 C.E., where Christianity spread and grew rapidly. (Acts 2:40-42; 4:4; 6:7; 11:19-21) Why might our congregation seem to be stagnant, going years with next to no growth, even actually losing ones that we already have? Why did so many Jews and then Samaritans and then Gentiles accept Christ and the kingdom back in the first-century, growing from 120 to over one million in just 10-years? – Acts 8:4-8; 10:44-48.

If one is to accept the good news of the kingdom, certain factors must take place. First, one must obtain an accurate, full, or true knowledge (Gr., epignosis) of biblical truths. (1 Tim. 2:3-4; Rom 10:14) After that, they must put faith in that knowledge of God. (Heb. 11:6) At that point, one will develop an appreciation for the Father's sacrifice of his Son as a ransom sacrifice and his loving-kindness toward humankind. It is like the apostle John expressed it, "In this the love of God was made manifest among us, that God sent his only begotten Son into the world, so that we might live through him. In this is love, not that we loved God, but that he loved us and sent his Son to be the propitiation for our sins." – 1 John 4:9-10.

These are the initial stages of one's accepting Christ. As they are taking in God's Word, putting faith in the things heard, they are also developing spiritual values. Jesus, said, "Blessed are the poor in spirit, for theirs is the kingdom of the heavens." (Matt. 5:3) The phrase "poor in spirit" can be difficult to understand. Let us look at GOD'S WORD Translation, which reads, ""Blessed are those who [are poor in spirit] recognize they are spiritually helpless ..." The Greek word ptochos means "beggar." The "poor in spirit" is an alternative literal rendering. The meaning is that the "beggar/poor in spirit" is aware of his or her spiritual needs, as if a beggar or the poor would be aware of their physical needs. Jesus went on to say in verse 6, "Blessed are those who hunger and thirst for righteousness, for they shall be satisfied." One who is self-satisfied and self-righteous, is unaware of the need to develop spiritual values, and is unreceptive to biblical truths. When this one is first told of the good news of the kingdom, he answers with something like, 'I am not interested. I do not believe in any religion.' Another one who is usually not receptive to biblical truths is the one who is deeply wrapped up in material pursuits. – Matthew 6:33-34; 7:7-8; Luke 12:16-21.

The one's that every Christian proclaimer of the good news is looking for are those that are receptive to biblical truths because they sense a spiritual need that they are lacking. When we are sharing the Word of God with unbelievers, how are we to identify such ones? First, we need to appreciate the fact that the Bible is often misunderstood and even the apostle Peter said the apostle Paul's letters were "hard to understand, which the ignorant and unstable twist to their own destruction, as they do the other Scriptures." (2 Pet. 3:16) Thus, our first concern is to take a book that is admittedly complicated and difficult to understand and make it easy to comprehend. How can we accomplish such things if we do not fully understand God's Word ourselves?

Whose Methods Were Effective?

When the apostle Paul wrote to the Corinthians for the first time, he told them that he was sending them Timothy, the young man that has been traveling with him for a few years, who would go on as his traveling companion for another decade. Paul told the Corinthians that Timothy was his "beloved and faithful child in the Lord, and he will **remind you of my ways** which are in Christ ..." (1 Cor. 4:17) What did Paul mean when he said, "remind you of **my ways**"? Some commentaries take "**my ways**" as referring to Paul's **ways** of living not just his ideas or his doctrinal positions being the same as Jesus Christ. However, we might notice the context, because after Paul told the Corinthians that Timothy would remind them of "my ways" he finishes the sentence by saying, "just as I teach everywhere in every congregation." Therefore, while his personal conduct is certainly a part of "my ways," his methods of teaching are the centerpiece. On this Kistemaker and Hendriksen write, "These ways relate to the work Paul performed while he was with the Corinthians: teaching, preaching, counseling, shaping, nurturing, and praying. They pertain to the work Paul accomplished on behalf of Jesus Christ and the building of the church."[67] It should be mentioned

---

[67] Simon J. Kistemaker and William Hendriksen, *Exposition of the First Epistle to the Corinthians*, vol. 18, New Testament Commentary (Grand Rapids: Baker Book House, 1953–2001), 146.

that the verse before these words, Paul wrote, "I exhort you, become imitators of me." (4:16)

Paul like Jesus had methods of teaching and proclaiming. Jesus took the Mosaic Law that can be complex and difficult to understand, which the ignorant and unstable Jewish religious leaders twisted to their own destruction and taught it to tens of thousands. Jesus conveyed the Hebrew Scriptures with simplicity, unquestionable logic, thought-provoking questions, and striking figures of speech, meaningful illustrations taken from things familiar to his listeners, and his reasoning from more than 120 Old Testament Scriptures recorded in the Gospels. Jesus was thoroughly at ease with God's Word. (Matt. 6:25-30; 7:3-5, 24-27) In other words, Jesus had methods of teaching; he did not just haphazardly go about teaching others. This effective teaching and preaching method he handed down to others, as he taught his apostles and later the seventy others he appointed. These methods will always be the most effective way of reaching the hearts of the receptive ones, who are aware or can be made aware that they have spiritual needs. – Luke 9:1-6; 10:1-11.

The First Obstacle to Our Being an Effective Evangelist

When we enter the pathway of walking with our God, we will certainly come across resistance from three different areas. **Our greatest obstacle** is **ourselves** because we have inherited imperfection from our first parents Adam and Eve. The Scriptures make it quite clear that we are **mentally bent toward evil**, not good. (Gen 6:5; 8:21, AT) In other words, our natural desire is toward wrong. On the other hand, prior to sinning, Adam and Eve were perfect, and they had the natural desire of doing good. This means that they literally had to go against the grain so to speak, like rowing up river, violating their perfect inner person. Returning to our current condition, the Scriptures further tells us of our inner person, i.e., our heart.

Romans 7:21-24 (UASV)

²¹ I find then the law in me that when I want to do right, that evil is present in me. ²² For I delight in the law of God according to the inner man, ²³ but I see a different law in my members, warring against the law of my mind and taking me captive in the law of sin which is in my members. ²⁴ Wretched man that I am! Who will deliver me from this body of death?

Jeremiah 17:9 (UASV)	**1 Corinthians 9:27** (UASV)
⁹ The heart is more deceitful than all else, and desperately sick; who can understand it?	²⁷ but I discipline my body and make it my slave, so that, after I have preached to others, I myself will not be disqualified.

We are all imperfect with human weaknesses, so we are our greatest obstacle in becoming a competent teacher and proclaimer of biblical truths. Maybe we feel uncomfortable, inadequate and not adequately educated for those whom we may strike up a conversation. While it is true that Jesus did not attend the rabbinical schools of his day, studying under persons such as Gamaliel, as Pau had, as Jesus was the Son of God, a perfect human being. Nevertheless, Jesus was still a student of God's Word.

When Jesus was twelve years old, the family had gone down to celebrate the Feast of the Passover, as they did every year, they accidently left Jesus behind. After a three-day search, they "found him in the temple, sitting in the midst of the teachers and listening to them and questioning them. And all those listening to him were amazed at his understanding and his answers." (Lu 2:46-47) This was a twelve years old. Now, many times in the Gospels, it is said that the people marvels at the way Jesus taught. Matthew tells us, "They were astonished and said, 'Where did this man get this wisdom and these mighty works?'" (Matt. 13:54, ESV) Even though Jesus was very wise as the Son of God and a perfect human, his methods of teaching were very practical and can be learned by anyone. We know the disciples imitated Jesus, so what was said of them. On one occasion, when called before the Jewish Sanhedrin (high court), it was said of Jewish leaders, "Now when they saw the boldness of Peter and John, and perceived that they were uneducated,[68] common men, they were astonished. And they recognized that they had been with Jesus." – Acts 4:13.

Why was Jesus so effective in his evangelism and proclaiming of the good news? Are we to believe that Jesus was like our modern day televangelists, who use exaggerated emotionalism to sway their audiences? No. Jesus was a man who always sought to do the will of the Father, but who also understood the Word of God very well, and taught it in a simple way. If a person failed to understand the simplified explanation, i.e., interpretation of the Old Testament, Jesus would offer even more of an

---

[68] This is not suggesting that Peter and John were illiterate, saying they could not read and write. This is saying they were not educated in the Rabbinical schools.

clarification, helping the listeners to grasp what was meant. When Jesus "came to Nazareth, where he had been brought up; and as was his custom, he went to the synagogue on the Sabbath day, and he stood up to read. "And the scroll[69] of the prophet Isaiah was given to him. And he unrolled the scroll[70] and found the place where it was written, 'The Spirit of the Lord is upon me, because he has anointed me **to proclaim good news** to the poor. He has sent me **to proclaim release** to the captives and recovering of sight to the blind, to set free those who are oppressed, **to proclaim the favorable year** of the Lord.' And he rolled up the scroll and gave it back to the attendant and sat down ..." This quote was from a prophecy in the book of Isaiah. Jesus then said, "Today this Scripture has been fulfilled in your hearing." – Luke 4:16-21.

The good news that Jesus came to earth to share first, with the Jews, and second, with the rest of humanity, was an offer to release them and us from bondage to sin and death and from the condemnation of Adamic sin.[71] He too was releasing us from our human weaknesses, while also waking us up to Satan's world

---

[69] Or a *roll*

[70] Or *roll*

[71] There are three main reasons for Jesus coming to earth. First, he came to bear witness to the truth about God. (John 18:37) Second, he came to suffer for us, leaving us an example, so that you might follow in his steps. (1 Pet. 2:21) Third, he did not come to be served, but to serve, and to give his soul a ransom for many. (Matt. 20:28; Rom. 5:12-21) As is made clear from the above paragraph, Jesus had many sub-accomplishments that went with these three main reasons for coming. For example, while he came to offer his souls as a ransom sacrifice for all, one of the results was a releasing of those who accepted that ransom from condemnation to sin and death.

that caters to the imperfect human flesh. When Jesus taught the Jews the ways of true worship and what was expected of them, they were released from the many twisted interpretations the Pharisees, Sadducees, Scribes and other Jewish leaders gave to the Scriptures. (Matthew 5:21-48) While the physical cures that Jesus performed were certainly greatly appreciated the being released from the captivity of false worship, the ruler of this world (Satan), and the condemnation to sin and death were of a far greater value. In other words, while Jesus may open the eyes of a blind man, this blind man recognizing Jesus as the truth and the way, leading to an opportunity at eternal life was of far more importance. (John 9:1-34; Deut. 18:18; Matt. 15:1-20) This being released will not be fully evidenced until the second coming of Christ. While our eyes are wide open to all that has been revealed within Scripture, we still live in a fallen world and a fallen condition, but we draw comfort in our hope that Jesus has given us.

1 Peter 3:15 Updated American Standard Version (UASV)

[15] but sanctify Christ as Lord in your hearts, always being prepared to make a defense[72] to anyone who asks you for a reason for the hope that is in you; yet do it with gentleness and respect;

Yes, our imperfect and human weaknesses can be a barrier in our work as an evangelist, but it can be overcome, as we will shortly see. Being aware of our imperfections and all that they entail is the only thing that will save us from the second greatest obstacle.

---

[72] Or *argument*; or *explanation*

The Second Obstacle to Our Being an Effective Evangelist

The **second greatest obstacle** is the **world of humankind that is alienated from God**. Its ruler, Satan, designs this world to cater to our fallen flesh. The spirit of this world comes from Satan himself, and if breathed in for too long, we will begin to adopt the same mindset, the same thinking, attitude, conduct, and speech that is opposite of God. This poisonous air will paralyze us quite quickly if we entertain it either by thinking on it, or worse still, engaging in it. – 1 Corinthians 2:11-16

1 Peter 4:3-4 Updated American Standard Version (UASV)

³ For the time that has passed by is sufficient for doing the will of the Gentiles, living in sensuality, lusts, drunkenness, orgies, drinking parties, and lawless idolatry. ⁴ With respect to this that you do not run with them into the same flood of debauchery, and they malign you;

This spirit of the world or rather the mental disposition of those alienated from God breeds a spirit of disobedience and rebellion that is contrary to God's will and purpose, his standards and values. This spirit is demonic and alienated from our Creator and is under the influence of the ruler of the world, namely, Satan (2 Cor. 4:3-4) Satan's world caters to our fallen flesh, placing these ones at odds with God. As we can see from the desires of the flesh from above (sinful and selfish), it runs counter to the fruitage of the Spirit. Just as being aware of our imperfections and all that they entail is of paramount importance, so too is our being aware of those who are alienated from God. The first two obstacles are what our third obstacle uses against us, hoping that we will fall away, abandon, or tire out, so as to not finish the race of life.

The Third Obstacle to Our Being an Effective Evangelist

The **third greatest obstacle** is **Satan the Devil and his demon army**. Yes, they are so powerful that one demon could kill hundreds of thousands of humans in very short order. That is why true Christians receive a hedge placed around them by God, protecting them from Satan and the demons. Yes, God's servants receive special protection from this powerful force. (Job 1-2) The only way to weaken that protection is to violate your conscience repeatedly, toy with demonic activities, like horror movies, rap and heavy metal music, games like the wigi-board or dungeons and dragons. However, we also weaken our protection from God when we repeatedly involve ourselves in the desires of the flesh. Below is a list by Paul, which covers the prominent works of the flesh, but it is not exhaustive. However, notice that he ends his list with the phrase, "and things like these." If we are carrying out a work of the flesh not listed and we think all is well because it is not on the list, we are sadly mistaken, because Paul includes all works of the flesh with the phrase, "and things like these."

Our human imperfections and the world that caters to them is with us 24/7. True, we can get control over our vessel by putting on the new personality, gaining the mind of Christ, and the help of Holy Spirit. However, it does not take much to drift away (Heb. 2:1), draw away (Heb. 3:12-13), fall away (Heb. 6:6), become sluggish (Heb. 6:12), shrink back from Christian responsibilities (Heb. 10.39), tire out (Heb. 12:3), refuse (Heb. 12:25), or

213

become hardened through deceptive powers (Gal. 6:9). We just need to entertain the wrong thoughts too long, without dismissing them, and then we are on our way. (James 1:14-15) Now, as far as Satan goes, Peter warns us in the extreme to, "Be sober; be on the alert. Your adversary the devil walks around like a roaring lion, looking for someone to devour." (1 Pet. 5:8) Paul also said that we are to,

Ephesians 6:11-12 Updated American Standard Version (UASV)

[11] Put on the full armor of God, so that you will be able to stand firm against the schemes of the devil. [12] For our struggle[73] is not against flesh and blood, but against the rulers, against the powers, against the world-rulers of this darkness, against the wicked spirit forces in the heavenly places.

Threefold Assistance in Our Being an Effective Evangelist

There is a threefold defense against this threefold opposition to our being an effective evangelist for God. **First**, we have **the Word of God**, which should come in the way of literal translations, like the Updated American Standard Version, the New American Standard Bible, and the English Standard Version. God gave us this special revelation to guide us through this wicked time. It has the power to make us stronger spiritually, as well as fortify us to accomplish his will and purposes. The apostle Paul tells us, "For the word of God is living and active and sharper than any two-edged sword, and piercing as far as the division of soul and spirit, of both joints and marrow,

---

[73] Lit., "wrestling."

and able to judge the thoughts and intentions of the heart." —Hebrews 4:12.

The Bible should be read daily, in conjunction with CPH's recommended Bible reading program.[74] We also need to use our Bible in all of our religious meetings. If a Scripture is being read, we need to look it up. We also need to use our Bible in our ministry, meaning that we need to formulate texts that can help us to teach others the good news of the Kingdom.

Deuteronomy 17:19 Updated American Standard Version (UASV)

[19] And you shall come to the Levitical priests and to the judge who is in office in those days, and you shall consult them, and they will declare to you the verdict in the case.

As we work our way through the Bible in our Bible reading program, let us not rush, but make sure we understand the author's intended meaning, and how we can apply that in our lives, as well as share it with others. We should be able to see our walking with God, come to life through the historical accounts found all throughout Scripture.

Joshua 1:7-8 Updated American Standard Version (UASV)

[7] Only be strong and very courageous, being careful to do according to all the law that Moses my servant commanded you; do not turn from it to the right or to the left, so that you may have success wherever you go. [8] This Book of the Law shall not depart from your mouth, but you shall meditate on it day and night, so that you

---

[74] http://www.christianpublishers.org/the-new-bible-study

may be careful to do according to all that is written in it; for then you will make your way prosperous, and then you will have good success.

Below in Psalm 1:1-3, you will notice in verse 1 that there is a progression of intimacy through walking in the counsel of the wicked, to standing with sinners, to sitting with scoffers. Each level is a sign of spending more time with, being more deeply involved. We should not be involved with any of these three, because this would never be in harmony with a Christian, who is walking with God. After that, the Psalmist in verse 2 helps us to appreciate where our delight is found, the law of Jehovah, to which we read and study in a meditative way, day and night, which simply means on a regular basis. Truly, verse 3 helps us to appreciate the result of avoiding certain ones, and cultivating a love for God's Word, endurance and a strong spiritual health. If we follow the counsel of verses 1-2, we will be able to weather any storm that may come upon us. Think, this is but three verses out of over 31,000 verses, which offer us the very knowledge of God.

Psalm 1:1-3 Updated American Standard Version (UASV)

¹ Blessed is the man
   who walks not in the counsel of the wicked,
nor stands in the way of sinners,
   nor sits in the seat of scoffers;
² but his delight is in the law of Jehovah,
   and on his law he meditates day and night.

³ He is like a tree
   planted by streams of water
that yields its fruit in its season,
   and its leaf does not wither.
In all that he does, he prospers.

Second, along with God's Word, are some of the best **Bible study tools** as well as the **Christian congregation**. Paul tells the Ephesians, "Look carefully then how you walk, not as unwise but as wise, making the best use of the time, because the days are evil." (Eph. 5:15-16) Moreover, the Apostle Paul exhorted "let us consider how to stir up one another to love and good works, not neglecting to meet together, as is the habit of some, but encouraging one another, and all the more as you see the Day drawing near." (Heb. 10:24-25) We need to have a personal Bible study for at least thirty minutes a day, every day of the week. Moreover, we need to prepare for the Christian meetings, so as to participate in them, whether it be answering at the Bible study classes or looking up Scripture and taking notes at those with lectures.

Third, we have to be effectively sharing God's Word with others. It is our sharing offensively and defensively that will keep us in battle mode, always prepared to defend the hope that we have, always taking in the very knowledge of God on a more deeper level, the every Word that is Spirit inspired, meaning always taking in and applying Spirit inspired, inerrant Word of God. The apostle Paul told the Galatians that if we can walk by the 'walk by the Spirit, we will not carry out the desire of the flesh.' How are we to walk by the Spirit? We do so by taking the Spirit inspired Word into our minds, so that we are inundated mentally by it, so that it becomes our way of thinking, and to do otherwise would trigger a warning from our Christian conscience.

Galatians 5:16-26 Updated American Standard Version (UASV)

[16] But I say, walk by the Spirit, and you will not carry out the desire of the flesh. [17] For the desires of the flesh

are against the Spirit, and the desires of the Spirit are against the flesh, for these are opposed to each other, so that you may not do the things you want to do. [18] But if you are led by the Spirit, you are not under the law. [19] Now the works of the flesh are evident, which are: sexual immorality, impurity, sensuality, [20] idolatry, sorcery, enmity, strife, jealousy, fits of anger, rivalries, dissensions, divisions, [21] envy, drunkenness, orgies, and things like these. I warn you, as I warned you before, that those who do such things will not inherit the kingdom of God. [22] But the fruit of the Spirit is love, joy, peace, patience, kindness, goodness, faithfulness, [23] gentleness, self-control; against such things there is no law. [24] And those who belong to Christ Jesus have crucified the flesh with its passions and desires.

[25] If we live by the Spirit, let us also walk by the Spirit. [26] Let us not become conceited, provoking one another, envying one another.

Those who follow the flesh will reap the results of such a course by having unattractive fruits. On the other hand, those who follow the lead of the Spirit will have fruitage that is attractive and beneficial for themselves, family, congregation, friends, and neighbors. One thing that we have to realize by looking at other related texts is, these fruits are not the results of our efforts, but rather they are the consequence of having an active faith in Christ, which makes us receptive to them. In addition, it is the fruitage of the Spirit, which is going to sustain us through a lifetime of proclaiming the good news, teaching the Word and making disciples.

While there are many enemies against or in opposition to our walking with God aright, the greatest is our own human imperfection, followed the world of humankind that is alienated from God, as well as Satan the Devil and his demon army. So too, there are many things that can keep us spiritually strong, but the most effective are the Word of God (preparing for Christian meetings and personal study), regular attendance and participation at Christian meetings, followed by effectively sharing our faith.

Therefore, we must trust in God by applying his Word with conviction in our lives, especially in being bold as we go about sharing the Word in these difficult times, just as was true of the apostle Paul and Barnabas in the first century. As these two, brought the Word of God to Iconium, their evangelism created a sharp division of feelings, thoughts and some opposition. On this, Kenneth O. Gangel writes, "As in Pisidian Antioch, the opposition came not from Gentiles but from unbelieving Jews. Luke uses poignant language to describe what happened—stirring up the Gentiles, the Jews **poisoned their minds**, literally 'caused their minds to think evil.' Not only against Paul and Barnabas, but against all believers there (**the brothers**). This time, rather than shaking off the dust of the city, Paul and Barnabas evidently decided that the persecution actually gave them a good reason to stay a **considerable time** in Iconium. They spoke boldly for the Lord (Luke surely intends us to understand "Jesus" here), and he confirmed the message through miracles (*semeia kai terata*). All this took place in Galatia, so we can understand this ministry in light of the Galatian letter. There Paul tells us that these mighty works of the Spirit certified that God approved his gospel (Gal. 3:4–5). Luke uses an interesting phrase—**the message of his grace**—to describe the gospel. The linking of the message with the accompanying miracle reminds us of Hebrews 2:1–4. Signs and wonders in Acts remind us of the transitional nature of this book. Barnhouse puts it well:"

These signs and wonders were specially given to the apostles and early Christian church workers because there was no written New Testament as yet. Not a line of the New Testament had been written at this point, and there was no solid authority to which the apostles could point and say, "See, we're preaching truth. You can check it in the Word of God!" There was no completed Word of God. So God enabled the apostles to perform wonders and signs to authenticate their ministry, but these wonders and signs would fade as God's Word came into being (Barnhouse, 126).[75]

We must remember as the United States of America, the last bastion of religious freedom on earth fades into an atheistic, socialist country, opposition to our work, as evangelists will grow, as we draw ever closer to the second coming of Christ. Nevertheless, just know that "this gospel of the kingdom will be proclaimed in the whole inhabited earth for a testimony to all the nations, and then the end will come." (Matt. 24:14, LEB) Each of us can do our part by evangelizing our communities, making sure everyone has an opportunity to hear, knowing that as the end draws near almost none will listen.

Rejection Will Be the Norm

Jesus the greatest evangelist to have ever live preached to and taught tens of thousands, yet only a few

---

[75] Kenneth O. Gangel, *Acts*, vol. 5, Holman New Testament Commentary (Nashville, TN: Broadman & Holman Publishers, 1998), 231.

hundred responded. The second greatest evangelist would be the apostle Paul. While it is true he set up congregations all over the then known world; nevertheless, only a fraction of the people he spoke to and taught accepted the truths he shared. For example, what kind of receptions did Paul receive when he preached in Athens? Luke tells us,

Acts 17:18-20 Updated American Standard Version (UASV)

[18] And certain ones of the Epicurean and Stoic philosophers were conversing with him. Some were saying, "What would this idle babbler wish to say?" Others, "He seems to be a proclaimer of strange deities," because he was preaching Jesus and the resurrection. [19] And they took him and brought him to the Areopagus, saying, "May we know what this new teaching is that you are presenting? [20] For you are bringing some strange things to our ears; so we want to know what these things mean."

We must understand that true conservative Christianity's greatest enemy is within, namely, liberal and moderate Christianity. We were clearly told by Jesus to be no part of the world, yet liberal Christianity is nine part world and one part Christian. On the other hand, moderate Christian scholars and church leaders are casting doubt on the Scriptures with their historical-critical method of biblical interpretation. The world and liberal Christian views the few remaining conservative Christians as relics of the past, knuckle-dragging Neanderthals, who refuse to adjust their grammatical-historical interpretation of God's Word with the times. It is imperative that we realize that the good news of the kingdom and all other Bible truths is repulsive to the world and so the media are certainly going to be in opposition to us. It seems now that the liberal progressive United States government is following in the footsteps off the liberal European governments as well as Canada and Australia, by suppressing religious freedom for conservative Christianity, while giving more freedom to Islam. As a result, most that we will witness to will have heard a very biased, heretical interpretation of what the Bible says and they will prejudge us and reject God's Word outright, with only a handful listening a little further before making a decision. Even then, that handful who listen a little further, most of them will mock the message in the end. This leaves us but a fraction of that handful, which will be won over by the truth. This is why we must understand well what we are sharing; otherwise, how else will we find those select few? Lastly, keep in mind those who reject the biblical truths are rejecting Christ not us, so let us not personalize it. – Acts 17:32-34; Matthew 12:30

Start Off By Building Rapport

If we are to reach the hearts of those select few that are receptive to biblical truths, we need to start by building rapport. When a complete stranger approaches us, we automatically have subconscious questions or thoughts going through our minds. We sigh, thinking, what do they want? Is this going to be some sales or marketing pitch? What do they want me to buy? Thus, when we begin a conversation with a person that we have never met before, we need to begin by putting their minds to rest by answering who we are and our intentions. How are we to do this? We can follow Jesus example, who said, "As you enter the house, greet it." Of course, we do not greet the house per se, but rather those who live in the house. If the persons there are

222

receptive, our blessing will remain with them, but if they were unreceptive, we leave with our blessing of peace. – Matthew 10:12-13.

What is meant by the translation that is more literal "let your peace come upon it [i.e., the persons of the house]"? It means that as we share the good news with others, our hope is to share the peace that we have found with all with whom we speak. In other words, the moment that we begin speaking, we want them to sense the Christ like personality that we project. Even today, the Jews greet people with "Peace be with you" or "Peace" ("*Shalom aleichem*" or "*Shalom*" in Hebrew. Of course, we do not need to follow that example, but our intention should be the same, to put the person at ease, so they will be more receptive the biblical truths that we wish to share. If we introduce ourselves with our personal name, and where we are from, it will evidence that we are local. Therefore, we might say, "hello, I am David and this is John, we are out sharing an important biblical message with our neighbors." We might add that while our biblical message these days is a bit apologetic (defending the Word of God and the Christian faith), we are not apologetic, as though we are embarrassed or ashamed of being out sharing God's message. – Mark 8:38.

Sadly, many are embarrassed to be seen talking with people carrying Bibles, so we need to be respectful of others. Jesus, although being a Jew, witnessed to Samaritans, people who were viewed by Jews as nothing more than dogs in the street. Therefore, most Samaritans would be very hesitant to be caught talking to a Jew. Therefore, Jesus was very discreet in his approach at talking with the Samaritan woman at the well. He made sure the apostles were away before the conversation was to take place, and chose a time of the day when the more prominent people would not be coming to draw water. Jesus was compassionate in his teaching of others. (John 4:5-30) Therefore, if we are witnessing on the streets, we do not want to be like those screaming doomsday comments, shaking their Bible around, trying to shame those who pass by. These ones are doing nothing more than drawing attention to themselves, not God.

Once we have introduced ourselves, made known we too are local, and have stated our purpose, we need to find common ground as quickly as possible. We need to identify with them on some level. We could talk about things that matter. We might start with, "I like to get your insight on something …" Here we can fill in the blank. First, everyone likes to share what he or she thinks. Make sure it is something in the news.

"I like to get your insight on something, 'what do you think of those who have illegally come into America?"

"I like to get your insight on something, 'what do you think the solution to this ISIS terrorist group?'"

"I like to get your insight on something, 'what do you believe is causing this extreme wickedness in the world today?'"

"I like to get your insight on something, how do you feel about Christian business owners, who refuse to make a wedding cake for same-sex couples?'"

"I like to get your insight on 1 John 4:8, which reads, 'God is love.' "Would you agree that the pain, suffering, old age and death, not to mention the wickedness of today, make it difficult to believe in a loving God?"

"I like to get your insight on something, "it would seem that everyone wants peace, why do you think we still have wars?'"

"I like to get your insight on something, "science has certainly improved our living conditions, but do you think it will ever get to the point of helping humans live forever?'"

"I like to get your insight on something, 'police officers have been called into question of late, do you believe the work they do has been covered well by the media?'"

What has been suggested in the above is only a start. What further can we do to reach those receptive ones before the end comes as Jesus put it? Moreover, what qualities are needed that will make us more effective in our sharing of the good news? The next chapters will address this and more.

Exercise

This week, find three opportunities at introducing yourself to a stranger as a Christian and share just one Scripture, Romans 12:17-18, asking them 'How can the counsel given here be applied in our dealings with neighbors?'

Review Questions

- What are some of the aspects involved in a person's accepting the Good News?

- How can nervousness and embarrassment be conquered in our witnessing to others?

- What should we try to accomplish when we introduce ourselves for the purpose of witnessing to another?

- How can Jesus and Paul's example help us in our approach to others?

CHAPTER 12 Rightly Handling the Word of Truth

2 Timothy 2:15 Updated American Standard Version (UASV)

[15] Do your best to present yourself to God as one approved, a workman who does not need to be ashamed, rightly handling[76] the word of truth.

One Greek-English Lexicon says of our Greek word orthotomounta (lit., straightly cutting), to give accurate instruction—'to teach correctly, to expound rightly.'[77] Om 2 Timothy 2:15, the *Holman New Testament Commentary* says, "God bestows his approval on the one who exhibits truth, love, and godliness in daily living, and who correctly handles the word of truth. The false teachers were mishandling God's words, using them for their own benefit. Timothy was commissioned to handle the words of God correctly. All preaching should present the truth clearly, cutting through erroneous ideas or inaccurate opinions."[78] *The New American Commentary* says, "Third, this same workman (specifically, Timothy but by application today all believers) was to be accurate in delivering the message of truth. The truth is the gospel. Paul showed concern that Timothy would present the

---

[76] Or *accurately handling* the word of truth; *correctly teaching* the word of truth

[77] Johannes P. Louw and Eugene Albert Nida, *Greek-English Lexicon of the New Testament: Based on Semantic Domains* (New York: United Bible Societies, 1996), 414.

[78] Knute Larson, I & II Thessalonians, I & II Timothy, Titus, Philemon, vol. 9, *Holman New Testament Commentary* (Nashville, TN: Broadman & Holman Publishers, 2000), 286.

gospel without perverting or distorting it.* He was not to be turned aside by disputes about words or mere empty prattle.

* Interpreters find a variety of possible sources for the derivation of the term [*orthotomeo*] ("handling aright the word of truth," ASV; "driving a straight furrow, in your proclamation of the truth," NEB). Lock presents the possibilities as a plow cutting a straight furrow, a road engineer's building a straight road, or a mason's squaring and cutting a stone to fit its proper place. He questions whether any one of these were consciously present in Paul's mind (The Pastoral Epistles, ICC [Edinburgh: T & T Clark, 1924], 99).

J. E. Huther properly suggests that the notion of cutting falls quickly into the background so that the meaning is "deal rightly with something so as not to falsify it" (Critical and Exegetical Handbook to the Epistles to Timothy and Titus (1884; reprint, Peabody, Mass.: Hendrickson, 1983], 234). Paul wanted Timothy to perform the task opposite that of a peddler of God's word (2 Cor 2:17).

The *New International Greek Testament Commentary* touching on the rendering, says, "The material that this worker is to handle correctly is 'the word of truth' [*ton logon tes aletheias*]. Only when he handles it correctly will he be unashamed [*anepaischunton*]. The rendering given in several of the modern translations, using a combination of the verb 'handle' and some adverb such as 'accurately' (NASB), 'rightly' (RSV), or 'correctly' (NIV), for the compound verb [*orthotomounta*] with the phrase 'the word of truth' as the direct object captures this relationship quite well."

The apostle Paul tells us, "For the word of God is living and active, sharper than any two-edged sword, piercing to the division of soul and of spirit, of joints and of marrow, and discerning the thoughts and intentions of the heart." (Heb. 4:12) "God's Word penetrates the **soul and spirit.** ... God's message is capable of penetrating the impenetrable. It can divide what is indivisible. ... God's message is discerning. **It judges the thoughts and attitudes of the heart.** It passes judgment on our feelings and our thoughts. What we regard as secret and hidden, God brought out for inspection by the discerning power of his Word."[79] As the Word of God is compared to a sword, it only seems reasonable that we would want to have skill in our use of it. This is why Paul told Timothy that he need be ashamed, "rightly handling the word of truth." Whenever we share or defend the Word of God, we want to do it in such a way that we arrive at what the author meant by the words that he used, accurately understanding what it says.

Context is the material surrounding a verse that we are reading is what will help us understand and apply it as it was meant to be applied. We need to keep in mind that the Bible is not just sixty-six books of fragmented, unconnected verses, gathered together haphazardly, and fitting for use under any situations as evidence of a point that we may feel, think or believe to be correct. It is sixty-six books written over about 1,600 years, by forty plus writers, who were moved along by Holy Spirit at the

---

[79] Thomas D. Lea, Hebrews & James, *Holman New Testament Commentary* (Nashville, TN: Broadman & Holman Publishers, 1999), 72.

direction of the Father. In other words, it is one book by one author, inspired and fully inerrant. Thus, we need to get the whole picture when we are considering what a verse or set of verses means. We need to consider the setting, who was the book written to, what the reason for writing the book was, and what these particular verses were meant to convey, i.e., is it a specific topic different than other parts of the chapter(s). This is important if we are going to "rightly handling the word of truth."

Some Examples

Let us use our main text for this chapter as our example, 2 Timothy 2:15, where Paul writes, "Do your best to present yourself to God as one approved, a workman who does not need to be ashamed, rightly handling[80] the word of truth." These words were written to Timothy in about 65 C.E. after Timothy had been Paul's traveling companion for 15 years. When Paul discovered young Timothy, in his late teens or early twenties in about 50 C.E. in Lystra on his second missionary journey, Timothy "was well spoken of by the brothers." (Acts 16:1-3) Moreover, Timothy was the son of a Jewish woman who was a believer, but his father was a Greek. Paul, in writing this letter, was "reminded of [Timothy's] sincere faith, a faith that dwelt first in [his] grandmother Lois and [his] mother Eunice and now, [Paul was certain, dwelled] in Timothy as well." (2 Tim. 1:1-2, 5) Therefore, the words to Timothy about handling the Word of God aright, were, in fact, written to a person that had been well-grounded in the Word of God

---

[80] *accurately handling* the word of truth; *correctly teaching* the word of truth

and who was caring out the will of the Father in major ways.

Therefore, the words of Paul to Timothy, in this second letter to him, were his telling Timothy how to give instruction to fellow Christians within God's congregations. While it is just as true that we need to 'handle the word of truth aright' when evangelizing unbelievers, Paul was not counseling Timothy on how to convert unbelievers to Christ. This is evidenced by Paul's first letter as well, where he writes to Timothy, "remain at Ephesus so that you may charge certain persons not to teach any different doctrine." (1:3) Later in that same first letter, Paul writes, "Keep a close watch on yourself and on the teaching. Persist in this, for by so doing you will save both yourself and your hearers." (4:16) In addition, Paul's direction at 2 Timothy 2:2, "what you have heard from me in the presence of many witnesses entrust to faithful men who will be able to teach others also." In other words, Timothy's was to use the word of truth rightly to benefit and guide his fellow Christian brothers.

Avoid Distorting God's Word

As Christians, we too, need to be cautious in our interpretation of and applying God's Word so that it is what the author meant by the words that he use, not what we feel, think, or believe it to mean. For example, take the King James Version at Isaiah 14:12-16, where it begins, "How art thou fallen from heaven, O Lucifer, son of the morning! how art thou cut down to the ground, which didst weaken the nations!" In the modern translations, the Hebrew word for Lucifer (*helel*), which means the "shining one," is rendered "day star" or "morning star." (ASV, ESV, LEB, HCSB, while the NASB renders it "star of the morning") Helel in this verse is not

231

a personal name or a title for Satan, but rather a term describes a brilliant position taken the dynasty of kings in Babylon, through the line of Nebuchadnezzar. On this the Baker Encyclopedia writes,

> There are many who believe the expression (and surrounding context) refers to Satan. They believe the similarities between Isaiah 14:12, Luke 10:18, and Revelation 12:7–10 warrant this conclusion. However, although the NT passages do speak of Satan's fall, the context of the Isaiah passage describes the defeated king of Babylon. The Babylonian king had desired to be above God, and so fell from heaven. His doom is pictured as already accomplished. Though defeat is certain for Satan, he yet continues his evil acts against God's people. Not until the final judgment (Rv 12–20) will his fate be sealed and his activity stopped. Isaiah, then, is not speaking of Satan in 14:12 but of the proud, and soon to be humiliated, king of Babylon. (Elwell, Baker Encyclopedia of the Bible 1988, Volume 2, Page 1361)

No, Lucifer in the King James Version is not a title or name for Satan the Devil. Helel is a reference to the King of Babylon as is evidenced from verse 4, which reads, "will take up this taunt against the king of Babylon." In addition, verses 15-16 of chapter 14 says, that this "day star" or "morning star" will be "are brought down to Sheol" i.e. the place where the dead are buried. Moreover, in verse 16, we read, "Those who see you [i.e., "day star" or "morning star." ("Lucifer," KJV)] will stare at you and ponder over you: 'Is this **the man** who made the earth tremble, who shook kingdoms," Clearly, no one would ever suggest that Satan is a man, rather he is a very powerful fallen angel of God. In fact, he is chief of the fallen angels.

Poor Proof Texting

Proof texting is using isolated texts, without regard for context, to establish a doctrinal belief. In many cases, the Scriptures used may not accurately reflect what the original author meant. Please note that this is not saying one cannot use appropriated selected texts from different parts of Scripture to support a doctrinal point. All Bible scholars do this, but each text that is selected has to be used within its original context and with the meaning the author meant to convey, namely, what the original author intended. In fact, we can turn to Jesus and the apostles and see that they used scattered texts to prove the biblical truth, but did this appropriately as mentioned in the above. However, even this needs to be qualified.

On many occasions, a New Testament writer would quote or cite an Old Testament Scripture. Many times the New Testament writer would be using the Old Testament text contextually, according to the setting, and intent of the Old Testament writer (observing the grammatical-historical sense). However, **at times** the New Testament writer would add to or apply the text differently than what was meant by the Old Testament writer (not observing the grammatical-historical sense). This is either a new or a progressive revelation of God, where he has inspired the New Testament writer to go beyond the intended meaning of the Old Testament writer, and carry out what is known as Inspired Sensus Plenior Application (ISPA). In this latter case, the New Testament writer is using the Old Testament text to convey another meaning to another circumstance. This does not violate the principle that all texts have just one single meaning. The

Old Testament text has one meaning, and the New Testament writer's adaptation of that text is not a second meaning, but another meaning. The New Testament authors were inspired, moved along by Holy Spirit, so they could skip over historical-grammatical interpretation to give an entirely new meaning, out of context, which is the subjective interpretation. However, what they meant to say with this new meaning is what God meant to say so that they can be subjective. However, we need to stay far from the shores of subjective interpretation, by either penning it or reading it.

Now, proof-texting is only wrong, if we pull the verses out of their context and apply them to a doctrinal position, which is giving them a meaning that the author did not intend. In Romans chapter 9, the Apostle Paul quotes eleven times from other parts of the Bible.[81] However, Paul is not using the verses that he pulls from different books of the Old Testament out of context. They are being used as examples of Israelite history, as it relates to the sovereignty of God: the example of Esau and Jacob, the example of Pharaoh, the example from Hosea, and the example from Isaiah. The concluding two points of Paul were, (1) **"Through faith the Gentiles have found righteousness without even seeking it** (9:30)." (2) **"Through the law Israel has not found righteousness even after seeking it** (9:31–33)."[82]

---

[81] The quotations are found in Romans chapter 9, verses 7 (Genesis 21:12), 9 (Genesis 18:14), 12 (Genesis 25:23), 13 (Malachi 1:2, 3), 15 (Exodus 33:19), 17 (Exodus 9:16), 25 (Hosea 2:23), 26 (Hosea 1:10), 27, 28 (Isaiah 10:22, 23), 29 (Isaiah 1:9), and 33 (Isaiah 28:16).

[82] http://biblia.com/books/outlnbbl/Ro9.6-29

The Meaning of a Text Is Often Within the Context

Some Christians have been guilty of misapplying verses within Scripture because many are confused by the *plain sense of the meaning* that is mentioned in some basic biblical interpretation books. For example, Elmer Towns writes that "the Bible should be interpreted literally, which means we should seek the obvious meaning, of words, context, and language."[83] While this is true, phrases like the *plain sense of the meaning* and *obvious meaning* can cause confusion. For example, one might read Proverbs 10:7 in support of the idea that the wicked will not receive a resurrection. It reads, "The memory of the righteous is a blessing, but the name of the wicked will rot." It is true that those guilty of gross wickedness will not receive a resurrection. However, Proverbs 10:7 is not a Scripture that could be used to make a case for the wicked not receiving a resurrection. Some might be asking why, it says, "the name of the wicked will rot," which seems quite *plain* and *obvious* to me. If we look at the context in Proverbs 10, we will take note of a series of contrasts, a wise son contrasted with a foolish son, a slack hand contrasted with the hand of the diligent, the wise of heart contrasted with the babbling fool and so on. However, nothing to do with the resurrection is discussed here. Therefore, it would be wrong to use this text as a proof text that the wicked will not receive a resurrection. Rather the point of verse 7 is that the good people will be remembered as a blessing, but the wicked will soon be forgotten. In other words,

[83] Towns, Elmer (2011-10-30). AMG Concise Bible Doctrines (AMG Concise Series) (Kindle Locations 1024-1025). AMG Publishers. Kindle Edition.

the name or reputation of the wicked is not a pleasurable memory, as the name of Adolf Hitler. Nevertheless, there are Scriptures that can be used as evidence that the wicked will not receive a resurrection. (Matt. 23:33; 25:46; Rev. 21:8) Notice that when towns spoke of our seeking the **obvious meaning**, he spoke of words, but he also spoke of context and language.

1 John 4:18 Updated American Standard Version (UASV)

[18] There is no fear in love; but perfect love casts out fear, because fear has to do with punishment,[84] and the one who fears is not perfected in love.

If we were to look at the context of 1 John 4:18, namely, verses 15-21, will help us get at what John meant. Verse 17 reads "By this, love is perfected with us, so that we may have confidence [Gr., *parresia*; Lit., "freedom of speech" "outspokenness"] in the day of judgment; because as he is, so also are we in this world." On this *The Complete Word Study Dictionary* writes, "Especially in Hebrews and 1 John the word denotes confidence which is experienced with such things as faith in communion with God, **fulfilling the duties of the evangelist**, holding fast our hope, and acts which entail a special exercise of faith. *Parresia* is possible as the result of guilt having been removed by the blood of Jesus (Heb. 10:19 [cf. vv. 17, 18]; 1 John 3:21; 4:17) and manifests itself in confident praying and witnessing (Heb. 4:16; 1 John 5:14)."[85] (Bold mine) However, we can see

---

[84] Gr., Kolasin (Lit., lopping off cutting off), the punishment is the fear of being cut off, i.e., not remaining in God's love on judgment day.

[85] Spiros Zodhiates, *The Complete Word Study Dictionary: New Testament* (Chattanooga, TN: AMG Publishers, 2000).

that in verse 18 we are continuing the discussion of having a "freedom of speech" that was spoken of in verse 17. However, John is not speaking about our **fulfilling the duties of the evangelist**. Rather, our "freedom of speech" is our speech toward God. This is made clear earlier in First John,

1 John 3:19-21 Updated American Standard Version (UASV)

[19] By this we know that we are of the truth and will persuade[86] our heart before him, [20] in whatever our heart condemns us; for God is greater than our heart and knows all things. [21] Beloved, if our heart does not condemn us, we have confidence [Gr., *parresia*; Lit., "freedom of speech" "outspokenness"] toward God;

Therefore, "God is love, and the one who remains in love remains in God, and God remains in him. By this, love is perfected with us" (4:16-17), and we can feel free to come to our heavenly Father in full confidence, i.e., with freedom of speech toward him. Because of Jesus' ransom sacrifice, our imperfection, and inherited sin do not deter us from coming to the Father, asking for help in doing his will. (Matt. 7:21; 1 John 2:1-2, 15-17) Just as a child would feel confident in coming to his loving human father, possessing freedom of speech toward him, knowing his father will help him, even if he has made a mistake. How much more so should this be the case with our heavenly Father? We should feel confident, free to say anything that is on our heart or mind so that we may remain in him, and he remains in us. We should not have some dark fear when it comes to our heavenly Father, thinking that God will seek justice from his imperfect, sinful human, condemning us because our being mentally

---

[86] Or *assure; convince*

bent toward sin in mind and heart. (Gen 6:5; 8:21; Jer. 17:9) Even so, this does not give us the permission to practice or live in sin, perpetually coming to God for forgiveness, in essence, and taking advantage of his love, mercy, patience and long-suffering. (1 John 3:9-10) Nevertheless, it does mean that if we **commit a sin**, no matter the gravity, we need not have some dreadful fear of going to our heavenly Father, with freedom of speech toward him, seeking correction for the wrongdoing we have committed, be it thoughts or actions. In fact, we know that nothing is hidden from the sight of God. – Psalm 139:1-3, 15-18, 23-24.

Now that we correctly understand 1 John 4:18, we can fully appreciate our remaining in love, meaning we remain in God, and God remains in us. This, love is perfected with us (4:16-17), because we have the freedom of speech, in prayer, toward God; therefore, we can be confident that he will direct us in the way that we should walk. Our being "perfected in love" means that the love of God is entirely complete in us, in that we are continuously seeking to do his will wholeheartedly. – Ephesians 3:12; Hebrews 4:16; 1 John 5:14

Avoid Abusing Prophetic Scripture

Fulfillment is the result of a prophetic message, prophecies that are fulfilled. Luke 24:27 tells us "And beginning with Moses and all the Prophets, [Jesus] interpreted to them in all the Scriptures the things concerning himself." Matthew especially, referenced many prophecies that were fulfilled in Jesus. Let us look at one from Hosea in Matthew.

Hosea 11:1 English Standard Version (ESV)

1 When Israel was a [boy], I loved him,

and <u>out of Egypt I called my son</u>.

Matthew 2:15 English Standard Version (ESV)

[15] and remained there until the death of Herod. This was to **fulfill** what the Lord had spoken by the prophet, "<u>Out of Egypt I called my son</u>."

Some argue that we need to see Matthew's meaning in Hosea. In other words, Hosea meant to convey the meaning that Matthew expressed. This just is not the case. Was Hosea meaning his words to be prophetic, or were they a reference to a historical event, to make a point to his current readers? His audience would have understood what Hosea meant, by their use of historical-grammatical interpretation. "When Israel was but a boy" is a reference to the nation's early beginnings, when they were young, while they were in Egypt. "I" is Jehovah God speaking through the prophet Hosea, their loving Father, who 'out of Egypt called his son.'

On many occasions, a New Testament writer would quote or cite an Old Testament Scripture. Many times the New Testament writer would be using the Old Testament text contextually, according to the setting, and intent of the Old Testament writer (observing the grammatical-historical sense). However, at times the New Testament writer would add to or apply the text differently than what was meant by the Old Testament writer (**not** observing the grammatical-historical sense). This is either a new or a progressive revelation by God, where he has inspired the New Testament writer to go beyond the intended meaning of the Old Testament writer, and carry out what is known as *Inspired Sensus Plenior Application* (ISPA). In this latter case, the New Testament writer is using the Old Testament text to convey another meaning to another circumstance. This does not violate the principle that all texts have just one single meaning.

239

The Old Testament text has one meaning, and the New Testament writer's adaptation of that text is not a second meaning, but another meaning.

Now, **(1)** was Matthew intending to interpret the message of Hosea, because it was supposedly prophetic, or **(2)** was he using Hosea's meaning of a historical reference, and giving it a *sensus plenior* meaning, by way of inspiration of Holy Spirit? It was the latter, number**(2)**. Hosea's meaning was a historical reference to the Israelite nation when they were in Egypt. Matthew's meaning is to take Hosea's words, and add new additional meaning to them, not suggesting at all that Hosea meant his new meaning.

Dr. John H. Walton's approach in dealing with this sort of circumstance is that we need to grasp the difference between **(1)**message and**(2)** fulfillment. The message of Hosea was not prophetic, and was understood by his audience. "Fulfillment is not the message, but is the working out of God's plan in history. There are no hermeneutical principles within the grammatical-historical model that enable one to identify a fulfillment by reading and analyzing the prophecy."[87] In other words, we need not concern ourselves with trying to shove a square peg into a round hole. We do not have to fit Matthew's meaning into Hosea, as though Hosea's meaning was prophetic, and this justifies Matthew's conclusions. We are not causing any ripple in Scripture, because these two have different meanings from each other. Walton is in harmony with Dr. Robert L. Thomas, with the exception of his seeing Matthew's use of Hosea's words as a **fulfillment**, while Thomas sees them as

---

[87] Page(s): 11, Inspired Subjectivity and Hermeneutical Objectivity by John H. Walton Master's Seminary Journal March 01, 2002.pdf

a **completion**, "some sense the transport of Jesus by His parents from Egypt **completed** the deliverance of Israel from Egypt that had begun during the time of Moses."[88] Bold is mine

It is difficult to see Matthew's use of Hosea's words as a fulfillment, because, Hosea's words were not prophetic. Without an intended prophecy, how can there be a fulfillment. We should see Matthew's use of Hosea's words as completing whatever historical reference Hosea was referring too. What we do know is that if Matthew assigns a different meaning to Hosea's words, it is his meaning and it is subjective. Which if we recall, we are perfectly fine with, because he has the authority to offer subjective meaning; he was an inspired Bible writer, who had been moved along by Holy Spirit. Matthew was not interpreting the message Hosea penned, he was giving us a *sensus plenior*, a completion to Hosea's words.

Therefore, we need to look at the Greek word behind fulfillment (*pleroo*). *Pleroo* has a range of meaning, and the context will give us which sense was meant. It can mean, "to fulfill, to complete, carry out to the full, accomplish, and perfect."[89] What is the sense that we find at Matthew 2:15 and other places that New Testament writers use it, when they are referring to an Old Testament Passage? Bible scholar Dr. Robert L. Thomas has this to say on the subject, "Most (if not all) English translations frequently render the Greek verb *pleroo* by the English word fulfill. In some instances,

---

[88] Robert L. Thomas. Evangelical Hermeneutics: The New Versus the Old (p. 263). Kindle Edition.

[89] W. E. Vine, Merrill F. Unger and William White, Jr., vol. 2, Vine's Complete Expository Dictionary of Old and New Testament Words, 8 (Nashville, TN: T. Nelson, 1996).

this is unfortunate because the two words do not cover the same semantic domain. In English, fulfill, when used in connection with Old Testament citations, carries the connotation of a historical occurrence of something promised or predicted. The Greek *pleroo*, however, covers more linguistic territory than that."[90] New Testament Scholar Douglas J. Moo adds,

> *Pleroo* cannot be confined to so narrow a focus [as referring to fulfillment of an Old Testament prophecy].... What needs to be emphasized, then, is that the use of pleroo in an introductory formula need not mean that the author regards the Old Testament text he quotes as a direct prophecy; and accusations that a New Testament author misuses the Old Testament by using pleroo to introduce nonprophetic texts are unfounded.'[91]

We can see that the context of Matthew 2:15 leads us to the rendering "This was to **complete** what the Lord had spoken by the prophet, 'Out of Egypt I called my son.'" In other words, "In the Matthew 2:15 citation of Hosea 11:1 Matthew uses [pleroo] to indicate the completion of a *sensus plenior* meaning he finds in Hosea 11:1."[92] As we have already said, the single meaning of Hosea 11:1 is not prophetic, but rather a historical reference to the time of Moses, when God called the Israelite nation out of Egypt. Therefore, to use the English rendering fulfill is "misleading." "Matthew's meaning is

---

[90] Robert L. Thomas. Evangelical Hermeneutics: The New Versus the Old (p. 262). Kindle Edition.

[91] Moo, Doulas J., "Problems of Sensus Plenior," 191

[92] Thomas. Evangelical Hermeneutics: The New Versus the Old (p. 263).

that in some sense the transport of Jesus by His parents from Egypt completed the deliverance of Israel from Egypt that had begun during the time of Moses."[93]

Now, it is time for a little warning. We should be very cautious of writers who give us interpretations of allegory, typology, and fulfillment that are not specifically given by a bible writer. No human writer at present, or that lived after the Apostle John died in 100 C.E., has the authority to give us fulfillment unless it was stated by a bible writer. Humans are very curious about what the future holds, especially Christians with the fulfillment of Scripture. This is why books by authors telling us they have unlocked Scripture or that they can explain the fulfillment of things that no Bible writer expressed as a fulfillment, are very dangerous. We cannot reproduce the interpretive skills of the New Testament writers, because they did not always follow the historical-grammatical interpretation (objective), they at times gave a message that was subjective. We do not have the authority to imitate them by our skipping over historical-grammatical interpretation to give revelations about allegory, typology, and fulfillments of Scripture. Therefore, let us stay far from the shores of subjective interpretation, by either penning it, or reading it.

New Testament Use of Old Testament

The New Testament writers used Old Testament writers in one of two ways. **(1)** The New Testament writer took the one grammatical-historical interpretation of the Old Testament passage. In this case, we are talking about a fulfillment of the Old Testament passage and we

---

[93] IBID., p. 263

are perfectly fine to word it that way. In other words, the Old Testament passage was written as a prophecy for that future event, not some immediate fulfillment. **(2)** The New Testament writer goes beyond what the Old Testament writer penned, assigning it additional meaning that is applicable to the New Testament context. In other words, the Old Testament writer's grammatical-historical interpretation would have been a fulfillment for him and his audience, not just a hope. The New Testament writer then made the information applicable to his situation, by adding to it, which fit his context. With number **(1)**, we have the New Testament writer staying with the literal sense of the Old Testament writer. With number **(2)**, we have the New Testament writer adding a whole other meaning.

Dr. Robert L. Thomas calls number **(2)** "inspired sensus plenior application" (ISPA), which we will adopt as well.[94] It is inspired because this is an inspired Bible writer adding the additional sense or fuller sense than what had been penned in the Old Testament.

When interpreting the Old Testament and New Testament each in light of the single grammatical-historical meaning of each passage, two kinds of New Testament uses of the Old Testament surface, one in which the New Testament writer observes the grammatical-historical sense of the Old Testament passage and the other in which the New Testament writer goes beyond the grammatical-historical sense in using a passage. Inspired sensus plenior application (ISPA) designates the latter usage. Numerous passages illustrate each type of New Testament use of the Old Testament.

---

[94] Robert L. Thomas. Evangelical Hermeneutics: The New Versus the Old (p. 242). Kindle Edition

The ISPA type of use does not grant contemporary interpreters a license to copy the method of New Testament writers, nor does it violate the principle of single meaning. The ISPA meaning of the Old Testament passage did not exist for humans until the time of the New Testament citation, being occasioned by Israel's rejection of her Messiah at His first advent. The ISPA approach approximates that advocated by John H. Walton more closely than other explanations of the New Testament use of the Old Testament. "Fulfillment" terminology in the New Testament is appropriate only for events that literally fulfill events predicted in the Old Testament.[95]

Most conservative evangelical scholars believe that some biblical prophecies possess more than the initial fulfillment, an extended fulfillment. This writer and many others would also point out that the prophecies in both the Hebrew Old Testament and the Greek New Testament had *meaning* to those who the prophecy was written to; it served as means of guidance for the initial audience, as well as for succeeding generation, down to our day. This is not to say that the prophetic message itself was applicable from then until now, but that its meaning is beneficial to all. In many cases, the *fulfillment* took place within that first generation.

At times, there are New Testament writers that give another fulfillment during the New Testament era, 02 B.C.E. up unto 100 C.E. In addition, there are some cases where a prophecy has a final fulfillment in what the Bible calls the "last days" or "end times," or even during the millennial reign of Christ. Revelation 21:1; Isaiah 65:17; 66:22; 2 Peter 3:13

---

[95] IBID., p. 241

Here I should qualify what I mean by having *meaning* to the initial audience and being *fulfilled* during the lifetime of the first audience. Isaiah 65:17 informs the initial audience, the contemporaries of Isaiah "I am about to create new heavens and a new earth, and the former things shall not be remembered, and they shall not come to mind." What do "new heavens and a new earth" mean, and when was this to take place?

> **65:17-19**. The new condition of salvation for only a portion of God's people could occur because God had created something entirely new. The new creation would differ greatly from the old one, being dominated by joy instead of mourning and weeping. The joy would be shared by the people and by God. This new creation would share some features with the old. It would still have both heavens and earth. And it would center in the holy city of Jerusalem.[96]

I certainly would agree with Dr. Trent C. Butler's assessment, but is this applicable to the time period of Isaiah's prophesying, c. 780-730 B.C.E.? The words can merely refer to the future in general, as opposed to what we think of as the last days or end times. In other words, the Israelites could place their hope in a bright future, but not knowing the day and the hour. There is nothing in Scripture where another inspired writer took Isaiah words, and gave them meaning of fulfillment. They could have taken place already, but we cannot speak of that in absolute terms, because as was stated earlier, we are not

---

[96] Anders, Max; Butler, Trent (2002-04-01). Holman Old Testament Commentary: Isaiah (p. 374). B&H Publishing.

inspired, to be able to speak of fulfillment. However, let us offer a possible time when they could have been fulfilled in the past, but after Isaiah was written.

It could have been fulfilled almost 200 years after Isaiah when the Israelites would come back from the seventy-years that they were going to spend in Babylonian captivity. Butler said, "The new condition of salvation [was] for only a portion of God's people." Only a small remnant of Israelites returned home from Babylonian captivity in 537 B.C.E. This would mean that there was no immediate *fulfillment* for the people of Isaiah's day, or even the next generation. However, there was *meaning* for the Israelites, because they knew destruction and desolation of Jerusalem was coming, but they also knew that a remnant was going to come through this, and purified worship would be restored to Jerusalem, which offered them hope.

As we grow in our ability to interpret correctly and understand God's Word because we have bought out the time from Satan's world, we will become more and more acquainted with its message of beauty and its meaning in our lives, comforted in the fact we are now sharing and defending what the authors meant to convey. Many times, we have likely looked to the prophecies in the Hebrew Scriptures regarding the blessings coming to what is referred to as the new heavens and the new earth (renewal of the present universe). We know this is the final redemption from the domination of sin (Matt. 19:28; Ac 3:31; Rom. 8:18-21), contemplating the paradise-like conditions that are to come under Christ's kingdom on this new earth.

However, sometimes we are slow to realize that the prophecies of Isaiah and the like had some fulfillment to those who heard it, or succeeding generations. Think of the words of Isaiah the prophet at 35:1, 7, "The wilderness and the dry land shall be glad; the desert shall rejoice and blossom like the crocus; the burning sand shall become a pool, and the thirsty ground springs of water; in the haunt of jackals, where they lie down, the grass shall become reeds and rushes." If we look at the context of this Scripture, it is all too clear that it applies to the returned Jews after their seventy years of Captivity in Babylon, under Governor Zerubbabel. In fact, verse 10 specifically says, "and the redeemed of the Lord will return and come to Zion with singing, crowned with unending joy. Joy and gladness will overtake them, and sorrow and sighing will flee." (HCSB) Jehovah saw fit to make the land of Israel a mini paradise for the remnant that was to return from their captivity. In essence, a land that had grown over for seventy years, was restored to paradise-like conditions. Those same miracles, acting on behalf of his people will pale in comparison to the renewed heavens and earth that are to come under the rule of his Son, the Lord Jesus Christ.

Only truly conservative Christianity can completely appreciate that "the word of God is living and active." (Heb. 4:12) Yes, God is very much alive and his speaks to his people today through the page of the living, inspired, inerrant Word of God. In this way, he gives power to his people and understanding of deep biblical truths as to his intentions for his servants. It is for this reason alone that every true Christian should have an internal desire to "handle the word of truth aright." We want to be efficient in our using it to proclaim, to teach, to defend and to make disciples as Jesus had commanded. Paul said to Timothy,

2 Timothy 3:16-17 New American Standard Bible (NASB)

¹⁶ All Scripture is inspired by God and profitable for teaching, for reproof, for correction, for training in righteousness; ¹⁷ so that the man of God may be adequate, equipped for every good work.

If we are to use the Word of God aright, what must we do? We must read it and study it, seeking the very knowledge of God. (Josh 1-8; Psa. 1:1-3; Deut. 6:4-9; Pro. 2:1-6) Such knowledge and understanding do not come easily, nor should we expect that it would. If we were going to become an attorney, to provide justice for the troubled of this world, would we do this by reading a law book once and a while for a few minutes? If we wanted to be a pediatric heart surgeon, to save the lives of children, would this happen by reading a few medical books here and there and sitting in a few medical classes? If we are to evangelize the Word of God aright, is it going to happen by occasionally picking up the Bible to read and sitting in church services ritualistically? No, we must buy out the time, by having a daily personal study, preparing for meetings, participating in meetings that allow such, and sharing what we learn regularly.

Proverbs 2:1-6 Updated American Standard Version (UASV)

2 My son, if you receive my words
   and treasure up my commandments with you,
² making your ear attentive to wisdom
   and inclining your heart to understanding;
³ For if you cry for discernment
   and raise your voice for understanding,
⁴ if you seek it like silver
   and search for it as for hidden treasures,
⁵ then you will understand the fear of Jehovah

and find the knowledge of God.
⁶ For Jehovah gives wisdom;
   from his mouth come knowledge and understanding;

Exercise

- Did Matthew at 1:23 use a literal treatment of Isaiah 7:14?

Review Questions

- What background information aids us in properly understanding 2 Timothy 2:15?

- What common explanation of Isaiah 14:12-16 has often been given, but what is the actual Scriptural explanation, and so who truly is the Lucifer of Isaiah 14:12-16, reflecting whose attitude?

- What is proof-texting and how can it be wrong? Whose examples help us to appreciate that you can use texts from different places within Scripture to make a particular point?

- What are some examples of the meaning being within the context?

- How can we avoid abusing Prophetic Scripture?

CHAPTER 13 The Reasoning Evangelist

Acts 18:19 English Standard Version (ESV)

[19] And they came to Ephesus, and he left them there, but he himself went into the synagogue and **reasoned with the Jews**.

If someone or a church evangelizes their community, one must be prepared to reason with any culture, and numerous religions, such as the Jewish, Buddhist, Muslim, Hindu, Shinto, Taoism, Confucianism, as well as atheists and agnostics, among others. This can seem overwhelming, but it is not as complicated as it sounds. There are many good Christian books out, which will give you the basics of the major religions in just one book, a chapter on each, and demonstrate how to reason with them.[97]

Reasoning with one, means that one uses Scripture, questions and illustrates logically, which causes the listener to think, and get the message in their mind and then in their heart. If someone uses a direct, rigid and unbending approach, one will close off the listener's mind and heart. Meanwhile, a reasoning manner uses logical thinking to get results or draw conclusions, which inspires discussions. The evangelist's desire must be for the conversation to weigh on the mind and heart of the listener, moving them to contemplate the discussion, so they are anxious to engage the evangelist in future discussions.

---

[97] http://astore.amazon.com/bibletranslat-20/detail/0736920846

While it is true that the truth will set one free, it must be received in such a way to do just that. Think of a conversation in terms of two people tossing a ball back and forth. If one tosses the ball so that it is catchable, the odds are better that it will be caught and received well. If one throws a ball like you are trying to take the other person's head off, it will not be received well, and few will catch it. Some people's beliefs remain dear to them, and to have them bluntly disclosed may not be received well.

James 3:17 English Standard Version (ESV)

[17] But the wisdom from above is first pure, then peaceable, gentle, **open to reason**, full of mercy and good fruits, impartial and sincere.

James says that "the wisdom from above is … open to reason." The Greek word here eupeithes "open to reason" means "easily persuaded," "compliant," or "congenial." Some translations render it "obedient," (LEB) "gentle" (HCSB, NASB). On this verse, the Baker New Testament Commentary says, "Another attribute of wisdom is consideration. The person who is 'considerate' is fair, **reasonable**, gentle in all his deliberations. He quietly gathers all the facts before he gives his opinion. He refrains from placing himself first and always considers others better than himself (Phil. 2:3; 4:5)."[98] (Bold mine.)

Acts 17:1-3 English Standard Version (ESV)

[1] Now when they had passed through Amphipolis and Apollonia, they came to Thessalonica, where there

---

[98] Simon J. Kistemaker and William Hendriksen, Exposition of James and the Epistles of John, vol. 14, New Testament Commentary (Grand Rapids: Baker Book House, 1953–2001), 122.

was a synagogue of the Jews. **²** And Paul went in, as was his custom, and on three Sabbath days he reasoned with them **[the Jews]** from the Scriptures, **³** explaining and proving that it was necessary for the Christ to suffer and to rise from the dead, and saying, "This Jesus, whom I proclaim to you, is the Christ."

The Apostle Paul studied under the renowned Pharisee Gamaliel, who was the grandson of Hillel the Elder (110 B.C.E.[99] – 10 C.E.), the founder of one of the two schools within Judaism. Paul describes himself as "circumcised on the eighth day, of the people of Israel, of the tribe of Benjamin, a Hebrew of Hebrews; as to the law, a Pharisee; as to zeal, a persecutor of the church; as to righteousness under the law, blameless." (Phil 3:5-6) He also states, "But whatever gain I had, I counted as loss for the sake of Christ. Indeed, I count everything as loss because of the surpassing worth of knowing Christ Jesus my Lord. For his sake I have suffered the loss of all things and count them as rubbish, in order that I may gain Christ" (Phil. 3:7-8) Thus, we note that Paul "reasoned from the Scriptures" when he talked to the Jews in the Jewish Synagogue. His listeners accepted the Hebrew Scriptures as an authority. Therefore, he began his witness with what they knew and accepted.

However, at Acts 17:22-31, we find Paul witnessing to the Greeks at the Areopagus in Athens; he did not turn to the Scriptures as his source of reasoning. "As in Lystra, so in Athens, it would have been futile to begin with the God of the Old Testament choosing a certain people, sending prophets, and promising a Messiah. That was a

---

[99] B.C.E. years ran down toward zero, although the Romans had no zero, and C.E. years ran up from zero. (100, 10, 3, 2, 1 ◀B.C.E. | C.E.▶ 1, 2, 3, 10, and 100)

message for synagogues or Jews gathering by a river. Paul began with the doctrine of God and launched his message with a local object lesson, the altar to *agnosto theo.* [unknown god][100] In "Establishing rapport with his Athenian audience, Paul quotes verbatim from two Greek poets. Both writers extol the virtues of the god Zeus ... By quoting these poets Paul is not intimating that he agrees with the pagan setting in which the citations flourished. Rather, he uses the words to fit his Christian teaching. From the Old Testament, he is able to draw the evidence that man derives his life, activity, and being from God (Job 12:10; Dan. 5:23)."[101] Paul used information familiar to his audience. Then, he took that information, and made a case for the Creator, the only true God. On this, Bible scholar John B. Polhill writes,

> As so often in the speeches of Acts, Paul began his discourse with a point of contact with his audience. In this case it was the altars Paul had already observed in the city (v. 16). One in particular caught his attention. It was dedicated "TO AN UNKNOWN GOD." This gave him the perfect launching pad for his presentation of monotheism to the polytheistic and pantheistic Athenians. Piety had no doubt led the Athenians to erect such an altar for fear they might offend some deity of whom they were unaware and had failed to give the proper worship. Paul would now proclaim a

---

[100] Kenneth O. Gangel, *Acts*, vol. 5, Holman New Testament Commentary (Nashville, TN: Broadman & Holman Publishers, 1998), 289.

[101] Simon J. Kistemaker and William Hendriksen, *Exposition of the Acts of the Apostles*, vol. 17, New Testament Commentary (Grand Rapids: Baker Book House, 1953–2001), 636-7.

God who was unknown to them. In fact, this God, totally unknown to them, was the only true divinity that exists.[102]

In the 1950s and 1960s, almost everyone that someone would talk to on the street possessed some knowledge of the Bible. If one said Old or New Testament, they understood. If an evangelist spoke of the apostles, the person knew what that meant. However, today billions have almost no knowledge about the Bible other than the name "Bible," and it is still regarded as a holy book. People who do not recognize the Bible, nor have any knowledge of the Bible, have **some commonalities** with Christians: they want to hope in something better. They see violence, pain and suffering, sickness, old age and death every day, the same as any Christian. They too want a better life for themselves and their children. Thus, the ability to reason requires finding common ground such as this. Then, open the Scriptures by explaining how we got here, and how there is a hope for something better in Jesus Christ. This reasoning might offer them a hope that they have not had, or a hope that is more real and legitimate than any they have now.

REVIEW QUESTION:

Who must we be prepared to reason with? What does reasoning mean? How is a conversation like tossing a ball? What did James mean by "open to reason?" Explain how Paul reasoned differently, depending on his audience. How did Paul use information differently, depending on his

---

[102] John B. Polhill, Acts, vol. 26, The New American Commentary (Nashville: Broadman & Holman Publishers, 1995), 371.

> audience? How do we find commonalities with people who have no knowledge of the Bible, or those who do not recognize its authority?

Even those who have a vast knowledge of the Bible, but who are atheists, agnostics or other critics of the Bible, have as their mission in life to evangelize their message, "God is dead!" In the last 50-60-years, atheists have made many disciples for themselves. There are millions of Christians and those from other religions who have become atheists because they have succumbed to the misleading propaganda of the books, videos, movies, websites, television shows, and other tools of the atheistic machine. We certainly must reason from the Scriptures, but with these enemies of the faith there must be more.

> God is rational, and he has created us as rational beings. The Bible urges us to give the reason for the hope that is in us (1 Pet. 3:15, NIV). Indeed, Jesus declared that the greatest commandment is: "You shall love the Lord your God with all ... your mind" (Matt. 22:37). The Apostle Paul added, "whatever is true, ... think on ...° (Phil. 4:8). Thinking is not an option for a Christian; it is an imperative.[103]

Ephesians 6:17 English Standard Version (ESV)

[17] and take the helmet of salvation, and the sword of the Spirit, which is the word of God,

---

[103] Ronald M. Brooks; Norman L. Geisler. *Come, Let Us Reason: An Introduction to Logical Thinking* (Kindle Locations 12-14). Kindle Edition.

2 Corinthians 10:4-5 English Standard Version (ESV)

⁴ For the weapons of four warfare are not of the flesh but have divine power to destroy strongholds. ⁵ We destroy arguments and every lofty opinion raised against the knowledge of God, and take every thought captive to obey Christ,

In Christian spiritual warfare, the mind can help us wield "the sword of the Spirit, which is the word of God." However, a blank mind will do us no good. If we have not taken in knowledge of God, there is nothing to recall that can be used in the battle for the Bible that lies ahead. Do we want to free those brothers and sisters by the tens of millions, who have been taken captive by the world? One could have the absolute best sword ever made, but if he or she does not have the skills to use it, the sword is worthless to use. My prayer is that all Christians will awaken from their stupor and join the fight that some have taken up these last few decades. May they make use of the mind that God gave them, to use their power of reason, to equip themselves to defend the faith.

Believers live in a time when certain critics of Christianity have abandoned all delicacy and decorum in debate. Rather than sticking to rational, carefully reasoned arguments, they have taken off the gloves to launch angry, sarcastic, and sloppily argued attacks. They lob their rhetorical grenades in hopes of creating the (incorrect) impression that belief in God is for intellectual lightweights who believe ridiculous, incoherent doctrines and who also are opposed to all scientific endeavor and discovery. These objectors are writing books—

indeed, best sellers—that tend to be more bluster and emotion than substance. New Atheists such as Richard Dawkins, Sam Harris, and Christopher Hitchens characterize this tone of debate. On another front, textual critic Bart Ehrman misleadingly raises doubts about the New Testament text's reliability, while novelist Dan Brown's Da Vinci Code and Jesus Seminar cofounder John Dominic Crossan mislead many into thinking that various Gnostic Gospels give us more reliable information about the historical Jesus than do the canonical Gospels. From various angles the public is being told that we cannot trust what the New Testament, and the Gospels in particular, say about Jesus of Nazareth.[104]

It is no longer a matter of preaching on Sunday and hoping that some new faces show up. It is as though most Christians hide in their fort, the Church, watching as lives are taken one by one, hoping that the enemy will go away or that they can hold out until the return of Christ. The enemy takes one life after the other, and few are lifting themselves to join the fight. There is a need for a knowledge of the deeper things of God's Word, a need to reason with the enemy and his victims, so that they can see that our message is more important, why it involves them as well, and just how they are going to be affected personally. If Christians prove effective in this, we must have the ability to reason with the enemy, defeating him on the battlefield, not hiding in the church waiting for dawn. One of the leading apologists of the

---

[104] Craig, William Lane; Copan, Paul (2009-08-01). *Contending with Christianity's Critics: Answering New Atheists and Other Objectors* (Kindle Locations 47-56). B&H Publishing. Kindle Edition.

20th and 21st centuries, Dr. William Lane Craig, wrote the following:

> This is a war we cannot afford to lose. The great Princeton theologian J. Gresham Machen warned on the eve of the fundamentalist controversy that if the church loses the intellectual battle in one generation, then evangelism would become immeasurably more difficult in the next:

> > False ideas are the greatest obstacles to the reception of the gospel. We may preach with all the fervor of a reformer and yet succeed only in winning a straggler here and there, if we permit the whole collective thought of the nation or of the world to be controlled by ideas which, by the resistless force of logic, prevent Christianity from being regarded as anything more than a harmless delusion. Under such circumstances, what God desires us to do is to destroy the obstacle at its root.[105]

> The root of the obstacle is to be found in the university, and it is there that it must be attacked. Unfortunately, Machen's warning went unheeded, and biblical Christianity retreated into the intellectual closets of Fundamentalism, from which it has only recently begun to re-emerge. The war is not yet lost, and it is one which we must not lose: souls

---

[105] J. Gresham Machen, "*Christianity and Culture*," *Princeton Theological Review* 11 (1913): 7.

.

of men and women hang in the balance. So what are evangelicals doing to win this war? [106]

REVIEW QUESTION:

Why is the Christian mind so important in spiritual warfare? Why are Bible critics getting away with offering misleading and false information? If Christians are to be effective in evangelism work, what ability do they need? Where are most Christians hiding today? What ideas are the greatest obstacle to one receiving the gospel?

Course Project D

Reasoning From The Scriptures: Using several Scriptures, effectively communicate why _____ is not biblical or is biblical. The director or assistant direct will assign a subject. [107]

Biblical and Christian Apologetics

When "false apostles, deceitful workmen, disguising themselves as apostles of Christ" caused trouble in the congregation in Corinth, the Apostle Paul wrote that

[106] Craig, William Lane; Copan, Paul (2007-10-01). Passionate Conviction: Modern Discourses on Christian Apologetics (pp. 8-9). B&H Publishing. Kindle Edition.

[107] The Evangelism Program Director or Assistant Director will select the topic.

under such circumstances, we are to *tear down their arguments* and *take every thought captive*. (2 Cor. 10:4, 5; 11:13–15) All who present critical arguments against God's Word, or contrary to it, can have their arguments overturned by the Christian who is able and ready to defend that Word in mildness. (2 Tim. 2:24–26)

1 Peter 3:15: But in your hearts honor Christ the Lord as holy, *always being prepared* to make a *defense to anyone* who asks you for a reason for the hope that is in you; yet do it with *gentleness and respect*.

Peter says that we must be prepared to make a *defense*. The Greek word behind the English "defense" is *apologia* (apologia), which is actually a legal term that refers to the defense of a defendant in court. Our English apologetics is just what Peter spoke of, having the ability to give a reason to any who may challenge us, or to answer those who are not challenging us but who have honest questions that deserve to be answered.

2 Timothy 2:24, 25: And the Lord's servant must not be quarrelsome but kind to everyone, *able to teach*, patiently enduring evil, *correcting his opponents with gentleness*. God may perhaps grant them repentance leading to a knowledge [*epignosis*] of the truth.

Look at the Greek word (*epignosis*) behind the English "knowledge" from above. "It is more intensive than *gnosis*, knowledge, because it expresses a more thorough participation in the acquiring of knowledge on the part of the learner."[108] The requirement of all of the Lord's servants is that they be able to teach, but not in a quarrelsome way, but in a way to correct opponents

---

108. Spiros Zodhiates, *The Complete Word Study Dictionary: New Testament*, Electronic ed. (Chattanooga, TN: AMG Publishers, 2000, c1992, c1993), S. G1922.

with mildness. Why? The purpose of it all is that by God, yet through the Christian teacher, one may come to repentance and begin taking in an accurate knowledge of the truth.

Some Christians see apologetics as pre-evangelism; it is not the gospel, but it prepares the soil for the gospel.[109] Others make no such distinction, seeing apologetics, theology, philosophy, and evangelism as deeply entwined facets of the gospel.[110] Whatever its relation to the gospel, apologetics **is an extremely important enterprise that can profoundly impact unbelievers** and be used as the tool that clears the way to faith in Jesus Christ. (Bold mine.)

Many Christians did not come to believe as a result of investigating the Bible's authority, the evidence for the resurrection, or as a response to the philosophical arguments for God's existence. They responded to the proclamation of the gospel. Although these people have reasons for their belief, they are deeply personal reasons that often do not make sense to unbelievers. **They know the truth but are not necessarily equipped to share or articulate the truth in a way that is understandable** to those who have questions about their faith. It is quite possible to believe something is true without having a

---

[109] Norman Geisler and Ron Brooks, When Skeptics Ask (Grand Rapids: Baker Books, 1996), 11.

[110] Greg Bahnsen, Van Til Apologetic (Phillipsburg, NJ: Presbyterian and Reformed, 1998), 43.

proper understanding of it or the ability to articulate it. (Bold mine.)

Christians who believe but do not know why are often insecure and comfortable only around other Christians. Defensiveness can quickly surface when challenges arise on issues of faith, morality, and truth because of a lack of information regarding the rational grounds for Christianity. At its worst, this can lead to either a fortress mentality or a belligerent faith, precisely the opposite of the Great Commission Jesus gave in Matthew 28:19–20. The Christian's charge is not to withdraw from the world and lead an insular life. Rather, we must be engaged in the culture, to be salt and light.

The solution to this problem requires believers to become informed in doctrine, the history of their faith, philosophy, logic, and other disciplines as they relate to Christianity. Believers must know the facts, arguments and theology and understand how to employ them in a way that will effectively engage the culture. Believers need Christian apologetics. One of the first tasks of Christian apologetics provides information. A number of widely held assumptions about Christianity can be easily challenged with a little information. This is even true for persons who are generally well-educated.[111]

---

[111] Powell, Doug (2006-07-01). *Holman QuickSource Guide to Christian Apologetics* (Holman Quicksource Guides) (p. 6-7). B&H Publishing. Kindle Edition.

The ability to reason with others will take time, practice and patience. For example, if someone reasons with others successfully, that person must be reasonable. In a discussion about the historicity about Jesus, a believer knows the other person denying the existence of Jesus is wrong. Moreover, believers possess a truckload of evidence to support this position. However, it is best sometimes to not unload the truck by dumping the entire load at a listener's feet in one conversation, or in one breath. Being reasonable does not mean that a believer compromises the truth because he or she does not unload on the listener.

The other person will likely make many wrong statements in the conversation, and we should let most of them go unchallenged; rather, focus on a handful of the most crucial pieces of evidence and do not get lost by refuting every wrong statement. He may make bold condemnatory statements about many Christian beliefs, but remain calm and do not make a big deal of those statements. Listen carefully to the other person, and stay within the boundaries of the evidence in the conversation. For example, in a conversation on the historicity of Jesus when the listener states, "The New Testament manuscripts were completely corrupted in the copying process for a millennium, to the point that we do not even have the supposed Word of God." The evidence for the historicity of Jesus rests in the first and second century, so it would be a fool's errand to get into an extensive side subject about the restoration of the New Testament text, which took place over the centuries that followed that millennium. There will be another day to talk about the history of the Greek New Testament, but today focus on the historicity of Jesus Christ.

God has given humanity free will, meaning each human has the right to choose, even if that choice is unwise. Believers have the assignment of proclaiming "the good news of the kingdom," as well as "making disciples" of redeemable humankind. Therefore, we must not pressure, coerce, or force people to accept the truth of that "Good News." Christians have an obligation to reason with them by overturning their false reasoning, in the attempt that being used by God to save some.

Joshua 24:15 Updated American Standard Version (UASV)

[15] "And if it is evil in your eyes to serve Jehovah, choose this day whom you will serve, whether the gods your fathers served in the region beyond the River, or the gods of the Amorites in whose land you dwell. But as for me and my house, we will serve Jehovah."

REVIEW QUESTION:

What are biblical and Christian apologetics? What does the Greek word (*epignosis*) mean? Christians who come into the faith outside of apologetics usually are unable to do what? Christians who believe but do not know why are often what? The solution to this problem is for believers to do what? When reasoning with others, why should we not unload all of the evidence?

Course Project D

Reasoning From The Scriptures: Using several Scriptures, effectively communicate why _____ is not biblical or is biblical. The director or assistant direct will assign a

Effective Questions

Luke 10:25 Holman Christian Standard Bible (HCSB)

[25] Just then an expert in the law stood up to test Him, saying, "Teacher, what must I do to inherit eternal life?"

A historical note here, "an expert in the law," or "lawyer" as some translations have it, is not a lawyer as we would think of one today. A lawyer was someone that was an expert in the Mosaic Law. However, this person would have the same level of education on the law as a lawyer would today, many years of study and memorization. Thus, this man would certainly know the answer to such an easy question as the one he asked. Now, if a believer is asked an easy Bible question, we might be tempted to just offer an answer. Certainly, as the wisest man ever to live, Jesus could have easily answered the question. Instead, Jesus wanted the man to offer his own thoughts, insights or understanding. However, Jesus knew this man was "an expert in the law," and he recognized the man would have had a certain perspective on his question. In other words, the man was not asked because he did not know. Thus, Jesus asked,

---

[112] The Evangelism Program Director or Assistant Director will select the topic.

Luke 10:26 Holman Christian Standard Bible (HCSB)

²⁶ "What is written in the law?" He asked him. "How do you read it?"

The man answered correctly,

Luke 10:27 Holman Christian Standard Bible (HCSB)

²⁷ He answered: Love the Lord your God with all your heart, with all your soul, with all your strength, and with all your mind; and your neighbor as yourself.

The conversation could have ended there. Again, the man knew the Mosaic Law, but seemingly wanted to see if Jesus would agree with what he knew. Jesus gratified him, letting him feel good, by giving the correct answer. Jesus responded:

Luke 10:28-29 Holman Christian Standard Bible (HCSB)

²⁸ "You've answered correctly," He told him. "Do this and you will live."

²⁹ But wanting to justify himself, he asked Jesus, "And who is my neighbor?"

Here again, the man looks to prove himself righteous, and Jesus could have simply stated the truth, even the Samaritan. However, Jesus having insight into the setting, the Jews detested the Samaritans; so, while he would give the correct answer it would be disputed in a long, back-and-forth conversation, and the Jews who listened would have sided with the man. Thus Jesus boxed the man into giving an answer by having him reason on an illustration.

Luke 10:30-37 Holman Christian Standard Bible (HCSB)

The Parable of the Good Samaritan

³⁰ Jesus took up the question and said: "A man was going down from Jerusalem to Jericho and fell into the hands of robbers. They stripped him, beat him up, and fled, leaving him half dead. ³¹ A priest happened to be going down that road. When he saw him, he passed by on the other side. ³² In the same way, a Levite, when he arrived at the place and saw him, passed by on the other side. ³³ But a Samaritan on his journey came up to him, and when he saw the man, he had compassion. ³⁴ He went over to him and bandaged his wounds, pouring on olive oil and wine. Then he put him on his own animal, brought him to an inn, and took care of him. ³⁵ The next day he took out two denarii, gave them to the innkeeper, and said, 'Take care of him. When I come back I'll reimburse you for whatever extra you spend.'

³⁶ "Which of these three do you think proved to be a neighbor to the man who fell into the hands of the robbers?"

³⁷ "The one who showed mercy to him," he said.

Then Jesus told him, "Go and do the same."

This man had to admit the elite in the Jewish religion, the priest and the Levite, had not been neighborly, but the Samaritan proved to be a good neighbor. Jesus moved him to reason out a new way of viewing exactly what "neighbor" meant. Instead of letting the man walk him into a long debate, Jesus made the man do all of the reasoning in the conversation, and moved him to admit something no Jew would ever utter,[113] as well as grasp a whole new understanding of what it meant to be a neighbor. Jesus took this approach because the circumstances called for it. However, on another occasion, a scribe, another expert in the law, asked him the same question and on that occasion, he chose to give the direct answer. (Mark 12:28-31) Circumstances vary.

What lessons can we take in from the example that Luke provided us? **(1)** Jesus **used Scriptures** initially to answer the man's question. **(2)** Jesus proved **perceptive** enough to **take notice** of the man's agenda. **(3)** Jesus did not simply answer the easy Bible question, but **shifted the responsibility** through **a question** of his own, by asking the man how he understood the law, giving him a chance to express himself. **(4)** Jesus **complimented** the man for a discerning with the correct answer. **(5)** Jesus made sure the man and the listeners **made the connection** between the initial question and the Scriptures. **(6)** Jesus **used an illustration** that was able to **reach the heart and mind**, where the answer was kept to the forefront. **(7)** Jesus moved the man **to reason** beyond his basic understanding of a neighbor.

Explaining and Proving

Acts 17:2-3 English Standard Version (ESV)

2 And Paul went in, as was his custom, and on three Sabbath days he reasoned with them from the Scriptures,**3 explaining and proving** that it was necessary for the Christ to suffer and to rise from the

---

[113] Notice the hatred ran so deep between Jews and Samaritans that when asked by Jesus, who was the neighbor I the illustration, he did not say, the Samaritan, but rather, "the one who ..."

dead, and saying, "This Jesus, whom I proclaim to you, is the Christ."

We have already spoken on the fact that Paul reasoned from the Scriptures. However, he did more, as one can see from the above, that he explained, proved, and made application. Many times you may read a Scripture to someone, and while it seems straightforward enough to you, but the listener fails to see the point. You may do as we mentioned previously, highlighting a word or phrase or a part of the text, and then explaining the verse. We are doing that with Acts 17:2-3, as we highlight **explaining and proving**. You could also offer to walk them through the context, like we also did previously with Acts 17:2-3, when we backed up to verse 1, to show that Paul reasoned from the Scriptures because he talked with Jews in the Synagogue, people, who would be familiar with the Hebrew Scriptures. Another option is offering them additional texts that support the one the evangelist used. If the listener does not grasp the text and the explanation, add an illustration like Jesus did over forty times. Then again, asking the right questions might get the listener to reason on things further.

The person who makes a claim has the burden of proving it by offering sound arguments. As stated previously, one must give evidence that reasonably satisfies any statements that made. Never be troubled over a listener asking for proof, as they have every right to do so. By thorough arguments, rational reasoning, and serious appeal, you can overturn any faulty reasoning of the one who is listening.

When the person an evangelist talks to makes a claim, he is then responsible to prove it. He may begin with a wrong proposition that forms the basis of his argument or from which a conclusion is drawn. Maybe, the sources he is using are biased, which can be pointed out to him. Additionally, you might point out that part of his argument is superficial. Moreover, many times, if you know the issue well enough, one may notice the listener offering evidence, yet failing to mention any facts that support his argument. Then again, one might point out that his evidence is not really evidence at all, but simply appeals to emotion, as opposed to reasons.

For Christians, the Bible is primary evidence, while other sources are secondary. However, as already stated, the majority of people no longer hold the Bible as an authority. Therefore, the evangelist must be versatile by being able to use both in conjunction with each other, or depend on the secondary evidence, until the listener begins to see the value and reasonableness of Scripture. For example, one may use the universe as evidence of a Creator.

> The universe reveals God's existence. It is evident that the things which constituted the universe could not have made themselves (see Cosmological Argument). There must be "a first cause eternally existing, of a nature totally different to any material existence we know of, and by the power of which all things exist; and this first cause, man calls God" (ibid. 26; cf. 28). Paine also argued from motion. Since the universe consists of matter that cannot move itself, the origin of the rotation of the planets is impossible unless there exists an external first cause which set them in motion. This First Cause must be God (Aldridge, 6:17). He also argued from design (see Teleological Argument). Since the "work of man's hands is a proof of the existence of man," and since a watch is "positive evidence of the existence of a

watch-maker," then "in like manner the creation is evidence to our reason and our senses of the existence of a Creator" (*Complete Works*, 310).[114]

If an evangelist witnesses to someone who sees the Bible as the word of man, not the word of God, how should one respond? Seeing what Bible scholars such as Dr. Norman L. Geisler or Dr. Gleason L. Archer have to say may be helpful. However, the evidence is not the fact that they are saying it is the Word of God, but rather what they provide as evidence. Support from someone that agrees with you, especially the like of the above scholars is evidence, but it is low-level evidence. One could use science by starting with what Scripture says first, and then use science to confirm or give support.

Regardless of whatever one attempts to prove, the level of evidence required will be dependent on the person to whom you are talking. The average person may not need more than Scriptural proof, with some outside sources. Some may require a tremendous amount of evidence. A few people will not be convinced as no amount of evidence is going to persuade them to change their mind. Their heart and mind is closed to the light of truth. They are mentally blind. The evidence that will satisfy this person may not be enough to satisfy another. Therefore, one must pay attention to the listener to meet their needs sufficiently.

One must appreciate that the evangelist seeks redeemable ones, one's who hearts and minds are open to truth, or can be opened to truth. Believers do not seek

---

[114] Norman L. Geisler, *Baker Encyclopedia of Christian Apologetics*, Baker Reference Library (Grand Rapids, MI: Baker Books, 1999), 573.

people with closed minds and hearts. Jesus said, "Do not give dogs what is holy, and do not throw your pearls before pigs, lest they trample them underfoot and turn to attack you." (Matt 7:6) One will recognize these after some experience in witnessing. One sign is they present a claim that that the Bible is the word of man, not God, and is full of errors and contradictions. Ask for one, and they provide one that they feel is the nail in the coffin of the Bible. The evangelist offers them a reasonable answer, which they cannot dispute, so they act as though they never raised that issue and go on to another. The evangelist then gives them a reasonable answer to that one, which they cannot dispute. Instead of showing appreciation that they have received answers to these supposed issues, they act as though they never asked and move on to the next. Therefore, the pattern will continue as they do not seek answers, as they have a closed mind and heart.

How can any Christian obtain or develop more fully the skill to reason from the Scriptures? Several things are important: **(1)** One must have an accurate understanding of what the Scriptures say and mean. One must prepare for Christian meetings that one regularly attends. Regular personal Bible study, every day is necessary. **(2)** One must have a complete picture of the history of the Bible from Genesis 1:1 to Revelation 22:21. This can be accomplished by studying through a book like the *Holman Bible Handbook* by David S. Dockery (Nov 2, 1992). **(3)** One must have an understanding of Bible difficulties, which run from Genesis 1:1 to Revelation 22:21. This can be accomplished by studying through *The Big Book of Bible Difficulties: Clear and Concise Answers from Genesis to Revelation* by Norman L. Geisler and Thomas Howe (Jun 1, 2008). **(4)** One must have an accurate understanding of Bible backgrounds of Bible

273

times. One can accomplish this by studying through *Nelson's New Illustrated Bible Manners And Customs How The People Of The Bible Really Lived* by Vos, Howard (May 15, 1999). **(5)** One definitely must understand how to interpret the Bible correctly. This can be accomplished by studying through *Basic Bible Interpretation* by Roy B. Zuck (Jan 1991). **(6)** One must meditate and ponder the things he or she learns, mentally exploring the information from various perspectives, and appreciating the significance of them. **(7)** While one studies the Bible, look for not only clarifications of Scriptures but also Scriptural whys and wherefores for those clarifications. **(8)** As one studies, consider how to use the verses, to explain biblical truths to different groups of people. **(9)** Contemplate and ponder what kind of illustrations might be used to make biblical points. All of this can be accomplished through the reading Bible study program in APPENDIX A of this book, and other programs.

REVIEW QUESTION:

How did Jesus use questions effectively? What lessons can one take in from the example that Luke provides in 28:25-37? Based on Paul in Acts 17, what more is needed than reasoning from the Scriptures? Who is responsible for providing the evidence? If the Bible critic makes a claim, what weaknesses may the evangelist look for being used? If one witnesses to someone who sees the Bible as the word of man, not the word of God, how should one respond? Why will someone have to provide different levels of evidence? How can any Christian obtain or fully develop

---

	the skill to reason from the Scriptures?

Course Project D	**Reasoning From The Scriptures**: Using several Scriptures, effectively

communicate why _____ is not biblical or is biblical. The director or assistant direct will assign a subject.[115]

---

[115] The Evangelism Program Director or Assistant Director will select the topic.

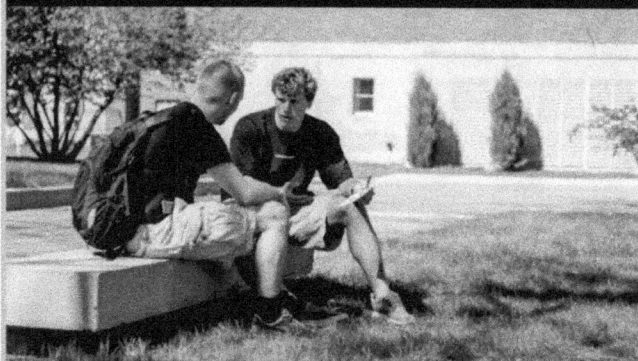

CONVERSATIONAL
EVANGELISM

Defending the Faith, Reasoning from the
Scriptures, Explaining and Proving,
Instructing in Sound Doctrine, and
Overturning False Reasoning

Edward D. Andrews

EDWARD D. ANDREWS

THE CHRISTIAN APOLOGIST

Always Being Prepared to Make a Defense

THE EVANGELISM STUDY TOOL

Basic Bible Doctrines of the Christian Faith

Edward D. Andrews

Bibliography

Aldrich, C Joseph. *Lifestyle Evangelism.* Portland, OR: Multnoma Press, 1981.

Anders, Max. *Holman New Testament Commentary: vol. 8, Galatians, Ephesians, Philippians, Colossians.* Nashville, TN: Broadman & Holman Publishers, 1999.

Andrews, Edward D. *THE EVANGELISM HANDBOOK: How All Christians Can Effectively Share God's Word in Their Community.* Cambridge: Christian Publishing House, 2013.

Archer, Gleason L. *A Survey of Old Testament Introduction (Revised and Expanded).* Chicago: Moody, 1994.

—. *Encyclopedia of Bible Difficulties.* Grand Rapids: Zondervan, 1982.

Bercot, David W. *A Dictionary of Early Christian Beliefs.* Peabody: Hendrickson, 1998.

Brand, Chad, Charles Draper, and England Archie. *Holman Illustrated Bible Dictionary: Revised, Updated and Expanded.* Nashville, TN: Holman, 2003.

Bromiley, Geoffrey W. *The International Standard Bible Encyclopedia (Vol. 1-4).* Grand Rapids, MI: William B. Eerdmans Publishing Co., 1986.

Bromiley, Geoffrey W., and Gerhard Friedrich. *Theological Dictionary of the New Testament, ed. Gerhard Kittel, vol. 4.* Grand Rapids, MI: Eerdmans, 1964-.

Brotzman, Ellis R. *Old Testament Textual Criticism.* Grand Rapids: Baker Academic, 1994.

Coleman, E. Robert. *The Master Plan of Evangelism.* Westwood, NJ: Fleming H. Revell Company, 1964.

Comfort, Philip. *Encountering the Manuscripts: An Introduction to New Testament Paleography and Textual Criticism.* Nashville: Broadman & Holman, 2005.

Cornwall, Judson, and Stelman Smith. *The Exhaustive Dictionary of Bible Names.* Gainsville: Bridge-Logos, 1998.

Eims, LeRoy. *One to One Evangelism.* Wheaton, IL: Victor Books, 1974, 1990.

Elwell, Walter A. *Baker Encyclopedia of the Bible.* Grand Rapids: Baker Book House, 1988.

—. *Evangelical Dictionary of Theology (Second Edition).* Grand Rapids: Baker Academic, 2001.

Elwell, Walter A, and Philip Wesley Comfort. *Tyndale Bible Dictionary.* Wheaton, Ill: Tyndale House Publishers, 2001.

Epp, Eldon J. *Textual Criticism.* Atlanta: Scholars Press, 1989.

Geisler, Norman L. *Defending Inerrancy: Affirming the Accuracy of Scripture for a New Generation.* Grand Rapids, MI: Baker Books, 2012.

Geisler, Norman L, and William E Nix. *A General Introduction to the Bible.* Chicago: Moody Press, 1996.

Geisler, Norman L., and Thomas Howe. *The Big Book of Bible Difficulties*. Grand Rapids: Baker Books, 1992.

Geisler, Norman, and David Geisler. *CONVERSATION EVANGELISM: How to Listen and Speak So You Can Be Heard*. Eugene: Harvest House Publishers, 2014.

Green, Joel B, Scot McKnight, and Howard Marshall. *Dictionary of Jesus and the Gospels*. Downers Grove, IL: InterVarsity Press, 1992.

Greenlee, J Harold. *Introduction to New Testament Textual Criticism*. Peabody: Hendrickson, 1995.

Harris, Robert Laird, Gleason Leonard Archer, and Bruce K Waltke. *Theological Wordbook of the Old Testament*. Chicago: Moody Press, 1999, c1980.

Hastings, James, John A Selbie, and John C Lambert. *A Dictionary of Christ and the Gospels*. New York, NY: Charles Scribner's Sons, 1907.

Hindson, Ed, and Ergun Caner. *The Popular Encyclopedia of Apologetics: Surveying the Evidence for the Truth of Christianity*. Eugene: Harvest House, 2008.

Kennedy, D. James. *Evangelism Explosion*. Wheaton, IL: Tyndale House Publishers, 1977.

Larsen, L. David. *The Evangelism Mandate*. Wheaton: Crossway Books, 1992.

Larson, Knute. *Holman New Testament Commentary, vol. 9, I & II Thessalonians, I & II Timothy, Titus, Philemon*. Nashville, TN: Broadman & Holman Publishers, 2000.

Manser, Martin H. (Managing Editor) McGrath, Alister E. (General Editor) Packer, J. I. (Consultant Editor). *DICTIONARY OF BIBLE THEMES: The Accessible and Comprehenssive Tool for Topical Studies.* Grand Rapids: Zondervan Publishing Company, 2009.

Mayers, Mark K. *Christianity Confronts Culture: A Strategy for Crosscultural Evangelism.* Grand Rapids : Zondervan, 1987.

McCue, Rolland. *Promises Unfulfilled: The Failed Strategy of Modern Evangelism.* Greenville, SC: Ambassador Group, 2004.

McRaney, William. *The Art of Personal Evangelism.* Nashville: Broadman & Holman, 2003.

Mirriam-Webster, Inc. *Mirriam-Webster's Collegiate Dictionary. Eleventh Edition.* Springfield: Mirriam-Webster, Inc., 2003.

Morgenthaler, Sally. *Worship Evangelism.* Grand Rapids: Zondervan Publishing House, 1995.

Mounce, William D. *Mounce's Complete Expository Dictionary of Old & New Testament Words.* Grand Rapids, MI: Zondervan, 2006.

Negev, Avraham. *The Archaeological Encyclopedia of the Holy Land.* Jerusalem: Jerusalem Publishing House Limited, 1986, 1990.

Osborne, Grant R. *BAKER EXEGETICAL COMMENTARY ON THE NEW TESTAMET: REVELATION.* Grand Rapids, MI: Baker Academic, 2002.

Packer, J. I. *Evangelism and the Sovereignty of God.* Downers Grove, IL: InterVarsity Press, 1979.

Posterski, C. Donald. *Reinventing Evangelism*. Downers Grove, IL: InterVarsity Press, 1989.

Pratt Jr, Richard L. *Holman New Testament Commentary: I & II Corinthians, vol. 7*. Nashville: Broadman & Holman Publishers, 2000.

Rainer, S. Thomas. *Evangelism in the Twenty-First Century*. Wheaton, IL: Harold Shaw Publishers, 1989.

Reid, Alvin. *Introduction to Evangelism*. Nashville: Boardman & Holmes , 1998.

Robertson, A. T. *An Introduction to the Textual Criticism of the New Testament*. London: Hodder & Stoughton, 1925.

Robinson, G. L., and R. K. Harrison. *The International Standard Bible Encyclopedia, vol. 2*. Grand Rapids: Eerdmans, 1982.

Schreiner, Thomas R. *The New American Commentary: 1, 2 Peter, Jude*. Nashville: Broadman & Holman, 2003.

Sisson, Dick. *Evangelism Encounter*. Chicago, IL: Victor Books, 1988.

Stein, Robert H. *A Basic Guide to Interpreting the Bible: Playing by the Rules*. Grand Rapids: Baker Books, 1994.

Torrey, Reuben Archer. *Difficulties in the Bible: Alleged Errors and Contradictions*. Chicago: Moody Press, 1907.

Tov, Emanuel. *Textual Criticism of the Hebrew Bible, Third Edition*. Minneapolis: Fortress Press, 2012.

Vine, W E. *Vine's Expository Dictionary of Old and New Testament Words*. Nashville: Thomas Nelson, 1996.

Wegner, Paul D. *A Student's Guide to Textual Criticism of the Bible: Its History Methods & Results*. Downers Grove: InterVarsity Press, 2006.

Wilkins, Don, and Edward D and Andrews. *THE TEXT OF THE NEW TESTAMENT The Science and Art of Textual Criticism*. Cambridge: Christian Publishing House, 2015.

Zodhiates, Spiros. *The Complete Word Study Dictionary: New Testament*. Chattanooga: AMG Publishers, 2000, c1992, c1993.